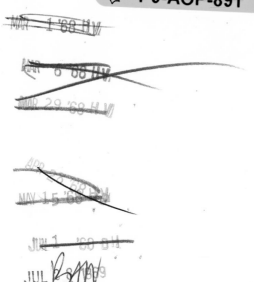

BUSINESS POLICIES
and
DECISION MAKING

ADMINISTRATION SERIES
Edited by Eugene E. Jennings
Michigan State University

BUSINESS POLICIES
and
DECISION MAKING

Raymond J. Ziegler
Merrimack College

New York

APPLETON-CENTURY-CROFTS
Division of Meredith Publishing Company

To my wife, Sue,

and my son, James

Preface

The study of business policies is undergoing rapid and substantial changes, some of which are reflected in the trend toward instructor and student involvement with many facets of name firms—histories, competitors, problems, and executive decisions. Real-world cases are still the focal point for studying business policies, but the research areas have broadened, giving the decision maker access to substantial information in order to analyze the firm's problem areas more effectively.

The author contends that it is doing a disservice to the student in trying to give him all of the information he might need. It is the author's purpose, rather, to encourage creative thinking on the part of the reader. These case studies provide the opportunity for the reader to develop his ability to analyze problems and situations—a basic requirement for the administrator, whose responsibility is setting policy and making decisions. Decision making is not a hit-or-miss affair. It presupposes a basic knowledge of sound business procedures. To meet the needs of the student researcher in this area, Chapter One has been included to provide information that is basic to an understanding of policy and decision making.

No real-world case is ever one hundred percent self-contained; the decision maker must gather much data on his own for problem solving. Whereas student research quickly meets a dead end with the X Manufacturing Company, a study of a company such as American Telephone and Telegraph Company enables the problem solver to avail himself of a myriad of primary and secondary sources simulating real-world decision making.

This collection of policy materials includes those of industry, merchandising, transportation, and communication. While each policy study is organized to acquaint the reader with the firm's background, industry setting, and basic problems, guidelines for research are afforded by the bibliography at the end of each case. These suggested readings indicate a starting point for research prior to decision making.

Special recognition is due Mrs. Elaine Mawhinney, who examined the entire manuscript and offered suggestions that I found valuable. Credit is also due Mrs. Anita Mazzaglia for typing the entire manuscript.

R. J. Z.

Contents

Chapter 5

Chapter 6

Chapter 7

Chapter 8

Chapter 9

Chapter 10

Chapter 11

Chapter 12

Chapter 13

Chapter 14

PART I

Policy Formulation and

Its Relevance to the Understanding

of Business Enterprise

The most important part of every business is to know what
ought to be done.

COLUMELLA

To ASSURE CONSISTENCY and uniformity of action, sound policy must
be formulated. Any situation which calls for such action can be remedied
because company policy clearly points out the direction the action ought
to follow. This also serves to promote unity and basic understanding
between employee and administration, which in turn brings about coordination of effort.

POLICY DEFINED

In business circles one frequently hears the word "policy" used. It is
a term often used loosely, as people generally assume a common meaning
for it. However, as it involves a vast gamut of principles and since it is
basic to the success of an organization, one cannot assume that others
share his interpretation of the word; therefore, there is need to define the
term. Arriving at a clear-cut definition of the word is a difficult task
since the area is nebulous. This is due not only to the many differences in
individual companies, but primarily to the lack of specific information
on companies, who are unwilling to part with such information because
of competition. Although the information made available to the public is
general and limited, there are some concepts that are common to any
business policy, and business authorities can agree on certain aspects of it.

1. *Policy is a necessity if a given business is to realize its objectives*. It is a
common misconception that objectives and policies are of the same nature.
To think clearly about a problem and to establish a sense of direction, we
must distinguish between the two.

1

An objective is the end; policy is the means to that end. An objective involves accomplishment; a policy involves the method. Objectives are the criteria for action; policies are part of that action. As an example, a particular firm might desire to produce and market only high quality products and retail them to customers with a minimum yearly income of $100,000. Its distribution policy, however, is to exclusively use low quality retail outlets; therefore, the firm's policy on distribution is not consistent with its quality objectives.

Forming objectives and setting policies are both the sole responsibility of those branches of a company whose business is decision making, for these are both types of decision making. This effort, then, is wholly the concern of the executive and administrative branches.

In working with the two, the administrator must be selective. He must be able to discard any methods that will not be effective in reaching a desired goal, and he must be able to eliminate objectives or goals that are unrealistic if the means to reach them are not feasible.

2. *Policy is a definite statement of purpose and procedure.* For a business to function effectively, administrators and executives must base their decisions on governing principles; because policy is basic to this effort, they cannot afford a hit-or-miss attitude. A definite statement of principle or procedure will bring about an understanding of requirements for effective action and administration. A firm may feel that it is desirable to have a definite statement relative to product policy. Policy will determine major product questions—for example, whether to undertake a new development project, to introduce a new product, or to eliminate an old one. These policies summarize the business characteristics which this firm's experience has shown successful products must have.

3. *Policy is a means by which company objectives are effectively reconciled with internal factors and organizational functions.* That objectives and decision making are contingent on internal factors cannot be disputed. Administration must set goals that are reasonable in accordance with internal factors—the company's resources and organizational functions—and which involve various sections such as purchasing and sales. A sales department, in taking orders, should consider internal factors, such as whether the company or organization can supply the needs of the customer on time. Thus, it must take into consideration the delivery date and the making of the material. Organizational functions such as production, scheduling, shipping, and loading would have to be considered. The sales policy should be formulated with these factors in mind.

Policy, then, is a statement of procedure or principle by which a company intends to realize its objectives. It insures proper direction to-

ward definite objectives of a business in the light of internal factors and organizational functions.

TYPES OF POLICIES

The function of the executive is leadership and guidance of a company. In order for him to lead and guide this company efficiently, he must set up policies for all levels—from the highest to the lowest.

GENERAL

General policies are statements of principles that guide the organization. As the classification suggests, they are broad and comprehensive; and they are basic to the direction of the company. They decide questions involving geographical location, product lines, product distribution, diversification, decentralization.

SPECIFIC

Major policies serve the major divisions and subdivisions of the organization, such as personnel, sales, finance, purchasing. When and in what quantities should goods be procured? At what prices should products be sold? What type and media of advertising will be used? How can union-management cooperation be insured? These questions are covered by major policies.

Minor policies are needed for the departments and sections within the major organizational divisions. Hiring or discharging employees, vacations, extension of credit to customers, restrictions on inventories, and insurance would all come under minor policies.

As each unit or department has its own objectives, the executive must formulate policy keeping these in mind.

PROCESS ANALYSIS OF POLICY

While there is no specific formula for policy formation, there is a general approach, which serves as a useful guide to the executive in policy making. Policies are adopted whenever there is a need to set specific rules to govern a particular type of activity.

1. *The policy is formulated by the organization's executive branch, which has the direct responsibility for accomplishing the objectives to which the policy applies.* Policy is formulated by the executive directly involved. Before putting the ruling into effect, he should consult his superior and

other executives who may be affected by the policy. In addition, any minor policy he formulates must be in harmony with any general policy covering that problem. He may also recommend via the president a general policy for consideration by the board of directors. Line and staff subordinates may help formulate policy subject to the executive's approval. The executive may refer policy problems to a committee of executives.

Policy-making committees are usually formed when the higher echelon feels that a committee is likely to be more competent in certain areas than an individual. These areas usually deal with major aspects of management such as planning, control, forming objectives, organization questions, and settlement of disputes. In overall planning a committee can be extremely helpful in presenting important facts and different views, especially if the members have varied backgrounds.

To ascertain that the policies currently being used are being effectively carried out and achieving the objectives for which they are intended, policy control is instituted. Because of the extensive information that may be required to check the effectiveness of these policies, it is often wise to form a committee to check on policy control rather than have an individual assume such a responsibility.

In formulating objectives the operating executive needs group meetings. During these meetings the executive is presented with various opinions, some from those more directly concerned with policy making and others from those representing various interest groups. Such meetings by reason of the group's composition and authority can sometimes better determine basic objectives than can the executives who are usually weighed down by habitual problems.

Again, a committee can study different plans of organization, review their comparative merits, criticize inharmonious details, and approve or recommend one of these plans in a more efficient way and in less time than an individual.

In decision making, committees often serve as excellent arbitrators in settling disputes. A decision of collective judgment can be more impressive than that of an individual and is more likely to be accepted as an impartial decision.

Policy-making committees are found particularly in larger companies, usually at the director's level. Whether individual or group policy making is more effective is a question that is determined by the organizational structure of the company.

2. A set of basic rules or principles must be devised which will govern and direct the company. In order to accomplish this, the executive or administrator must understand the objectives and requirements necessary for the growth of the company. In order to select basic rules or principles that will be in accordance with the objectives, the executive must merge knowledge of the actual operation of the company with the objectives the company has in mind; he must have conclusions based on a thorough analysis of the objectives before he can determine how to accomplish them. He must also carefully consider the concrete and abstract factors that would affect the accomplishment of the company's objectives. Policy for hiring employees, for example, would have to take into consideration the experience and skills of the individual related to the demands of the industry.

3. *The policy should then be set down in writing, clearly, logically, completely, and signed by the executive involved.* To prevent misinterpretation, administrators should state policy in terms that are definite and simple. Failure to do this can bring about lack of confidence in administration, thus lessening the policy's effectiveness. Policy associated with a production process, for example, would have to be clearly defined as to the basic process to be used and the extent of specialization and mechanization. The executive cannot assume that the policy is stated in such a manner that it is readily understandable and is not open to question of its intent. If the executive has taken the time to carefully think through his policies and state them specifically and concisely, personnel will be able to function more efficiently and confidently.

4. *The personnel involved are then informed of this policy and briefed on it in order to prevent misconceptions.* That various people can read the same policy and come up with different interpretations is understandable. Such a situation, however, takes away from the very effectiveness which the policy is supposed to effect. When a policy is known but not understood, the group that must conform to this policy will not accept it and will only give it superficial acknowledgement.

What can the executive do to educate his personnel in regard to policy? He must first clarify the meaning and significance of a policy as it relates to particular situations. The explanation is then the responsibility of the immediate superior of the individual having difficulty with the interpretation of the policy. Finally, interpretations of policies should be put in writing. If the executive has allowed sufficient time for education of personnel on the policy and its objectives, he will undoubtedly have eliminated numerous misconceptions which may have arisen, thereby facilitating the implementation of the policy.

5. *The effectiveness of this policy is then determined in the light of its specific objectives.* The effectiveness of any policy is determined by whether or not the personnel have conformed to it. This determines the success of the policy—a success which should be realized on the basis of the objective involved.

If the executive has followed these basic rules, then he has eliminated many of the common policy problems in business today.

POLICY RELATIVE TO ORGANIZATIONAL STRUCTURE

In order to better understand policy formulation, it is necessary to review organizational hierarchy from the point of view of policy.

Policy will vary to some extent according to organizational structure. In line organization, in which the direct flow of authority goes through specified channels and the responsibility returns through these same channels, policies are adopted at the top. This is the most basic of all organizational structures, usually used in small firms which have no need of a specialized form of organization. In a small firm the flow of authority originates at the top and is passed down to the foreman or foremen and then on to the workers. The authority in each department is individual and does not overlap with other departments. Because of the basic structure of straight-line organization, carrying out a policy follows the same route. Any policy handed down comes from one source, the executive, who passes it on to the foreman, who assures the execution of this policy.

Because the structure of line organization is so simple, it is clearly understood. However, some companies, because of the complexity of their organizational structure, cannot employ this form of organization. They must use one of two other methods: functional or staff.

In functional organization the activities of the business are assigned to specialists; in addition, the flow of authority is greatly modified. Therefore, each of these specialists exercises authority not only over his own group, but also in any area where that activity in which he specializes takes place. This feature is referred to as functional authority. To illustrate, a company may have a specialist in charge of material handling. Regardless of where the material is moved—production department, shipping department, or storeroom—authority over this activity will be in the hands of the specialist. A policy, then, handed down from the top level, given to material handling, affects more than just the specific foreman and his workers. It now affects any foreman and worker involved in the section in which the material is moved.

A combination of line and functional organization is staff organization. Here the flow of authority proceeds from the top of the organization to the bottom along fixed lines. (See General Motors p. 84). The need for specialists, as is seen in the functional type, is here accommodated by the creation of staff divisions. However, the authority given to the specialist here is restricted to his own department. Each function of the business requiring the services of a specialist is assigned to a staff under the control of the specialist. The staff solves the problems associated with the particular function wherever in the business the problems arise. Once a solution is reached, the staff informs the supervisor of the division in which the problem exists. Then the supervisor exercises his authority as necessary to see that the corrective procedure is put into effect in his work area. (It is worth noting that the foreman exercises immediate authority over his workers as in line organization.) Policy here would originate from the top of the organization from specified committees and would be handed down to the individual staff groups, which in turn carry out the policies in accordance with their responsibilities. In General Motors, for example, top management policy is formulated by the Board of Directors and by the Financial and Operations Policy Committees. They would thus establish structural directives for administrators and executives for determining the activity of any or all departments and their interrelationship. These could include such policies as establishment of production schedules or price lists for automobile divisions. The responsibility for administering these policies rests to some extent with the president and the executive vice-presidents through the administration committee and the policy groups. These policy groups could be line or functional. Line-policy groups would include general engine, household appliance, Canadian, and overseas. The specific staff functions are covered by functional-policy groups, which include manufacturing, engineering, personnel, employee relations, public relations, and distribution.

CHARACTERISTICS OF POLICY

There are certain policy characteristics which are necessary to the solving of policy problems: flexibility, comprehensiveness, coordination, ethics.

FLEXIBILITY

Most important, perhaps, is flexibility. A flexible policy must, of course, be based on a satisfactory degree of stability. In order to maintain a sense of direction, policies should have stability; moreover, instability can result in a lack of confidence in executive leadership because of its inability to follow a definite path. Therefore, there should be stability based on ability to properly analyze objectives and situations. However, in order to cope with the variation in business, policy must have a sufficient degree of flexibility. "How deep the ruts of tradition and conformity," said Thoreau. This is precisely what can happen to a company whose policy fails to anticipate the future and relies too heavily on tradition. By maintaining rigid standards it can fall into a "rut," bringing progress to a standstill. Policies must change in accordance with changes in our society and in the world in general. Because of its scope, flexibility can cope equally efficaciously with periods of depression and prosperity. In order to sustain changing business trends, good strategy is important. Timing is the foundation of strategy. For example, if a company's standard purchasing policy is to buy on a daily basis and a strike threatens raw materials that are used, the company would buy a large quantity of this material to sustain it during the strike.

We can see, therefore, that broadness in policy, or flexibility, is necessary to keep up with a wide range of situations and ever-changing business conditions. This must, of course, be tempered with stability, which is needed to insure continued growth and effectiveness in business operation.

COMPREHENSIVENESS

Policy should have not only a reasonable stability or flexibility, but also should be comprehensive, containing the smallest number of broad, fundamental statements of principle that is practicable. Deviations from plans are then prevented, because good policies provide the means to an intelligent understanding of the project, its intentions, and plans toward their fulfillment.

Policy should be comprehensive enough to cover difficulties which develop in business. If these are not prepared for, an emergency situation would probably be handled under pressure, injuring the efficiency and effectiveness of the business operation.

COORDINATION

Coordination involves time and order of performance. If an organization is to function effectively, there must be a coordination of the activities among the organizational elements. This lends direction to the achievement of specified goals. Without a goal there is no functional organization—only a collection of elements assembled together without a unifying bond. Unless they feel they are working to attain a common goal, the individual elements may direct their efforts toward unrelated tasks. By guiding through policy, thereby providing the necessary coordination, the executive is fulfilling his responsibility. In order to insure coordination, specialists are often maintained to determine the effectiveness of current policies and degree of conformity. It is their responsibility to correlate the action with the policy.

ETHICS

Policy must be based on sound principles; they must conform to generally accepted standards of business conduct. The most important factor is service to the public. This discounts all endeavors of which the main objectives are purely of a material nature and of personal gain. Much depends on the fortitude and integrity of the individual executive as to whether or not he leads his company to violate certain ethical standards. The matter here seems to be definite; the answers seem obvious. However, many situations are borderline cases, as far as whether or not they are ethical. Does a company have the right to move out of a community, leaving it without employment? Whether it is ethical or not depends on many things. Is it the only major company in the area? Did it move so that it could get employees at a lower wage rate? Were transportation facilities poor? Obviously, the truth can only be reached by honestly answering the question, "Does the end justify the means?"

RELEVANCE TO DECISION MAKING

Policies are sometimes confused with decisions that are ready-made to resolve a given problem. As stated previously, policies are guides to action; therefore, they serve only to give direction to decision making. However, they do facilitate the making of a decision since decisions are made within the framework of policy.

Of the different types of decision making, policy decisions are the most important. They are born at the very start of the business where principles are needed to direct its conduct. Of less importance, but also significant, are the administrative decisions. These decisions are based on policy statement; they are made within the framework of policy. Therefore, while policy itself is concerned with principles, administrators are concerned with action based on these principles. Finally, executive decisions are more immediate, being made where the actual work is being done. These decisions are contingent on both policy and administrative decisions.

An understanding of the part policy plays in decision making can be furthered by knowledge of two decision-making techniques: programmed and nonprogrammed. While there are two types, there are relatively few decisions which can be classified at either extreme. The majority are a combination of both types and the foundation policy provides can be seen.

Programmed decisions are those which are repetitive and routine. For example, habits are programmed decisions; they allow an individual to minimize the expenditure of mental effort in deciding among the myriad of alternatives which present themselves every day as he performs familiar tasks. In an industrial setting, rules are programmed decisions specifying the alternatives which serve to guide individual actions in the direction of achieving the organization's goals. From a managerial point of view, the decisions made by the first-line supervisor and by the middle manager are largely programmed. There are preselected "best" alternatives to be chosen for most of the recurring problems with which managers at these levels are faced. The managers' primary decision-making function, therefore, is the recognition of a particular problem and the choice of the related specified alternative.

Nonprogrammed decisions, just as the name implies, are the antitheses of programmed decisions. They are unique decisions arising from novel situations in which there is little, if any, prior experience to guide the decision maker toward an optimum solution. It is in making nonprogrammed decisions that a person must apply judgment and imagination. To the business firm, nonprogrammed decisions are basic. They are applied in the formulation of policy and they are decisions which must be made before lower level decision making can be initiated.

CONTRIBUTIONS OF POLICY

Policy may be summarized as a guidepost for objective direction. It is basically a control function and may be organized according to the element that it is to control. To be functional, it must be clearly expressed in writing, broad and flexible, and acceptable to those who are governed by it. Along with objectives, policies are essential to, and provide the working paper of, effective and profitable decision making.

Policy, then, is formulated as an aid to the administrator in guiding the company, promoting its objectives, and making decisions. For the executive, policy enables him to consistently follow a straight path in his course of action. He is able to plan and determine far-reaching effects of objectives and decisions. To personnel, policy gives that confidence and direction needed for cooperation and coordination of action. On both levels policy provides an understanding of the basis for effective action in the operation of the company. It is necessary to determine the soundness of a plan of action. Finally, it is necessary for total integration of functions in a company.

PART II
Case Studies

"I reverence the individual who understands distinctly what he wishes; who unweariedly advances, who knows the means conductive to his object, and can seize and use them."

Goethe

CHAPTER I

Hilton Hotels Corporation

WITH AN INVESTMENT of $5,000 in the Mobley Hotel in a small oil-gushing Texas town, Conrad N. Hilton, in 1920, fresh from the First World War, began his hotel career which was to eventually form his world famous hotel empire.

A few years before the great depression young Hilton and his investment friends were buying and remodeling old run-down hotels throughout Texas. By 1929 the small buying group had sizable investments, and in the face of the oncoming depression Hilton built his first million dollar hotel.

Like many other businesses the Hilton Hotels did not escape the effects of the depression, but against mounting debt Hilton pitted a determined and stubborn effort which prevailed. In 1937 Hilton moved on to new horizons and the Sir Francis Drake in San Francisco, California. The San Francisco move proved to be only a stepping stone for further expansion across the United States. Among many other purchases during the war period, Conrad Hilton negotiated the purchase of two of Chicago's most famous hotels—the Palmer House and the Stevens (now the Conrad Hilton). Postwar found Hilton's chain stretching from California to New York, and in 1946 the Hilton Hotels Corporation was formed to consolidate the previously formed investment syndicates, which had provided the capital for the early hotel investments.

Shortly after the war Hilton Hotels International, a wholly owned subsidiary, was formed to expand the Hilton Corporation abroad. Since its inception, with the Caribe Hilton in Puerto Rico in 1947, the Hilton International has been highly successful. Undoubtedly, the success can be attributed to Conrad Hilton's basic overseas policies. First, hotels abroad are built and owned by the native government or foreign investors, with the Hilton Corporation providing the management. Second, Hilton maintains 20 to 25 year lease options and retains one-third of the profits.

In 1949 the Hilton Corporation acquired the most famous of all hotels, the Waldorf-Astoria. The Waldorf-Astoria not only enlarged the Hilton chain but also brought recognition to Hilton as owning one of the finest and most successful innkeeping corporations in America.

In 1955 Conrad Hilton topped his previous financial dealings when he bought controlling interest of the Statler Hotel chain, which consisted of ten notable hotels, at a cost of approximately $111 million. The importance of the Statler purchase, and thus the great expansion of the Hilton chain, is significant in that it brought the two largest hotel chains, Hilton and Sheraton, into direct competition. Since the Statler purchase, Hilton and Sheraton have been engaged in what one writer has termed ". . . a giant-scale game of checkers." The competition has been so intense that Sheraton and Hilton compete for business in 17 major U.S. cities.

The furious competition that Hilton faces from both Sheraton and the motel boom have brought new expansion of the traditional downtown hotel as well as the new Hilton Inn (motel line).

From the Texas Mobley to the present expansive international Hilton Hotel Corporation, Conrad Hilton's business guides of *esprit de corps* and maximum utilization of space have given the Hilton Hotel Corporation the reputation of excellence and luxury both in the U.S. and abroad.

Within the setting of the worldwide hotel industry, the Hilton Corporation is first, operating more rooms than any other chain. One of the basic measurements used to determine hotels' relative position in comparison to the industry is occupancy or the yearly percentage of rooms occupied. Hilton's average occupancy for domestic units declined again in 1962 to 61.6% compared with the previous 1961 rate of 63.8%. Hilton remained above the industry average rates for 1961 and 1962, which were respectively 62% and 61%.

With labor costs running at an all-time high for the hotel industry, 45% in 1963, Hilton was able to keep his cost level at 40%. In this year Hilton executive survey teams found cost savings amounting to two million dollars.

The bulk of operation revenue for the corporation comes from rooms and food and beverages; respectively, these two areas provide 42% and 45% of the company's operating revenue, with the remaining 13% divided among such areas as store and office building rentals, interest, and other services. Of prime importance to the hotel in drawing its revenue is the convention trade which accounts for approximately 30% of the occupancy of the corporation. The industry itself as a whole grabs off well over 50% of the convention business, which forms a substantial portion of hotel profits, accounting for 37% of the hotel occupancy.

The Hilton International Hotels have become an integrated part of Hilton's success plan. In 1961 overseas revenue only accounted for 18% of the total; in 1962 international revenue equaled 30% of the Hilton Corporation's total operating revenue (Figure 1.1). At the end of 1964, Hilton Hotels International showed an unprecedented lead over its closest overseas rival, Intercontinental Hotels, with 19. The Hilton International Hotels provide a substantial portion of business both domestically and abroad. In fact, this multiplier effect appears to be a dominant theme in Hilton's success plan: location of excellent hotels around the world to increase the business for all Hilton Hotels.

In 1962 Hilton's profits reached an all-time high of $17½ million.

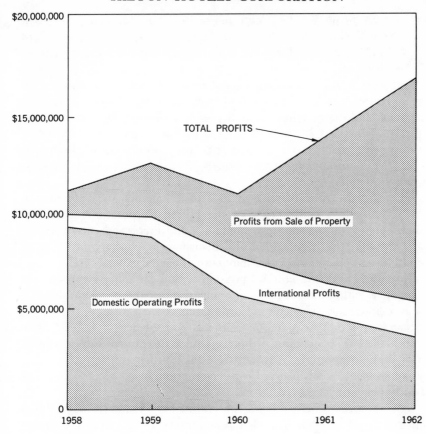

Figure 1.1
Profit Breakdown Analysis

SOURCE: *Forbes,* "Harried Host," May 1, 1963, p. 13.

However, $12 million came from nonoperating profits by sale of proper-
ties. This left Hilton's real operating profits down 6% of 1956 and 59%
lower than the operating profits in the peak year 1959. This large diver-
gence in percentages indicates the fact that Hilton's "net profits" in recent
years have been largely from nonoperating revenue. With industry profits
on the decline as a whole, Hilton book value per common share of stock
reached a new high of $30.28 because of profits on the sale of such
properties. By 1964 net profit from operations had declined to $4,402,549,
although it was an increase from $2,622,044 of 1963.

The high net profits that Hilton has been able to show coupled with
strong earnings per share and asset base per share because of the sale of
assets have increased the number of shareholders of the 3,843,000 shares
of outstanding common stock from 9,500 in 1961 to 12,000 in 1962. How-

ever, by 1964 the number had decreased to 10,500. Hilton's common stock on the New York Stock Exchange reached a new high of 18½ per share in April, 1964. By June, 1965, the stock was selling close to the high at 19⅞ per share.

The corporation's working capital in December, 1964, showed an increase from $22 million in 1963 to $32 million in 1964. In 1962 long-term refinancing and the merging of the Statler Corporation had increased the long-term debt from $86 million to $138 million. This heavy increase in long-term fixed debt, however, permitted the corporation to dispose of any of the nonprofitable Statler Hotels. By 1964 the long-term debt reached $150 million.

The earned surplus increase in 1962 to $75 million over $65 million in 1961 is largely a consequence of the Hilton Corporation's conscious financial policy of reducing asset holdings and increasing the operating capital through the lease option and management contract in order to extend Hilton's operations with a minimum of capital expenditures.

Any analysis of the Hilton's position within the industry would not be complete without at least a brief comparison of the corporation to its greatest competitor, the Sheraton Corporation.

Sheraton Hotel Corporation is the largest owner of hotels, while Hilton is the largest operator of hotels. Under the present rate of expansion of both corporations, it is hard to estimate their respective sizes because of so many hotels planned for construction, being constructed, and presently being finished.

The net profits before taxes for Hilton for 1962 were $27 million compared to $31 million for Sheraton. However, the after tax profits showed Sheraton at a loss after pushing the bulk of his earnings into depreciation using a double declining balance to provide a tax shelter for his profits. Hilton profits paid $1.50 per-share dividends in comparison to Sheraton's $.60 per-share dividends.

Occupancy trends for the two competitors for 1963 have shown Sheraton with a distinctively higher rate. In 1961 Sheraton maintained 70% compared to 64% for Hilton; in 1962, Sheraton occupancy declined as did both Hilton and the industry, but dropping farther and closing the gap between Sheraton and Hilton.

Sheraton and Hilton depend heavily upon the convention business for their revenues but theirs is substantially less than the industry average of 37%. Sheraton draws 25% of his business from conventions compared to Hilton's dependence upon approximately 30%. It should be noted that both corporations in their current building are providing large facilities for convention trade.

Over the past five years, Hilton and Sheraton have been divergent in their financial policies. Hilton has chosen to reduce his asset investment and operate hotels on a lease basis, spreading his chain internationally while maintaining high dividend payments to his stockholders. Sheraton, just getting started internationally, continues to increase his asset base by plowing back profits (instead of large dividends) and providing a tax cover by rapid depreciation. It has been stated that the competition between Sheraton and Hilton involves deploying assets and exercising innkeeping skill.

As the Hilton history reveals, the corporation has owned and/or operated some of the largest and most famous hotels in the world. Within the industry Hilton has maintained a reputation as the leader in its field mainly because of its flexibility in dealing with the problems at hand. The objectives of the Hilton Corporation remain the same, but a change is detected in the Hilton management policy as stated by Conrad Hilton:

As we are primarily hotel operators, we are endeavoring to increase return on invested capital by spreading available investment dollars over the largest number of suitable properties in a world-wide network. This goal can be furthered through partnerships, leaseholds, and management contracts rather than concentrating investment dollars in large equity ownerships in major hotels. This principle has been proven by the fact that the corporation receives its highest percentage return on invested capital from those hotels abroad which are built by others to Hilton's specifications and operated for a percentage of the profits.

Presently, Hilton Corporation faces many problems—those which are inherent to the industry and those peculiar to the corporation itself.

Basically, the accommodations industry, including both hotels and motels, is suffering from overexpansion. The recent expansion and upgrading of motels and motor courts have greatly increased the competition for the hotel industry. A tremendous amount of building has been taking place within the industry. In order to meet the competition the hotel industry has built new hotels in order to increase available rooms. Between 1948 and 1964 about 616,000 rooms have been added to the hotel-motel market, but on the average less than 2,500 additional have been sold each day.

The overexpansion caused an industrywide occupancy decline for both hotels and motels up to 1963. Hotels, hardest hit, dropped from a high in 1946 of 93% to 61% in 1962 but increased to 63.5% in 1963 and 64.3% in 1964. Motels, feeling the effects also, declined from 74% in 1957 to 69% in 1962 and to 64.8% in 1963, but increased to 65.7% in 1964. Total rooms available were 2,470,000 with average occupancy at only 1,578,000 (Figure 1.2).

The importance of high occupancy rates for Hilton to maintain successful operations is self-explanatory; however, overexpansion of the industry is not the full story of recent occupancy declines. The modern jet

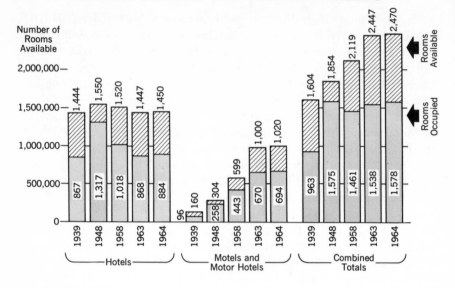

Figure 1.2
The Increase in Available Rooms and the Trend of Occupancy Showing in Thousands Average Number of Rooms Available and Occupied per Day
Source: Harris, Kerr, Forster & Company, *Trends in the Hotel-Motel Business,* 1964, p. 2. Based on U.S. Census Bureau Data with 1964 Estimated by H.K.F.

age has cut executives' hotel stays as businessmen are able to make swift flights and quick connections.

The convention trade, inadvertently accounting for 37% of hotel business, is now being grabbed off by many convention sites being built by local cities. A prime example is Chicago's McCormick Place which has cut into convention trade for both the Conrad Hilton and the Palmer House. The facts are that 20 years ago there were only 32 major convention cities. Today there are at least 62—with an increase of only 10% in the number of conventions. To Hilton, who derives 30% of his business from conventions, the competition has become extremely vigorous.

The recent tax laws concerning expense accounts have also reduced hotel food and beverage income. In addition, fewer businessmen are traveling in groups. This legislation cuts deeply into Hilton's food services, which account for 45% of his revenue.

The problems of overexpansion and increased competition will undoubtedly cause the failure of many of the older hotels, particularly those not supported by sound capital structures. Many of the hotels will, as the profit squeeze becomes more severe, become "residential" or semi-apartment buildings. It is estimated that at least one-fourth of the 80,000 hotels and motels will fold before the industry as a whole is stable once again.

The hotel industry is in a peculiar dilemma. The years after the Second World War brought huge profits which were not plowed back into capital improvements. With the declining physical plants of many downtown hotels and the population trend toward the suburbs, the new and modern motel has found a place in the accommodation market. Presently, the prevailing attitude of the public demands renovation of the many downtown hotels when the profits of these hotels are being strained. Not only are many hotels in need of renovation, but they must also provide more and more services to meet the motel competition.

The Hilton Corporation faces certain problems which are peculiar to the corporation itself and not necessarily inherent in the industry. Occupancy, and consequently profits, has declined as the industry has outstripped the market. Hilton has traditionally operated some of the largest hotels in cities all over the United States. Today, the larger hotels are finding it harder to maintain high occupancy rates because of the larger number of rooms to fill (Table 1.1). It is true that the larger hotels hold quite an edge in total occupancy, but this does not negate the fact that the larger hotels are in a weaker position compared with the smaller ones and must spend greater sums to attract a proportionate percentage of customers. Certainly Hilton's larger size hotels contribute to his occupancy problems and may in part explain his occupancy lag compared to the Sheraton Corporation. Hilton domestic hotels average 750 rooms to 500 rooms per Sheraton Hotel.

The problems of occupancy have a multiplied effect on Hilton corporate profits as a whole when it is realized that occupancy generates food and beverage income, which, as noted before, accounts for 45% of the revenue of the corporation. For every $1 earned in rooms, $1.06 is brought in from foods and services; and conversely, for every $1 lost in occupancy, $1.06 is lost in food and beverages. Hilton Corporation employs thousands of skilled food personnel and has millions of dollars invested in equipment. In order to maintain profits on this side of the corporation, Hilton must devise ways of drawing the dining market to its restaurants during periods of declining occupancy.

The importance of the convention trade to Hilton has already been cited as accounting for a very high percentage of Hilton's profits. In the recent expansion by the corporation, modern and up-to-date convention facilities have been incorporated to increase the chain's share of convention business; however, with the growing competition Hilton has been losing a portion of this important revenue. Hilton must either maintain his present volume of convention trade, which seems improbable, or find other uses for his facilities.

Perhaps one of the biggest problems facing Hilton Hotels is that of greater geographical competition. One factor which has made the competition keener is our modern transportation facilities. More important, how-

Table 1.1
OCCUPANCY AND ROOM RATES
Large Hotels Compared With Small Hotels

	Average No. of Rooms Per Hotel	Percentage of Occupancy			Average Rate Per Room Per Day		
		1964	1963	Variation	1964	1963	Variation
163 Hotels with more than 300 Rooms per Hotel	661	64.1%	62.7%	+2.2%	$12.70	$12.37	+2.7%
137 Hotels with 300 Rooms or less per Hotel	179	58.7	58.9	– .3	9.13	8.88	+2.8
Total for 300 Transient Hotels	441	63.1%	61.9%	+1.9%	$12.08	$11.75	+2.8%

SOURCE: Harris, Kerr, Forster & Company, *Trends in the Hotel-Motel Business*, 1964, p. 18.

ever, are the peripheral motels which are even moving into the downtown areas. The modern motel poses a special threat to Hilton because of the comparative low cost of building the appealing "inns." With the cost of building motels greatly reduced compared to that of hotels, the prospects of avoiding competition with them are few. With smaller financial backing required, motels will undoubtedly become more numerous and siphon some of Hilton's business, even though the hotels may provide greater services at more nominal costs.

All of this only tends to increase the necessity for the renovation and face lifting of some of Hilton's older hotels. Along with this the corporation recognizes that some of the older hotels must be sold and new structures erected in strategic positions in order to keep up with the changing attitudes of the public.

In the realm of finances Hilton has become more and more dependent upon profits and has come to rely less on large capital assets. The modern hotel strategy, revolving around the "lease" and management contract which Hilton employs, does not require the tremendous asset backing but depends more upon hotel operating skill—and hence profits. Although the corporation's current position is very sound, the outstanding long-term debt could pose difficult refinancing problems if occupancy and profits continue to decline. It seems evident that there is a definite need to reduce these fixed obligations to meet the prevalent declining profit situation (Table 1.2).

Three important comparison ratios pinpoint Hilton's financial problems. First, the operating ratio, the proportion of operating expenses to sales, indicates an increase in operating expenses from 95% in 1961 to 96% in 1962. This indicates that even though Hilton is cutting costs, his proportionate costs are rising.

Second is the ratio of long-term debt to total assets, which shows the percentage of senior claims against the entire business. This important ratio, although not an indicator of earnings, may indicate the declining credit position of the corporation.

The equity ratio, or "risk-bearing" ratio (net worth to total assets), indicates to some degree the risk involved in Hilton's methods of financing. In general, the lower the ratio of net worth to total assets, the greater the risk in the method of finance. Certainly to stockholders and future buyers this will act as a deterrent. More important, however, are the prospects of corporate failure.

The future of the Hilton Hotels Corporation is certainly founded on the basis of the world economy. Domestically, the occupancy problem cannot be overlooked, and Hilton must find new ways of maintaining the corporation's share of the market. The competition for convention trade has become so intense that Hilton is in no position to try and compete with the new and modern municipal facilities. Perhaps the manage-

Table 1.2
HILTON HOTELS FIVE-YEAR SUMMARY

Operating Results for Years Ended December 31,	1964	1963	1962	1961	1960
Gross revenue	$183,899,810	178,490,877	189,286,833	202,688,769	202,100,170
Operating costs and expenses	141,890,541	137,789,965	143,784,601	152,596,874	150,651,231
Lease rentals	7,837,648	7,703,140	7,612,736	13,196,475	12,439,828
Depreciation and amortization	14,280,720	13,182,419	12,584,759	11,077,492	10,802,755
Interest expense (net)	6,461,277	6,495,899	5,948,591	3,243,229	2,799,717
Property taxes	8,469,318	8,152,409	8,476,036	8,470,241	7,959,818
Corporate expenses, etc.	1,772,152	1,598,431	2,495,972	2,936,703	2,880,148
Income from Hilton Credit Corporation	1,583,143	767,811	—	—	—
Profit before income taxes	4,771,297	4,336,425	8,384,138	11,167,755	14,566,673
Income taxes	—	1,804,957	4,269,028	6,187,154	8,521,760
Minority interests profit (or loss)	368,748	(90,576)	(72,509)	(3,553)	—
Net profit from operations	4,402,549	2,622,044	4,187,619	4,984,154	6,044,913
Earnings per common share*	1.24	.74	1.03	1.18	1.46
Net profit (or loss) from property sales	(2,268,820)	890,021	11,932,372	7,177,422	2,247,028
Earnings per common share including profit (or loss) from property sales*	.60	.99	4.13	3.07	2.06

Financial Position at Year End	1964	1963	1962	1961	1960
Current assets	56,419,178	53,610,278	50,235,168	40,746,160	46,399,029
Current liabilities	23,550,340	31,416,655	26,921,756	24,658,177	24,820,530
Working capital	32,868,838	22,193,623	23,313,412	16,087,983	21,578,499
Fixed assets	193,048,121	192,005,229	196,818,766	147,768,623	144,408,751
Total assets	276,920,030	274,377,367	273,344,990	219,910,361	221,891,466
Long term debt	150,135,219	142,826,191	133,238,935	86,386,861	87,003,105
Common shareholders equity	99,683,400	95,571,965	108,716,274	98,735,318	85,963,747
Equity per common share	28.13	26.97	28.28	26.04	23.04

General Information at Year End					
Number of common shares outstanding	3,544,066	3,544,067	3,843,612	3,790,988	3,731,228
Number of common shareholders	10,500	11,773	11,740	8,663	7,456
Number of hotels	33	34	33	33	29
Number of employees	20,500	19,800	20,900	23,800	23,500

° After preferred dividends paid.

ment contract for operating these facilities might be a more profitable policy. The next five years of operations for many hotels will be a period of retrenchment and to some extent economic retreat as the industry waits for the occupancy rate to catch up with the present accommodations available. In spite of the many problems of competition and occupancy, however, Hilton Hotels Corporation has the inherent advantage of a large size chain and can weather industrywide difficulties with greater ease as compared to many of the smaller chains and independent hotels.

	Percentage of Occupancy			Average Room Rate		
	1962	1961	Variation	1962	1961	Variation
Hotels With More Than 300 Rooms	64.3%	66.1%	−2.7%	12.11	11.92	+1.6%
Hotels With Less Than 300 Rooms	58.3%	58.9%	−1.0%	8.41	8.31	+1.2%
Totals	63.0%	64.6%	−2.5%	11.39	11.22	+1.5%

Figure 1.3
Occupancy and Room Rates—Large Hotels Compared With Small
SOURCE: Harris, Kerr, Foster & Company, *Trends in the Hotel-Motel Business*, 1962, p. 18.

FOR DISCUSSION

1. What is the dilemma facing the hotel industry?
2. What are the specific causes of occupancy decline in Hilton Hotels?
3. How has Hilton been able to maintain an increase in book value?
4. What administrative decisions were made to solve the problem of competition? Do you agree with the decisions?

SUGGESTED READING

Annual Report 1964.
"By Golly," *Time*, July 19, 1963, pp. 66-68.
"Harried Host," *Forbes*, May 1, 1963, pp. 13-14.
"Too Many Rooms at the Inn," *Time*, January 11, 1963, p. 83.
"Will There Be Tourists To Keep Them All Full," *Business Week*, November 2, 1963, p. 108.

CHAPTER 2

General Electric

GENERAL ELECTRIC COMPANY is by far the largest domestic manufacturer of electrical equipment. It also holds a strong position in the fields of electronics and atomic energy. Through Canadian General Electric and International General Electric, representation is world-wide.

General Electric dates back to October, 1878, when a group of investors joined together to finance Thomas Edison's experiments with the incandescent lamp. The original Edison General Electric Company was formed to finance innovation. This emphasis on innovation has remained a hallmark of the company since that time. On April 15, 1892, a number of pioneer companies in the electrical field were incorporated as the General Electric Company. Their headquarters were at the former Edison General Electric Company in Schenectady, New York.

An interesting measurable yardstick for the company's growth in the past is the growth curve of the use of electricity in the U.S. Statistically, the use of electricity has doubled every decade since the 1880's and has grown three times as fast as the nation's economy. Instead of leveling off after over 80 years, the electrical industry is actually growing faster than ever. Ralph J. Cordiner describes this growth as "the benign circle of electric power." He goes on to explain:

A turbine generator installed in a power station makes possible the sale of more lamps, appliances, motors, and other users of power. And as more people buy lamps, appliances and so on, they create the need for another turbine generator and more transmission equipment. Thus, each new use of electricity accelerates the turn of the circle—creating a bigger potential market for General Electric products, not only in end use equipment, but in equipment to produce, transmit, and distribute electric power.

It is not hard to see why General Electric became a diversified product company early in its history.

Up until 1939 the company was able to operate efficiently under a highly centralized form of management. During the Second World War, however, G.E. began a period of almost explosive growth resulting in a change in organizational structure. The need to develop capable leaders for the future, the need for more friendly and cooperative relationships between managers and other employees, the need to stay ahead of competition in serving customers, and the need to make the work of a manager at all echelons of the organization more manageable resulted in decentralization. The company's work is carried on by over 100 decentralized product manufacturing departments (each equivalent to a $30 or $40 million company). The man chiefly responsible for the "new General Electric" was Ralph J. Cordiner, who retired as an officer and director in December, 1963. The director's salute to Mr. Cordiner from the *1963 Annual Report* seems to best express his work for the company:

The company has been strengthened by his planned decentralization of its organizational structure and by his planned diversification into new markets and technologies. With modern facilities, sound organization, dedicated employees, and intensively trained leadership, the "new General Electric" built by Ralph Cordiner is positioned for continued profitable growth and service.

Newly-appointed Fred J. Borch now occupies the position of president and chief executive officer of General Electric with Gerald L. Phillippe as chairman of the board.

Due to the company's wide diversification, it competes with hundreds of large corporations. In 1963 four product categories showed the following percentages of sales:

Consumer products	26%
Industrial components and materials	28%
Heavy capital goods	24%
Defense and aerospace products	22%

In the diversified electrical equipment market G.E. is a leader in profitability, its major competitors being Radio Corporation of America, Westinghouse, and McGraw-Edison. The January 1, 1965, issue of *Forbes* ranks these three companies in terms of growth, profitability, and trend. The following table lists the results:

GROWTH (5-year compounded rate)

	Sales	Earnings	Group rating
G.E.	2.9%	0.4%	1
Westinghouse	1.8%	Decline	2
McGraw-Edison	7.2%	Decline	3
R.C.A.	7.5%	10.5%	4

PROFITABILITY (5-year average)

	Return of equity	Cash flow to equity	Operational profit margin	Group rating
G.E.	15.5%	22.9%	12.6%	1
R.C.A.	12.0%	21.3%	7.8%	2
McGraw-Edison	9.1%	13.8%	11.2%	3
Westinghouse	6.6%	12.2%	7.8%	4

TREND (latest 12 months vs. 3-year average)

	Earnings	Net profit margin	Group rating
R.C.A.	+56.4%	+1.3%	1
McGraw-Edison	+27.1%	+0.5%	2
Westinghouse	+16.9%	+0.2%	3
G.E.	+ 7.2%	+0.3%	4

The color television market controlled by R.C.A. is just one example of why General Electric can never let down its rigid policies of cost control and research and development. R.C.A. and Westinghouse are both after the same prize, surpassing G.E. in performance. Other General Electric competitors include Zenith, Magnavox, Admiral, Motorola, Whirlpool, and Sunbeam, which are mainly appliance producers. Among specialty producers, Minneapolis-Honeywell Regulator, McGraw-Edison, and Singer are its main competitors.

General Electric's 1964 sales were up 4% over those for 1963. This is a new peak for the third consecutive year. Sales for 1964 totaled $4,941,-352,000 with a profit of $237,333,000.

Sales of consumer goods in 1963 captured 26% of total sales. Two main reasons were customer acceptance of new products, such as the electric slicing knife, lightweight portable T.V., attractive new designs in appliances; and increasing confidence in General Electric as a source of reliable products backed by "good after-sale service." In addition, warranty service calls declined for the fifth straight year.

The industrial components and materials area of the company's business maintained the 28% of sales from the previous year. Newer businesses, such as computers, advanced controls for machine tools, Lexan plastics, and silicone chemicals swelled the volume of sales that had been built on such established lines as component motors, appliance controls, and lamp ballasts.

Sales of heavy capital goods, both to the utilities and to industry, increased 1% in 1963 over 1962, despite the continuing downward pressure from further lowering of price levels at which sales were billed. Constant pressure from foreign producers, who were enjoying low labor costs, resulted in strict competitive pricing. General Electric strives for quality with reductions in cost of operations rather than reducing quality to meet competition.

Volume of defense business dropped almost 8% mainly because of government cutbacks in the aerospace field. This resulted in about a 2% drop in total sales which was 22% in 1963 and 24% in 1962.

Net earnings increased to $270,638,756 or $3 per share of stock. The 1962 net earnings were approximately $265.8 million or $2.97 per share of stock. Low price levels continued to hold down earnings improvement;

but cost-saving programs kept earnings from percentage of sales at 5.5% in 1963, the same as in 1962.

On November 15, 1963, the Board of Directors declared a dividend of $.55 a share payable on January 25, 1964. This brought 1963 dividends declared to $2.05 a share. The $.55 quarterly dividend is equivalent to an annual rate of $2.20 per share. Total 1963 dividends declared were a record $183.1 million. Dividends paid in 1963 were $2 per share.

The problems confronting the big corporations, such as G.E., are vast and often baffling. We can start with General Electric's planned diversification. With each of the four product areas contributing roughly a quarter of total sales in any given year, one obvious reason for diversification is evident. Short-range downturns for any one business area have not kept the company from continuing its overall growth and momentum. There are, however, other less evident reasons. "The benign circle of electric power" is one of these reasons. Along with a vast commercial product market General Electric carries on a vast program of technical research in the defense and aerospace market. The highly technical and risk enterprises of the space programs are often too much for a small enterprise. G.E.'s size and scope give it a certain invulnerability to occasional failure that might be ruinous to a smaller company, but work in space projects even confronts General Electric with problems of spacious magnitude both in science and management. The scientific aspect is self-evident; but the key to success lies in a smooth integration of the work of physicists, chemists, mathematicians, astronomers, engineers, and other scientists often working in physically distant laboratories. Their work must be planned and controlled so that all the pieces of research fit together for the achievement of a common end.

G.E. must also solve the problems of communication between management and the scientist. Some of the company's middle rank and experienced managers wonder whether these new-bred scientists can be managed and then learn to manage, or whether they will simply go on enhancing their specialized knowledge and vocabulary until they can converse only with computers.

General Electric limits space and defense work to one quarter of total business both for financial reasons and the maintenance of its independence of government. While government research and development contracts allow a fee of between 5 and 7%, half of that goes for taxes. Net profit for government work runs to no more than 2 or 3%. General Electric has no intention of getting in the position of North American Aviation, which engaged almost entirely in defense work making a profit of 2.2% on sales in 1961. Research and development contracts commonly provide a cost-plus-fixed-fee arrangement. The fee is fixed in advance. If costs overrun estimates, the government pays. This arrangement tends to slow up completion of work, and companies often underbid knowing that the government will cover the added expense. General Electric prefers competitive contracts in which close cost control determines the margin of profit. Despite the drawbacks and booby traps in space projects, the company has done very well in this market.

Moving to another problem area, the great "Electrical Conspiracy" has been a well-publicized facet of G.E.'s history. No company has suffered more in public esteem. There is little to say about the price-fixing incident that hasn't been said before. At present, all pending antitrust damage suits brought by the government have been settled; and based on price adjustments used in these agreements, the company is in the process of settling cases with electric utility customers.

Another baffling problem confronting General Electric is the unusually low prices of most of General Electric's products. The past few years have seen erosion in prices so that in 1963 producer goods were, on the average, selling at the 1953 price levels and consumer goods at 1950 levels. Since 1950, however, compensation per employee has risen 104% and the price of materials 35%. Despite aggressive cost reductions, earnings have been held back. General Electric strives for cost reduction, not by cuts in quality, but rather by managerial and technical innovations aimed at more productive work performance and more efficient use of materials.

Still another problem, partially linked with the previously mentioned one, is foreign competition. Foreign competitors enjoy lower labor costs, tax, and other differentials. Costs at General Electric must be scaled down proportionately. New steps are being taken toward increased automation. A stronger link is being established between research and development and the wants and needs of customers.

The final problem confronts every company—large or small. The January, 1963, issue of *Dun's Review and Modern Industry* asked a number of top executives the basic question: What do you consider is the prime task of management today in order to keep a well-managed company going? Their near unanimous choice of prime tasks was "developing more men of judgment, imagination, and ambition to staff the middle ranks of management and perhaps become the leaders of tomorrow." Employee development will always be a major task of management at General Electric. The extensive training programs and rigorous advanced management courses for executives prove this point to be true. Competent middle-management leaders are especially crucial to a decentralized corporation like this one.

In essence, the principal problem areas of diversification, competition, and management will require more attention as the American economy increases its demands for more electrical products and equipment.

FOR DISCUSSION

1. What was the nature of the executive decisions which were necessary after 1939? Why do you think these were necessary?
2. What are the general problems peculiar to any large corporation such as General Electric?
3. What are the specific objectives of General Electric's limitation of space and defense work?
4. In your opinion, what is General Electric's most pressing problem? Would you say that the firm is proceeding in the proper manner toward a solution?

SUGGESTED READING

Cordiner, Ralph J., *New Frontiers For Professional Managers*, New York, McGraw-Hill, 1956.
"General Electric Astride Two Worlds," *Fortune*, June, 1962, pp. 126-133.
"Incredible Electrical Conspiracy," *Fortune* (Part I), April, 1961, pp. 132-137; (Part II), May, 1961, pp. 161-164.
"The Ten Best Managed Companies," *Dun's Review and Modern Industry*, January, 1963.

Honeywell, Incorporated

In 1964 HONEYWELL commemorated its 79th year in business. The company traces its inception back to an invention of Alfred Butz. He created a gadget to operate the dampers of a coal-fired furnace or boiler in response to the demands of a room thermostat. After working over two years on the device, he came up with a workable version. In 1885 the patent was granted and immediately the Consolidated Temperature Controlling Company was organized by a group of investment-minded backers. Even though the Butz patent was valid, there was the possibility of patent litigation and infringement battles; so the new company decided to buy the bothersome ones outright or enter into a cross-licensing agreement. They bought most of them. Later, an eastern competitor was found who had a mechanical part that would greatly improve the Butz device if it could be incorporated into it. Consequently, in 1890 they bought the Guion Automatic Heat Regulating Company.

During this period, the name of the company was changed to the Electric Thermostat Company. It concentrated on damper motor units and bought the thermostats in partially assembled parts and completely assembled them in Minneapolis. From two to five people were employed.

The company, however, was steadily losing money. This was mainly because furnace manufacturers were, in general, not making lift dampers that could be easily adapted to the new innovation; and there was little inclination to change just to oblige an upstart industry.

Then W. R. Sweatt arrived on the scene and changed the small company's future. Sweatt, a banker, took the position of secretary-treasurer (without pay). He completely reorganized the company in 1894 under the name of Electric Heat Regulator Company. He also went personally to the furnace manufacturers to persuade them to change their design, the results being that all were providing dampers suitable for regulators within a few years. The company started to grow and expand. In 1920 a new era was initiated. Previously, the major emphasis of the company was on coal-fired equipment; but from 1920 on it was on controls for automatic firing with coal, gas, and oil.

An interesting note at this point is that as early as 1920, the company (today known as Honeywell) was by far the sales leader in the industry. Their sales of damper controls were more than 300,000 units. The combined sales of all other competitors were only about 75,000 units. This lead has never been lost.

In 1927 another significant event took place that affected the company and the entire heating industry. The Minneapolis Heat Regulator Company (the name had been changed again) and one of its competitors decided to merge into a single company—Minneapolis-Honeywell Regulator Company. The competitive company was the Honeywell Heating Specialties Company of Wabash, Indiana. It was started in 1906 by Mark Honeywell and by the early 1920's was offering stiff competition to the Minneapolis firm.

Both companies had enjoyed sound growth and profitable operations. At the time of the merger, Minneapolis Heat Regulator Company sales totaled about $3 million a year and Honeywell Heating and Specialty Company's about $1,500,000. This growth was continued after the merger along with diversification. The number of Honeywell's employees has grown from 1,500 at the time of the merger to about 49,000 in 1963. The Minneapolis home office has mushroomed to factories in 12 American cities and 7 foreign countries; 116 sales and service offices in the United States, 50 in the rest of the world; and distributors in 46 foreign countries.

Today, the world views Honeywell (in August, 1963, Minneapolis-Honeywell was shortened to Honeywell) as the largest and most sophisticated manufacturer of automatic control systems. It turns out 13,000 products so diverse that they encompass a $.60 microswitch and a $3 million electronic data processing system. It makes controls for chemical production, oil refining, food processing, nuclear reactors, dry cleaning, medicine, and aircraft and missile design. Basically, Honeywell's products fall into four principal categories: (1) controls for residential heating systems; (2) instruments for indicating, recording, and controlling process variables such as flow, humidity, pressure, and temperature; (3) high-speed computers and electronic data processing equipment for business, industrial, scientific, and government use; (4) various controls and inertial guidance systems for missiles and space vehicles and automatic electronic flight controls for manned aircraft. Even though Honeywell is subject to active competition in all lines of products, it is the largest producer in the United States of number 1 and 2 listed. Its competitors are, generally speaking, engaged in business on a nationwide scale.

Honeywell's position in the industry is not an easy one to specifically classify. The United States Commerce Department lists several categories in the controls industry such as; "control equipment, electric"; "control panels, electric"; "control transformers," etc. However, there is no all-encompassing category for automatic controls; hence, it is virtually impossible to gauge the size of the industry from government statistics. The absence of any trade association which would normally compile statistics is also a handicap in putting a dollar size on the industry.

By extrapolating and making assumptions from data compiled by *Electronics Magazine*'s Market Service Department, the following "total sales" for 1962 have been compiled.

Electronic hardware for control systems	$ 780,000,000
Controls and control systems for the Fed. Govt.	$ 4,800,000
Mechanically and pneumatically operated controls and systems	$1,300,000,000
Design construction and installation charges	$ 24,000,000
Industry total	$2,108,800,000

The near $596 million sales of Honeywell in 1962 shows the company capturing about 28% of the total market. When compared with chief competitors like Controls Company of America and Taylor Instruments, it is quite a substantial portion. Controls Company sales for 1962 were about $53 million or about 2.5% of the industry; Taylor Instruments with $42 million showed only 2% of the industry totals.

Thus, it appears that Honeywell is by far the largest in the industry. No one will dispute that it is the largest; however, one must be quite cautious of just how large these figures show it to be. Since Honeywell is so widely diversified, some of their products can be classified in other areas. Also, the total dollar sales of the entire industry are a variable estimate; therefore, only relatively general relationships should be made from the above figures.

A breakdown of Honeywell's 1962 sales shows about 40% going to the military and 60% to nonmilitary areas. Of the 60% nonmilitary, one-third of the sales were heating controls.

Most of the problems of Honeywell today are also the problems of the whole controls industry. There is a rapidly growing trend toward decreased size and increased complexity of controls. In simple household appliances, for example, the complexity has moved from "on-off" to "spin," "agitate," "lukewarm," and "tepid." Space capsules magnify a thousand-fold these complexities. The implication of decreased size and increased sophistication for manufacturers of automatic control devices are potentially higher profit margins, but higher labor costs and more costly research and development expenditures will be incurred too.

Thus, a major problem facing Honeywell as well as the entire industry is who is to pay for the lengthy studies which entail highly skilled and paid talent. Research at Honeywell has produced such new developments as infrared sensing tubes that can detect a frying pan's heat from five miles away. Previously, something like this would then be sold to the government for use in antimissiles or the like; but today, the trend is away from the companies selling the results of their research and toward user-sponsored studies. For example, a chemical company may hire a designer of control systems to work out a complicated array of instruments to run a fully automated plant. This technique seems to be working well, but more time is needed to get an accurate evaluation of its worth.

Honeywell has had few problems with government interference. The only trouble in the last few years has been a conviction in late 1963 on price fixing. Honeywell, Johnson Service Company of Milwaukee, Powers Regulator Company of Skokie, Illinois, and five of their executives were convicted on charges of conspiring to fix prices and restrict competition in the pneumatic temperature control field. Fines totaled $180,000. Of that amount, Honeywell's fine was $40,000 and two of their executives were fined a total of $35,000. Since the conviction was against only one division of Honeywell, it had little effect on the company as a whole.

Today, Honeywell sees its greatest future in automation. Its computers division represents the biggest single investment in a product Honeywell has ever made, but this division has also caused more trouble than any other division in the past. For example, in 1962 alone, $15 million in computer revenues covered only 55% of the $27 million cash expenditures; and 1962 showed much higher computer revenues than previous years even though expenditures have been rather constant. Honeywell's caution with its computer division has held cash investments in computers to $27 million yearly.

Investments to the end of 1963 were just under $150 million. Since it takes years to put enough computers out on lease to generate a profitable operation, capital burden was anticipated by Honeywell's board; however, bearing the burden alone was not. In 1955 Honeywell joined forces with Raytheon to organize Datamatic Corporation. In 1957 Honeywell was forced to buy out its data processing partner because, to quote the treasurer of Honeywell, Russel Laxson: "We weren't sure from one month to the next if they would come up with the needed cash." Since 1957 Honeywell has had to float $80 million worth of debentures, $50 million in 1957 and $30 million more in August of 1963. This increasing capitalization to invest in a losing division has diluted earnings.

	1959	1960	1961	1962	1963	1964
NET INCOME	29.4	26.2	24.9	26.9	34.7	41.4
SALES	381.4	426.2	470.2	595.9	648.5	667.1
$\dfrac{\text{Net Income}}{\text{Sales}}$	7.8%	6.2%	5.3%	4.5%	5.3%	6.2%

Net income and sales are expressed in millions of dollars.
SOURCE: *1964 Honeywell Annual Report.*

The figures for 1963 (above) indicate a possible end to the computer drain on profits. Figures for 1964 reflect more positive evidence of advances in sales and earnings level of computer systems.

In examining the other computer manufacturers, it becomes evident that Honeywell is not alone with computer troubles. As a matter of fact, only IBM has made money in the computer business. This is mainly due to their volume advantage resulting from patents which just recently expired. At the end of 1962 Honeywell, as far as number of computers sold was concerned, did not outdo its competitors by any means.

Industrial process computers show Honeywell in a rather poor position too. From 1958 to 1962, 205 industrial computers had been installed worldwide. Honeywell with 8 was seventh behind leaders like Thompson Ramo Wooldridge (56), GE (42), and IBM (22).

The future is looking better for Honeywell though. EDP operations in 1964 showed major gains. Total computer systems shipments exceeded $100 million in sales value, the highest annual figure yet achieved by this division. Contributing to this growth was the Honeywell 200 system, which was announced in late 1963 and which has already achieved a high level of sales success in this competitive industry. Recently, this division announced a new large-scale computer called the H-2200, compatible in programming with competitive computers made by International Business Machines Corporation. (It has also added a new Honeywell-developed card reader that features high-speed, improved reliability, optical sensing, and table-top accessibility; a full complement of communication controls; an array of family interface switches that permit peripheral devices to be switched between computers; and control units for magnetic ink character reading devices.) In addition, under the Honeywell concept of one family of peripheral devices for all systems, total computer capability can be expanded conveniently and efficiently in two directions: vertically, by adding new computers, such as the H-2200; and horizontally, by adding new peripheral devices and capabilities. These announcements represent a significant advance in Honeywell's line of data-processing equipment, establishing Honeywell as a major influence in electronic data processing.

Thus, Honeywell's strong position in growing areas and its ability to benefit from the trend toward industrial automation make Honeywell's future look very attractive. However, the company is still facing a tremendous capital investment problem through its decision to diversify into the computer-system field accompanied by the internal problem of decreased size and increased complexity of their controls.

FOR DISCUSSION

1. Many of Honeywell's problems are shared by the whole controls industry. What are these problems?
2. What problem does Honeywell face as a result of its increased research?
3. In what does Honeywell's strength lie?
4. Evaluate the solutions management has come up with for specific problems. Can you suggest any other solutions?

SUGGESTED READING

"Honeywell Offers Debentures," *Commercial & Financial Chronical*, August 12, 1963, p. 572.
"Just Plain Honeywell," *Time*, August 30, 1963, p. 57.
"New Challenge to IBM," *Business Week*, December 7, 1963, p. 30.

Hallicrafters Company

FOUNDED BY WILLIAM HALLIGAN IN 1933, the Hallicrafters Company was originally a one-man operation—manufacturing amateur radio equipment. Up until the beginning of the Second World War, Hallicrafters produced short-wave equipment for amateur radio operators, the Federal Communications Commission, airlines, and police forces. During the war, Hallicrafters changed over to the production of special military equipment. Since then, the company has been primarily interested in the production of military and aerospace equipment.

Because the company was consistently losing money, the Halligan family sold Hallicrafters to the Penn-Texas Corporation in 1956. The company was operated as a 100% subsidiary of Penn-Texas until December, 1957, when all common stock was sold back to the Halligan family for $2 million. After taking over for the second time, William Halligan instituted a rigid quality control system. The company has consistently shown a profit since then.

Hallicrafters' administrative, research, and engineering facilities are located in Chicago, Illinois. Also located in Chicago are separate plants for the production of large military equipment, short-run military equipment, and commercial products. In addition, Chicago is the site of the Quick Reaction Capability Support Laboratory. At this plant, facilities are placed at the disposal of the Air Force for the performance of high-priority contracts on short notice.

Military electronic forms the base of Hallicrafters' activities. In 1962 government contracts accounted for approximately 75% of net sales. The nucleus of the Military Communications Division is Manson Laboratories, Incorporated, a subsidiary which was acquired in 1961 (other divisions—Figure 2.1).

The earnings pattern of the Hallicrafters Company is unstable. For the fiscal year ending August 31, 1963, net income was about $1,500,000—a drop of 17.6% from the previous year. Up to this time net income had been increasing consistently since 1958. For the third quarter of the fiscal year ending May 31, 1964, earnings fell to $105,000, or $.04 a share, from $550,000, or $.21 a share, a year earlier. Sales of the producer of electronic equipment and electric organs declined to $9,824,000 from $15,072,000. In the first nine months of 1964, the company had a $758,000 loss because of a sizable deficit in the first half. This compares with a profit of $1,529,000, or $.60 a share, the year before. Sales dropped to $28,896,000 from $49,204,000.

In the middle of 1963 Hallicrafters borrowed $3,400,000 under a seven year 4¾% note from the First National Bank of Chicago. The company also arranged for $4 million of unsecured credit at the same bank. The loan was used to retire a previous V loan—a government loan on business contracted to Hallicrafters. The long-term debt has gone from about $80,000 in 1962 to over $3 million in 1963. Total assets did not differ significantly in these two years.

The price of Hallicrafters' stock reached an all-time high of $29 a share in 1961. The low for the period between 1953 and 1962 was $10 a share; however, the price in June, 1965, was only $8½ a share. This sharp drop in price is not characteristic of just the Hallicrafters Company. Most electronics stocks are deflated in comparison with their peak of a few years ago; for example, Texas Instruments a few years ago hit a high of 256¼ compared to the recent price of $81 per share.

The Bureau of Labor Statistics predicts a 7% annual growth rate for the electronics industry. The growth rate over the last ten years has been 15% per year. This decrease in the growth rate will come about because of a decrease in demand for electronics products by the government. The high growth rate for the industry over the last ten years has been a result of the cost of getting the missile program off the ground. The government will probably discontinue some of its crash programs for space projects, causing a slower growth rate.

Most electronics firms do at least some business with the government, and many of them are very largely dependent on such sales. In 1963 this market amounted to nearly $8.4 billion of the industry's total volume; however, while profits on most government business have always tended to be smaller than on comparable civilian work, the prospect is for still narrower margins because of the recent cost clamp-down by the Defense Department. Procurement policies have been given a complete overhaul, with much greater emphasis now on competitive bidding and contractor performance. Thus, the overall impact on the industry is bound to be adverse from an earnings standpoint.

Decreased profit margins and decreased government spending on electronics products are not the only problems facing electronics firms like Hallicrafters. Price-cutting within the industry itself has also affected earnings.

The shake-up in the stock market actually began in 1960 when sales of transistors jumped 35%. Dozens of firms sprang up almost overnight to share in this bonanza; subsequently, production capacity doubled, but the demand for electronics products stayed the same. Increasing importation of Japanese transistors and other components have contributed to even more intense competition. Price-cutting was inevitable and its result has been a sharp decline in profits.

Hallicrafters has more problems to face than decreasing profit margins and cutthroat competition. The company also has the problem of securing government contracts in the future. On August 31, 1963, the total order backlog for both commercial and military contracts was $23 million. The backlog for the previous year was $40 million. This decrease of 40% in the backlog of orders was mostly the failure of the company to secure new government contracts. However, Robert Halligan, president, has stated that progress is being made toward achieving a more favorable balance between commercial and government business. New business in June, 1964, exceeded $5.2 million, with 55% represented by nonmilitary orders.

High research and development costs for new products is another problem Hallicrafters faces. Financing research and development activities has become a problem in the electronics industry for these reasons: (1) fewer companies have the money to bear the growing costs of research and development; (2) increased competition makes a loan for research and

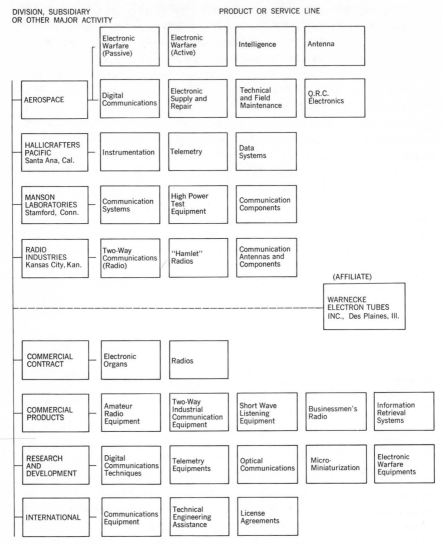

DIVISION, SUBSIDIARY OR OTHER MAJOR ACTIVITY

PRODUCT OR SERVICE LINE

	Electronic Warfare (Passive)	Electronic Warfare (Active)	Intelligence	Antenna
AEROSPACE	Digital Communications	Electronic Supply and Repair	Technical and Field Maintenance	Q.R.C. Electronics
HALLICRAFTERS PACIFIC Santa Ana, Cal.	Instrumentation	Telemetry	Data Systems	
MANSON LABORATORIES Stamford, Conn.	Communication Systems	High Power Test Equipment	Communication Components	
RADIO INDUSTRIES Kansas City, Kan.	Two-Way Communications (Radio)	"Hamlet" Radios	Communication Antennas and Components	

(AFFILIATE)

WARNECKE ELECTRON TUBES INC., Des Plaines, Ill.

COMMERCIAL CONTRACT	Electronic Organs	Radios			
COMMERCIAL PRODUCTS	Amateur Radio Equipment	Two-Way Industrial Communication Equipment	Short Wave Listening Equipment	Businessmen's Radio	Information Retrieval Systems
RESEARCH AND DEVELOPMENT	Digital Communications Techniques	Telemetry Equipments	Optical Communications	Micro-Miniaturization	Electronic Warfare Equipments
INTERNATIONAL	Communications Equipment	Technical Engineering Assistance	License Agreements		

Figure 2.1
Hallicrafters Organization Chart

SOURCE: *Facilities and Capabilities,* published by Hallicrafters Company.

development purposes harder to get; (3) investors have been unwilling to buy up bonds issued for research and development purposes.

The electronics industry favors such giants as General Electric, Western Electric, Radio Corporation of America, and Sylvania. These large companies have the advantages of sheer mass and integration. Smaller electronics companies like Hallicrafters cannot afford to spend as much for research and development as these large companies.

The emphasis at Hallicrafters and in the industry in general is shifting from scientific skills to the management art of cost-cutting. Transitron Company, for example, has initiated a new centralized inventory control system. Hallicrafters has reorganized management policy to give line managers more authority. A few years ago Hallicrafters was strictly a two-man setup controlled by William and Robert Halligan. Since then, the company has decentralized. Decision-making authority is now delegated to other top-level managers and even down to supervisors. This training in decision-making is solving the problem of lack of management depth that the company has had in the past.

Hallicrafters' problems, then, revolve around government contracts, research and development costs, price-cutting in the industry, and the industry growth rate. Robert Halligan has stated that efforts are being directed toward diversification in new fields of commercial leisure-time products and industrial electronics as well as those in which it is currently engaged. The company is hoping that through aggressive management, concentration on specialty products, and expanded distribution, Hallicrafters and its electronics market will continue to expand.

FOR DISCUSSION

1. Explain the recent sharp decline in profits.
2. What policies should be formulated to cope with existing problems?
3. Discuss the benefits of decentralization in a company such as Hallicrafters.
4. How much emphasis do you think should be placed on diversification in the new fields of commercial leisure-time products and industrial electronics?

SUGGESTED READING

"Electronics; Deflated Group," *Financial World*, October 9, 1963, p. 4.
"Glamor Industry Takes Its Lumps," *Business Week*, November 11, 1961, pp. 109-110.
"Honeymoon's End," *Newsweek*, October 2, 1961, p. 72.

Collins Radio Company

THE COLLINS RADIO COMPANY grew out of the early amateur radio activities of its founder and president, Arthur Collins. At a time when most amateur equipment was crude and unreliable, Mr. Collins designed and constructed an amateur station with which he maintained successful daily contacts with the 1925 MacMillan Arctic Expedition. National recognition of the achievement created a demand for similar equipment and eventually led to the formation of the company.

Though founded to manufacture higher quality and more reliable amateur equipment, the young company soon received as one of its first contracts an order for transmitters to be used during the 1934 Antarctic expedition. Subsequent response from government, commercial, and other communications customers prompted the company to pursue further research and new product development; this occurred despite the financially uncertain atmosphere that shrouded the early 1930's.

The development of single-sideband transceiving equipment under Navy and Marine contracts catapulted Collins' star to the forefront of the military electronics field. Within its first ten years of operation, Collins was firmly established in the amateur, fixed station, and broadcast markets. It had only one entry, however, in the field of airborne communications, the field it was later to dominate.

After twenty years of operation in Cedar Rapids, Iowa, the company's research and development programs had spurred a natural increase in project and product diversity, thus broadening its experience and promoting its industrial growth. Collins Western Division was established in 1948 with manufacturing facilities at Burbank, California. It was relocated in 1961 to new facilities in Newport Beach, California. The Dallas Division, now located on a 200-acre site at Richardson, Texas, was organized in 1952.

International sales at Collins date back to the founding of the company. With the rapid postwar recovery of the economies of Europe, Latin America, Asia, and Africa, the international division was established with principal sales and service installations in Zaandam (Netherlands), London, Paris, Geneva, Frankfurt, Beirut, Tokyo, Melbourne, and Rio de Janeiro. In all, more than seventy dealers and company sales offices are located throughout the free world.

Today, major manufacturing, research, and development installations have expanded to include Collins Radio Company of Canada, Limited, Toronto, Ontario; Information Science Center, Newport Beach, California; and Components Division, Santa Ana, California. In addition, Texical, Incorporated, the company's real estate subsidiary, was merged into the parent company on May 31, 1963. Similarly, Alpha of Texas, Incorporated, the company's construction subsidiary, was merged into the parent company in the 1964 fiscal year.

One of the most complete published yardsticks measuring the status of the military electronics industry and major component companies of that industry is the report published in *Moody's Stock Survey* of April 29, 1963, which stated in reference to Collins:

The market now seems to have taken into account Collins Radio's disappointing operating record of the 2 years and its recent announcement of a $12.5 million convertible bond issue. And there is better news on the horizon.

The company has made progress in cost-cutting, and its rapidly growing order backlog reflects expanding participation in space communications. It is doing well overseas too. Most of the expense of readying a new line of special-purpose data communication computers are behind it, though a heavy leasing business could be a drain on earnings for a while. Profits should be up about 30% in the current fiscal year, however.

With this note of reserved optimism in mind, let us take a look at the industry as a whole as brought out in the April 29, 1963, report by *Moody*. There it is pointed out that for the major firms included in the report, the average annual sales gain slipped from an impressive 11.3% for the four years through 1960 to 5.6% after 1960; and the annual rise in net income dropped from 6.4% to 1.5% in the same respective time periods.

These drops were attributed to increased competition from large companies, such as Minneapolis-Honeywell; greater sophistication in design; higher costs of drawing up contract proposals and developing new products; and higher interest costs for working capital and expansion. In addition, the Pentagon expects to cut annual outlays and to insist more and more upon fixed price contracts instead of the rich cost-plus-fixed-fee contracts of the past. In conclusion, *Moody's* feels that after-tax profit margins will not deviate much from the present 2½% and that important deviations from this trend will hinge upon the civilian portions of the business of the companies involved.

Referring specifically to Collins Radio, *Moody's* points to Collin's past history of sharply fluctuating margins and considerable convertible debt financing. It is pointed out, however, that financial and operational controls have been improved and that the order backlog has climbed substantially in the past couple of years. *Moody's* looked for a sizable improvement in profits and listed Collins stock as an "interesting speculation."

With the afore-mentioned ideas in mind, it is important to look at Collins' future in its major product line as postulated in its annual report of August 2, 1963.

In military and aviation system Collins has enjoyed a broad diversity in product line (Collins, in 1963, made deliveries on over 1,000 separate government contracts, no single one of which accounted for as much of 10% of the total) and has recognized competitive superiority in each product. Performance in this field should continue at least as well as it has, although the total market is not sufficiently large to provide more than a segment of the balanced activity desired.

In telecommunications Collins has surmounted the obstacle of building an extensive organization capable of estimating, selling, engineering, and constructing telecommunication systems of any size anywhere in the world.

In the critical area of computer systems, Collins has aimed specifically at the area of telecommunications systems and data processing. Computer-system design has exceeded expectation; in addition, performance and reliability are excellent. Market acceptance to date has been gratifying due to worldwide attention that has been focused on this highly developed, specialized computer application. Original budgets have been exceeded, however, and some programming is as much as six months behind schedule; but feasible limits have not been surpassed.

In the crucial area of commercial contracts, Collins has increased its commercial business to such a point that it now comprises 30% of the total dollar sales, compared to only 10% of four years ago.

Finally, the projected results of cost-reduction programs currently in effect point to drastic reductions in indirect manufacturing costs, thereby considerably enhancing the company's competitive position.

The annual report for 1964 shows that 72% of total sales from all principal market areas were sales to U.S. government agencies. The contributions of these areas to total sales were: aviation, 32.1; specialized military, 22.9; telecommunication, 16.5; space, 12.3; service, 10.2; other products, 6.0. This has resulted in increased earnings of $780,000 on sales of $63 million as of October 30, 1964. This shows a sales increase of 12% from 1963-1964.

Collins faces many manufacturing problems; one problem is the poorly defined lines of responsibility, particularly at the foreman level. This problem was easily detected when jobs went undone. One foreman assumed that another foreman had done the job; communications between them were not adequate.

In an attempt to solve this problem, Collins engaged the services of A. T. Kearney management consultants. These consultants immediately set up a training school which all foremen were required to attend. The training sessions consisted of two hours per session for two sessions per week for two months. This program has been going on for a year in an effort to eventually retrain all the company's foremen. Training is conducted along the lines of a directed conference, with outside reading and other homework required. After a man has completed this training, he must then assist in training the next group, thereby further reinforcing his own knowledge by practical application of the subject matter that he has just studied.

The second step that was taken was to institute a preforeman training program along the lines of that successfully in use at the Ford Motor Company. Collins hired the director of the program at Ford to set up and direct the program at Collins. Under this program, potential foremen are selected from among the line personnel. If they desire to participate in the program, they are taken off their job on the line and are assigned to work with a foreman for six weeks at the same pay that they received while working on the assembly line. After serving his six weeks "apprenticeship" under a foreman, the worker is returned to his original job on the line. If, however, an opening appears at the foreman level, Collins will fill that vacancy with one of the "apprentices." This provides Collins with a constant pool of foreman applicants, who are already quite familiar with the company and with their particular area. It serves as an incentive to both the line workers and to the present foremen, and it increases the efficiency of the present foremen by providing them the opportunity to pass their knowledge on and to review forgotten techniques.

Exorbitant overhead costs are another problem. These high overhead costs were threatening the competitive position of the company, thereby causing loss of potential sales.

To reduce these costs, Collins established a central-data system. This system consisted of a high-speed digital computer and several tape storage units. Microwave towers were set up to link the various manufacturing centers at Cedar Rapids, Iowa; Newport Beach, California; Santa Ana, California; and Toronto, Canada, to the computer center at Dallas, Texas. The computers were then programmed to receive and analyze data from the various facilities concerning payroll computations, accounts receivable, and accounts payable; for example, the Cedar Rapids division transmits all of the data from the employees' time cards via microwave to the computer center at Dallas. The computer calculates the hours worked and the salary earned for each of the approximately 10,000 employees at Cedar Rapids. It then transmits all of the salary and deductions data for each employee back to Cedar Rapids where it is immediately printed out automatically on payroll sheets. The payroll checks are also printed out automatically. In less than twenty minutes the whole weekly payroll is completed, so that employees can get paid on Friday for work through the preceding Thursday. The microwave equipment is used for many other purposes, so its entire cost cannot be charged off to indirect manufacturing. At the present time, the payroll department has virtually disappeared from Collins. The cost-control department has been reduced to 60% of its former size, and the accounting department has been reduced to 40% of its regular size. Collins is about one-third of the way toward its goal to be the first completely computerized company. It was their efforts in this area that brought Collins into the computer field.

Collins also faces business losses due to slow through time. In this particular industry it is common to spend from twenty to thirty weeks filling a particular order. Very small, highly specialized electronics companies became a threat by specializing in a particular instrument and thereby reducing through time.

To remain competitive, Collins instituted a program of progressive mixed assembly. First, the company was split into product lines; then a new system of mechanical drawings of all assemblies and subassemblies was instituted. Under this new drawing system, all parts were classified as either unique or common. A supply of unique and common parts was then manufactured and stored. All of the common parts were combined into subassemblies and stored. Since these subassemblies were composed of common parts, they could be used in one of several different instruments simply by attaching different sets of unique parts to them; thus, many products are one-half to two-thirds completed before an order ever comes in. Also, because the common-part subassemblies can be used for several instruments, there is little risk of obsolescence.

At the present time, through time has been reduced to about six weeks on many items. The ultimate goal is to reduce through time to four weeks.

Under this new system there is a larger in-stock inventory, but in-process inventory is drastically reduced as is finished-product inventory. One very definite side benefit that evolved from this system was a significant reduction in taxes due to the reduction in finished-goods inventory, since finished goods are taxed a lot higher than are subassemblies and raw materials.

Another area of concern is the poor method of predicting costs. Collins was running into difficulty in government contracts because of its inability to accurately predict costs. This resulted in loss of some contracts and in underpricing on some contracts which they did receive.

To alleviate this problem, Collins went to a predetermined standard-data system for calculating labor costs. The particular system selected was the Methods Time Measurement system as it seemed to offer broader diversification in its data and services. Most estimators and industrial engineers went to an accredited Methods Time Measurement school. The estimators went for six hours per week for six weeks. The industrial engineers went two hours per week for eight weeks. The product-support function was enlarged to provide manuals of standard practice and manuals of data for each industrial engineer to use. Time studies were increased to supplement the standard data that was available. The forementioned manuals were and are audited periodically at least once a month. Production is checked very closely so that if anything goes out of control, corrective training programs can be instituted.

Finally, Collins was hit with a rash of industrial accidents. In particular, there were several bad eye accidents. After a thorough inspection of the manufacturing facility, it was decided that most of the accidents were due to attitudes and acts of carelessness on the parts of the employees, rather than to unsafe working conditions. Immediately a formal campaign was initiated to increase employee awareness of safety and to improve employee attitudes. Movies on safety were shown in those departments which had a bad record; posters were made and distributed throughout the plant. In addition, safety training was incorporated into the foreman pretraining program, which was previously mentioned.

Because of the unusually large number of serious eye injuries, all employees were required to get a pair of safety glasses. Collins subsidized the cost of prescription safety glasses for those who needed them. All employees are now required to wear safety glasses when on the production floor.

With the improvement of financial and operational controls, Collins can concentrate its efforts on what is essentially its biggest problem—competition—from giants like Minneapolis-Honeywell to other electronics specialists.

FOR DISCUSSION

1. Evaluate Collins' program of progressive mixed assembly.
2. How did Collins solve its problem of lack of communication between foremen?
3. What are the objectives of the central-data system? Is this system adequate to produce the results Collins wants?
4. Can you suggest any procedures which could cope with the company's problem of competition?

SUGGESTED READING

Moody's Stock Survey, January 4, 1963, and April 29, 1963.
Research and Development, Collins Radio Company, Cedar Rapids, Iowa, 1963.

Litton Industries, Incorporated

IN 1963 LITTON INDUSTRIES' ANNUAL REPORT was titled, *Era of Opportunity*—a particularly appropriate theme for this company. On November 2, 1964, Litton celebrated its eleventh anniversary, and there was no question that Litton had taken advantage of all available opportunities in its climb to the top.

Today, Litton markets 200 products that range from hulking nuclear submarines to tiny electronic tubes; recently, it has been acquiring a new product almost every week, widely expanding its scope of operations. Litton produces and markets electronic brains, trading stamps, gyroscopes, calculating machines. Litton is first in sales of sound-recording equipment, first in seismic explorations (its Western Geophysical Division), second in the field of cash registers (its Svenska Dataregister Division), and third in the United States in private shipbuilding (its Ingalls Division).

Its activities range from mapping underground volcanic activity in Hawaii, to searching for oil beneath the North Sea, to scouring the jungles of Surinam for precious minerals.

However, diversification is not the entire story; the timing of acquisitions is at least as important. *Fortune* says that Litton has "made a practice of doing what other companies are not doing, and of not doing what everyone else is doing."

When competitors were scrambling for contracts for whole military systems, Litton concentrated on electronic components and it made profits to prove its point. While competitors have been producing big, general purpose computers, Litton has opened up a new market with its Monrobot XI, a compact desk-size computer at the relatively low price of $25,000. Currently, competitors have been fighting to take over outer space. Litton, feeling that there is not enough room in space for everyone, has started exploring the sea.

In the last eleven years Litton has developed into one of the most remarkable growth companies of the age. Litton now ranks as the nation's one hundredth biggest corporation, and by 1965 its sales should surpass the billion dollar mark and put it among the top fifty United States companies. What or who is responsible for this company's fantastic growth? The answer to this question lies in "Tex" Thornton.

Thornton, Litton's chief executive officer, attended Texas Technological College, where he found himself more interested in business than engineering studies; so he changed to Business Administration for a B.C.S. degree. At twenty-eight he became a second lieutenant in the Air Force, but for only forty-eight hours. After a series of whirlwind weekly promotions he became one of the youngest colonels in the United States Air Force. Thornton was in charge of bringing modern business planning and central systems to the Air Force. At one point, Colonel Thornton had 2,800 officers all over the world under his command. After the war he went to work for the Ford Motor Company, taking with him nine very bright young Air Force officers. They hired out as a group and became known in Ford as the "Whiz Kids." Thornton left Ford in 1948, since he felt that his chances for a top management position had been dimmed considerably. When Henry Ford II put Earnest Breech in the top spot and Breech brought in people trained in the car business to assist him, Howard Hughes offered Thornton the job of building up Hughes Aircraft. After he reorganized Hughes Aircraft and brought its sales from $1,500,000 to $200 million in five years, Thornton decided to quit and form his own company because the advisers balked at spending extra money to keep up the pace.

Roy Ash, whom Thornton had lured to Hughes from a post as top statistician at the Bank of America, and Hughes' engineer Hugh W. Jamieson agreed to join Thornton in his new venture. In 1953 Thornton persuaded Lehman Brothers, Wall Street's prestigious investment house, to back them with the sum of $1,500,000 in buying out a small California producer of microwave tubes. The company carried the name of its engineer-owner, Charles Litton. He suspiciously refused to take any stock in the new company, instead demanding $1 million in cash (today stock in that amount would be worth $85 million). With stock, cash, credit, and persuasive argument, Thornton and his friends began buying a series of little-known outfits that made printed circuits, computers, communications and navigational equipment. Thornton felt that Litton had to grow big in a hurry to survive the jolt of changing technology—but he had a reason behind every move.

Many men in both business and government consider Thornton to be the most outstanding executive in the U.S. today. Deeply involved in technology, Thornton is neither a professionally trained engineer nor a technician, and though he is a great believer in running things under tight control, he places little reliance on electronic logic in making management decisions. He takes his time about making up his mind. Thornton is a dreamer and a visionary who talks constantly about the way-out future, yet is also an intensely practical man who has made realities out of many of his early dreams. Far from being a lonely decision maker in an isolated executive suite, Thornton shows his true executive quality in his ability to pick good men and give them free rein. He has surrounded himself with an intensely loyal group of managers, who are independent thinkers, not afraid to question his judgment or to lunge at opportunities without waiting for his nod.

Litton president Roy Ash, forty-five, and Thornton, fifty, have come to work together as smoothly as if they were held on course by one of Litton's guidance systems. Thornton is the man with the intuition and the flair for the right deal at the right time; Ash is the lively and witty coordinator who keeps a day-to-day watch on Litton's ever-expanding activities. Perhaps Thornton's greatest contribution to the company is his superb sense of timing and intuitive dead reckoning that tells him when to move with a product and when to hold back. Thornton and Ash feel that keeping their men well-informed and making their responsibilities clear is the best way to get the most effort from them. "Our system works," Ash says, "only because the individuals and the system work together." Thornton was one-time boss of such talent as Defense Secretary Robert McNamara and present Ford president Arfay Miller. Litton's success has made Thornton a millionaire forty times over. It has also made millionaires out of twenty other Litton executives.

Probably, Litton's success in many of the highly competitive fields has been possible through the application of Thornton's dynamic personality.

Litton was just one of many firms with which Thornton could have started towards his goal of leadership in the electronics industry. He believed that this industry would behave very much like the auto industry; that is, many companies would go through the growing stages, but only a few dominant ones would survive the competition. Thornton and Ash developed a three-part plan which they have continuously followed.

Buy time. Thornton has said, "We either bought a product, a market, a research team, a management, or a plant—things that would have taken years to build from scratch." Litton Industries, Incorporated, receives about eighty feelers a month from firms wishing to be taken over by or merged with Litton. However, Thornton is so highly selective in his corporate acquisition that only three or four firms a year realize their desires.

Dr. Henry Singleton came to Litton from North American Aviation because he was granted a stock option. After being with Litton only three years, he solved one of the Pentagon's toughest problems: an inertial guidance system that was light enough to steer the most sophisticated missiles. This is an example of excellent timing in acquiring a man already established in research.

Another acquisition of an already established market was Westrex Corporation in 1958. It was a communications firm with outlets in thirty-five foreign countries. (The trustbusters forced Western Electric to sell.) Its system for recording phonograph records has long been the most widely used in the recording industry, but Litton still continues research. The recently developed model of Stereo Disk Recorder for making stereophonic records gives improved uniformity and stability.

Vertical strength. Merger with Monroe Calculator Machine Company gave Litton a chance to apply its electronic talents to the business machine field with a head start of an established name. The Monrobot XI computer—a compact, desk-size computer ideally suited for invoicing, computing taxes, taking inventories, and performing other accounting duties—was developed. It is the most widely used small scale business computer in the world. Research developed the new memory drum which has twice the memory capacity of the standard drum. The computer can also use a magnetic input and output into small, inexpensive computers for the first time.

The Stockholm, Sweden, based Svenska Dataregister was acquired in 1959. This is a point-of-sale recorder, which is compact enough to be installed in conventional checkstands and can be linked to the computer for instantaneous inventory control.

In January of 1961 Litton acquired the A. Kimball Company, which makes equipment that links the point-of-sale recorder to the computer. It also makes merchandising tags and tag punching and marking machines.

Simon Adhesive Products, acquired in June of 1961, completed the cycle by making adhesive for the tags. Senior Vice-President Sullivan says: "We now make everything at point-of-sale except the money that goes into the cash register."

Diversification. There is purpose in the acquisition policy so that something is always kept. Litton is diversified into areas where "we can capitalize most on the new technologies." The products fall into four main categories: space, sea, atmosphere, and earth. In the fiscal year 1963 Litton had a contract from National Aeronautics and Space Administration to design and build a hard space suit which the space-sciences laboratory fulfilled. The Ingalls Division installs its intricate electronics systems in its nuclear-attack submarine, the Barb. In the atmosphere category, Litton has developed a telescope which can be mounted directly on a miniature inertial platform in the Air Force aircraft to take sightings of the stars according to instructions sent by the system's computer; it then reports back to the computer. Aerial mapping and exploration for natural resources is a new field of interest. Litton has been conducting electromagnetic surveys in both hemispheres. The trend this past year has been towards the military with 55% of the sales in that area. However, no major commitment to any one military product has been made. In 1963 Litton reported the biggest and best year in its defense contract history.

Litton has companies from Utah to Virginia and from the Netherlands to Italy, with seventy-one plants in the United States and nine in foreign countries. The probing Litton radar antenna, set up in Turkey, reportedly keeps tabs on Soviet missile firings. Across the far north of Canada and Alaska, Litton klystron tubes generate radar beams for the Distant Early Warning Line.

The various products of the five divisions mentioned are used in many different market areas. Airports use the antennas to help control flight; universities use the digital-desk computers; government needs missile supplies; business makes use of the procedures for recording, storing, retrieving, transferring, communicating, and analyzing quantities of information; and entertainment firms use the systems of recording phonograph records. According to Litton's Annual Report: "From the world of commerce to the area of man's health to the arena of his entertainment, the opportunities are infinite."

Litton recognizes and makes opportunities and then follows through with its three-part plan: buy time, vertical strength, and diversification. This is the era of opportunity and Litton makes opportunity its business.

Litton's management structure is very informal. Roughly speaking, the only formal aspect is that the president, Roy Ash, runs the day-by-day internal affairs of the company, while chairman of the board, Tex Thornton, handles the external affairs for deciding on new acquisitions. However, this by no means states the matter precisely, as these two men are like interchangeable parts and work together very closely.

Thornton says: "No division reports to me directly, but the point is that any of our key men can walk into Roy's office or my office any time." Ash has often compared their situation to a barbershop. He says it is like a barbershop with two barbers and lots of customers. The first barber finished with a customer takes the next one to walk in off the street.

The result is a freewheeling and informal style of management that keeps everyone in rapid motion. It combines centralization, where major investment decisions are concerned, with decentralization in the day-to-day operations. Litton's headquarters staff includes only about 114 people and there are no standing committees. One reason for this is that Thornton likes to turn ideas over in his mind and finds large groups with their rapid-fire exchange somewhat daunting. "When you get a lot of staff," says Thornton, "then you question able authority with no responsibility."

In a sense, the fact that Thornton has a hand in most decisions makes the management autocratic. Conversely, however, the strong decentralization into five autonomous groups lends an air of "laissez-faire" to the management.

Another aspect of the informality of the management structure is that there are no written reports or memos. All communication is done by telephone or in person. Ash feels that there is a great deal of mutual understanding in the company without written reports. There are many entrepreneurs in Litton; and this type of person, with his own job security built right into him, does not develop the posture of people in institutional organizations. He does not have to keep things to himself to keep his job. He freely exchanges information laterally. Ash himself has been called "the switchboard" of Litton, and enormous amounts of information pass through him. He is on the phone constantly. Says Ash:

When you have information flowing, the problem of exerting control takes care of itself. You only have to step in when changes have to be made. Control shouldn't mean domination or imposition. If you have a good flow of information, control tends to be a part and parcel of communication.

At the same time that Thornton turned over some of his responsibility to Ash, he began creating a new layer of executive responsibility by setting up groups of divisions. As Figure 2.2 shows, there are five such groups now. Each of these groups is run autonomously from the home office in Beverly Hills. Each group has a head who is responsible for all divisions under him.

At the top of the chart is the Board of Directors; but this is composed of Thornton, Ash, and a few other members of the staff plus a couple of outsiders. Actually Thornton and Ash at the top of the chart handle all big matters. Each of the five groups is in close contact with Thornton and Ash and yet is run separately by each group head.

These 5 market areas encompass 36 divisions that are scattered through-

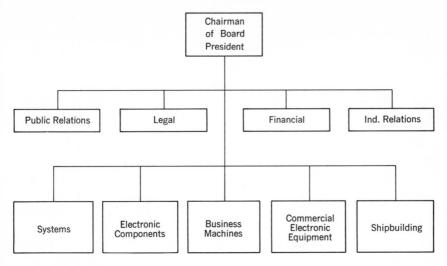

Figure 2.2
Litton Industries

out 87 plants in the U.S. and twelve foreign countries. The fastest growing is the electronic systems. As of July 31, 1963, this group generated
$200 million of sales or about 37% of the corporate total (Figure 2.3).
The business-machines group, headed by Svenska Dataregister and Monroe, generated $157 million or 29%. The shipbuilding group, headed by
Ingalls, generated $85 million or 16%. Finally, the electronic components
group and the commercial electronics group each generated $49 million
or 9% of the corporate total.

These totaled sales of $540 million and constituted a 40% increase over
the 1962 volume and a very steep rise over the $9 million volume of 1954.
The estimated sales for 1964 are $750 million and current figures indicate
Litton is well on its way to that goal. This is considered rather spectacular
growth, even in today's big business economy.

Litton's general financial condition is stronger than ever before. Earnings for 1964 rose 28% to reach $29 million; that is about $2.77 per share
to the 10 million shares of common stock outstanding, as compared to
$.09 per share in 1954. Its ratio of current assets to current liabilities is 2.7
to 1, which is considered a stable relationship. So far, Litton has issued
four stock dividends, but no cash dividends.

As of July 31, 1964, Litton achieved increases of 24% in sales and
28% in earnings. Sales for the year rose to a new peak of approximately
$685 million from $553,146,239 in fiscal 1963. The company's sales now
are at an annual rate of over $750 million. Net after-tax earnings achieved
a new record of approximately $29,700,000—up from $23,296,107 in the
previous fiscal year.

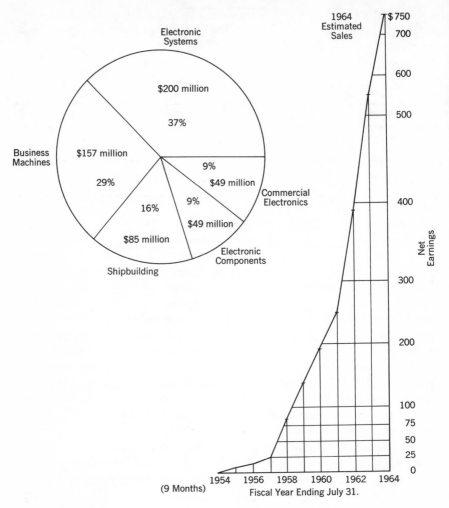

Figure 2.3
Litton Boom
In Millions of Dollars

Could Litton, which is similar to Rapid-American-McCrory structure in that they have closely related backgrounds and also low return on earnings, follow the same path of bankruptcy?

It is true that Rapid-American and Litton have similar backgrounds. Both companies have been dominated by one man: Rapid-American by Meshulan Riklis and Litton by Tex Thornton. Both started out by borrowing to acquire one company and used debt financing to build their empires.

Riklis went wrong when a couple of his companies started losing money. He started selling his acquisitions to help finance his losses; thus the chain of debt financing to build an empire started working backwards and tore down his empire. In his chain he found one or two weak links that lost money and started him in the reverse direction.

It is possible that this could happen to Thornton and Litton. However, it is not too probable. Riklis bought a lot of his companies simply for the sake of acquiring more. Thornton buys all of his acquisitions with a definite purpose in mind. He will use a research team from one company, a production department from another, or possibly a marketing team from a third. Thornton does not buy blindly. He makes sure why he wants a company and uses it accordingly. He has unusual foresight and has planned ahead for each acquisition in order not to fall into the same trap as Riklis did. Also Riklis put most of his time, money, and effort into one particular company, trying to get control of McCrory. On the other hand, Thornton has five distinct groups with several separate divisions in each one. He does not have his whole effort tied up in one idea which will make him or break him. True, Litton could follow the footsteps of Rapid-American, but it is highly unlikely.

Haphazard acquisition, as Riklis practiced, could lead to diversification problems. Litton's product diversification, however, is not haphazard because the company has stressed vertical growth. Although there are many different products, each tends to be related to one or more other products made by Litton. The products in such an instance are all manufactured at the point of sale; therefore, having many products does not keep one from being able to obtain a product where he needs it and also assures time saved for the customer and a selling advantage for Litton. Even with a large quantity of products, they fall easily into only five major divisions.

Because of such wide diversification, effective communications became extremely important. The very informal communications at Litton seem to pose some problems. Telephone calls and personal conversations do not provide an accurate record for future reference; also, the spoken word can be more easily misconstrued or forgotten than a written report. However, this problem is minimal. Litton has operated with free-flowing communications for ten years with no sign of strain. The lateral flow and freedom from burdensome reports outweigh any disadvantages. Of course, to some degree, the system should fit the key individuals; and if the top personnel of the company changed radically, the system might need to be tighter and more formal.

The most obvious and potentially upsetting problem is: What would happen if Thornton left? How dependent is Litton on the leadership of Thornton?

The company itself is in good financial condition. Long-term debt is low and sales are high and climbing. From that standpoint the company could withstand a change and even run on its own steam for a while.

The close interaction between Ash and Thornton makes Ash the prime candidate to take over. He has the necessary experience, particularly in day-to-day operations which he already directs. The singular intuitive flair might be missing, but Litton could easily slow down its growth and concentrate on current operations.

However, the specific, carefully thought out Master Plan really makes it reasonable to assume Litton could go on growing and acquiring companies without Thornton. Ash was intimately involved with drawing up the plan and is surely capable of continuing it. Even someone else would have an advantage by referring to the Master Plan.

What other leaders are available? The heads of the five groups are experienced men. They are not merely specialists; several were presidents of successful companies before Litton bought them out and they have continued to have wide responsibility and authority. Also, the free, lateral communications have kept these men advised of company direction and conditions.

Litton appears to be remarkably free of serious problems. The company is still young, but after ten years its survival is reasonably certain. The test now is to see if the high rate of growth will finally start to pay off with the 20% profit return Litton is shooting for.

FOR DISCUSSION

1. Explain the statement in *Fortune* that Litton has "made a practice of doing what other companies are not doing, and of not doing what everyone else is doing."
2. What are the strengths of the company?
3. What could be the possible effects on Litton if Thornton left?
4. What policies are necessary in diversification of an industry?

SUGGESTED READING

"Appetite for the Future," *Time*, October 4, 1963, pp. 104-108.
"New Line-ups," *Newsweek*, September 18, 1961, pp. 86-87.
Reiser, C., "When the Crowd Goes One Way Litton Goes the Other," *Fortune*, May, 1963, pp. 114-119.

Fansteel Metallurgical Corporation

FANSTEEL METALLURGICAL CORPORATION was originally incorporated in the state of Illinois in 1907 as the Pfanstiehl Electrical Laboratories. The corporation was formed to develop processes to produce quantities of the refractory metal tantalum for use in capacitors and rectifiers. Pfanstiehl Laboratories was one of the earliest producers of tantalum in commercial quantities. The corporation was reincorporated in 1914 in the state of Delaware as the Pfanstiehl Corporation, and again in New York in 1917 under the same name.

Only July 5, 1918, the corporate name was changed from Pfanstiehl Corporation to Fansteel Products Corporation and continued as such until September 3, 1935, when the present title of Fansteel Metallurgical Corporation was adopted. The corporation expanded as new uses were discovered for tantalum in the growing electronics industry and as processes were found to produce other refractory metals as a demand for them arose in the electronics and other industries.

Fansteel's principal activities came to revolve around four rare refractory metals: tantalum, columbium, tungsten, and molybdenum, and any special alloys incorporating one or more of them. The corporation strove also to develop new uses for these metals, and Fansteel research was successful in developing many new products.

In 1940 the Fansteel Mining Corporation, wholly owned by Fansteel, was dissolved and its tantalum mines in South Dakota and its tungsten mines and other assets were transferred to the parent company. Also in 1940 the Ramet Corporation of America, which was another wholly owned subsidiary, was dissolved and its assets taken over by the parent company. The Ramet Corporation owned and controlled patents and licenses for hard-carbide cutting, drilling, grinding tools, and dies. These consolidations were effected to gain greater coordination and efficiency of corporate effort.

In 1942 it organized the Tantalum Defense Department to help in the war effort in the manufacture of needed tantalum. This division merged with the parent corporation in 1958.

In July of 1947 Fansteel purchased for cash all of the stock of Weiger-Weed and Company of Detroit. This acquisition was made to improve Fansteel's competitive position, since Weiger-Weed was a major manufacturer of refractory alloys, resistance-welding dies, water-cooled electrode holders, and accessories used in the welding process. Operations were continued by Weiger-Weed Alloys, Incorporated, until 1958 when the operations were completely merged into the parent corporation.

To further strengthen its competitive position, Fansteel in 1948 increased its holdings of Vascoloy-Ramet Corporation from 66⅔% to 100%. Vascoloy-Ramet manufactures a broad line of carbide products and investment castings for various uses, including working the refractory metals that Fansteel produces; the acquisition opened new fields for Fansteel.

In 1961 it acquired Wesson Tool Corporation for $6.3 million. Wesson was made a subsidiary of Vascoloy-Ramet Corporation in order to bolster the cutting-tool roster of that corporation. Wesson adds cutting tools for such metals as Fansteel now produces, and the hope is that this merger will broaden operations and give Fansteel a competitive advantage.

The most recent move made by Fansteel to expand its operations was initiated on December 31, 1963, when it purchased Stauffer Chemical's refractory metalworking equipment, electron-beam furnaces, and related laboratory facilities. This move was made to enable Fansteel to produce tantalum and columbium of increased quality at lower prices.

The primary value of the refractory metals lies in their unique ability to withstand terrific heat levels. Most have melting points well in excess of 2,000 degrees Centigrade. As the need has grown for these refractory metals in the electronics industry, so also has Fansteel grown. Today, it is said to be the leading producer of tantalum, tungsten, molybdenum, and columbium; and it also fabricates a portion of its refractory-metal output into various product lines.

The corporation is listed on the New York Stock Exchange and has its general offices in North Chicago, Illinois. It has plants in North Chicago and Muskogee, Alabama. Its subsidiary, Vascoloy-Ramet Corporation, is located in Waukegan, Illinois. Wesson Corporation, a subsidiary of Vascoloy-Ramet, has plants in Ferndale and Brighton, Michigan; in Lexington, Kentucky; and Toronto, Ontario. Operations are also carried on by Fansteel A. G. in Zug, Switzerland, and by Vascoloy-Ramet (Europa) N. V., Zwolle, Holland.

Fansteel is divided into four operating divisions: the Chemical and Metallurgical Division; the Electrical Contacts and Specialties Division; the Rectifier-Capacitor Division; and the Carbide Products Division, composed of the Vascoloy-Ramet and Wesson Tool corporations.

Its customers span a broad cross-section of corporate activity. A large portion of the output, however, ultimately does go for governmental usage. Its 1961 major direct markets were the electronics industry, comprising 24% of sales; automotive, 17%; electric power, 14%; aero-space, 14%; metalworking, 12%; and the defense industry, 5%. Sales in 1962 by markets show several significant changes in its customer roster, considering that the change occurred in the course of one year. Sales in 1962 by markets were metalworking, 29%; electronics, 26%; automotive, 13%; electric, 13%; aero-space, 10%; petroleum and mining, 4%; chemical, 2%; export, 2%; and miscellaneous, 3%. These major changes in market percentages indicate one of the problems facing the company and the reasons for these changes will be discussed more fully later.

The production statistics are incomplete for the refractory metals, so Fansteel's production cannot be easily compared with that of its competitors. However, the annual production in pure form of refractory metals is small, ranging from around 1,250 tons of pure molybdenum to 1 ton or less of rhenium. In 1960, 700 tons of pure tungsten were produced in the form of wire rod and sheet, and pure tantalum produced reached a peak of 125 tons. In 1960, 65 tons of pure columbium were produced. The total output, then, of all of the refractory metals, apart from their use as alloying elements, can be seen as only a small fraction of 1% of the combined tonnage produced of all ferrous and nonferrous metals. However, since their production involves complicated chemical processes, the refractory metals' sales dollar value is considerably higher than their physical volume; in fact, the sales of just three—columbium, tantalum, and tungsten—jumped 50% between 1958 and 1960 to an estimated total of $45 million, and this sales volume is continuing to rise at a rapid rate. Much of this increasing sales volume is attributable to the heat-resistant properties of these metals, which place them in demand for use in the rapidly expanding missile and aero-space program.

The production of refractory metals among many corporations obviously accounts for their widely varying percentages of business. The operations are not expansive in many of these corporations, since many only produce refractory metals for their own use; however, some of these corporations do account for large percentages of the refractory metal production. Fansteel is the major producer of four of the refractory metals; another leader in the field is American Metal Climax, Incorporated, and its division, Climax Molybdenum, which produces over 60% of the world's supply of molybdenum. Stauffer Chemicals was another notable producer until Fansteel acquired its equipment. In addition, Union Carbide is completing a new plant to increase its production in this rapidly expanding field. These listings show that although Fansteel is presently a leading producer of refractory metals, it still is beset with increasing levels of competition from many other producers who want to increase their share in this growing market.

Fansteel's refractory-metal fabrications are also encountering intense competition, and it is safe to say that Fansteel's fabrications in general comprise only small percentages of the market. However, it does still manufacture more automotive breaker-point assemblies than any other manufacturer and also markets the most complete line of carbide-cutting products.

Fansteel earnings over the years generally have been very good; however, earnings recently have been declining since 1956 when peak earnings of $3,306,323 were obtained on a new sales volume amounting to $32,256,153. In 1962 a peak sales volume of $37,599,492 was achieved; but the net earnings had declined to only $1,333,319, which was equivalent to earnings of $.96 per share of stock. The 1963 new sales volume dropped from the 1962 level to $33,787,613, which left a net income of only $70,381, or about $.05 per share of stock. The drop in sales volume definitely accounted for part of this, but some of it is probably attributable to the purchase of Stauffer Chemical's facilities for an undisclosed sum of cash on December 31, 1963. Net sales in 1964 totaled $38,089,568 while consolidated net earnings amounted to $353,261, or $.26 per share. This showed an improvement in operating earnings due in large part to the increase in sales volume and earnings of the V/R Wesson Division (carbide tools) and the Electrical Contacts Division, which offset a continuing deterioration in the profitability of its refractory metals and tantalum capacitor business.

Fansteel Metallurgical in recent years has been passing through a difficult stage in its development. Profitability has decreased for a variety of reasons. The large profits potential in the electronics industry has inevitably resulted in a marked increase in the number of electronics producers. This has inevitably resulted in areas of overproductivity in the industry. This overcapacity has caused stiffer competition among producers resulting in decreasing prices and a cost-price squeeze which have drastically reduced profitability. The cost-price squeeze also has been tightened as products have matured; they are now manufactured by all of the producers rather than being specialty items. Currently there is no sign that this trend has run its course; overcapacity still exists and will continue to exist for a considerable length of time, since new producers are steadily entering the field.

Fansteel has been hit hardest by this overcapacity and price deterioration in its rectifier and capacitor product lines. As products matured, the prices fell drastically; at first the company tried to overcome this by increasing the sales volume. Since all of the producers stepped up production, the result was only to further depress prices. Because Fansteel did not feel that it was commercially sound to market products at or below cost and as it did not want to reduce the quality image of the product, it had to, in several instances, withdraw products from the market. An excellent example of this situation is Fansteel's silicon rectifier diode, which it hoped to market successfully to the automotive producers for use in the new alternator system. Fansteel forecasted a large sales volume of these items and set up its productive facilities accordingly in 1960-1961. Sales at first were disappointing since all of the automotive manufacturers did not immediately switch over to equipping their cars with the alternator; then, as other producers entered the field and all of the automotive producers switched to the alternator, Fansteel found that it could not produce and market a unit at a price that would yield a reasonable profit. As this condition emerged, it was forced to suspend production in this area even though substantial commitments in plant facilities and marketing effort had been made; consequently, the company incurred a large loss in this area, thus depressing overall profits. Fansteel hopes to make up for this loss by further developing the silicon rectifier diode for general industrial applications where the competition is not as fierce and where sales and profitability are more stable.

Similarly, Fansteel has suffered from this decline in profitability in its tantalum capacitor line and its semiconductor devices, which for years were its most profitable items. Not only has the sales price deteriorated rapidly on these items, but the price of tantalum has risen rapidly and production of tantalum ore has been at times chaotic. The company's major source of tantalum ore for processing is Katanga Province in the Congo, and the political upheaval there in recent years has greatly disrupted and threatened the steady supply of ore. Now, although the pressure has eased and shipments are back to normal, the price of ore is rising rapidly and is far above levels of previous years. Fansteel is striving to overcome these price increases through more efficient processing of the ore and by increasing the sales volume of existing products. It is also working to steadily introduce new tantalum products to keep ahead of the market.

Fansteel has been least affected by price deterioration in its Carbide Division and its Chemical and Metallurgical Division, although the increasing demand for these metals is causing large increases in the amount of competition in these areas. Prices on these products have been kept up by product differentiation which was not possible in the cases of tantalum capacitors and silicon rectifiers. It has steadily introduced new alloys and powder forms of the refractory metals and carbide cutting tools, keeping on a par or ahead of competition in this manner and through better processing techniques, which have reduced costs of production.

Fansteel's Electrical Contacts and Specialties Division has always shown fair profitability, but there is only small growth potential in these markets. Although it is the largest producer of automotive breaker points, it can only increase profitability in this area by lowering costs of production since the market is relatively fixed. Fansteel's line of "Cricket" switches has not as yet shown profitability since production is not yet stable, and it has not developed a complete line of commercially acceptable switches.

Fansteel has also encountered rapidly increasing costs of research and development in recent years as products have matured, and it has sought to improve the quality and marketability of existing products, at the same time developing a steady stream of new products to replace those that have become unprofitable. Since it is imperative for the company to develop new products as well as to improve existing ones and find more efficient methods of production, it has steadily had to increase the amounts set aside for research and development in recent years. Although this has increased costs and thereby lowered profitability, it is entirely necessary if it is to pass through this difficult stage in its development and expand.

In recent years Fansteel has taken many steps to overcome its problems of competitive pressures and price deterioration, stepping up its expenditures for research and development in an effort to find and develop new products to enable the company to keep ahead of competition. This has been successful in several cases, but as of today the increased costs of research have more than offset the profitability of the improvements made. However, in the future when the research really begins to pay off in a steady flow of new products, this move will undoubtedly increase future productivity; moreover, this cost cannot be avoided, since new products will determine the future growth of Fansteel in this overly-competitive industry.

Another major step taken by Fansteel to lessen competitive pressures has been to acquire competing companies, using their equipment advantageously to lower costs and increase efficiency or using their products to fill out its product lines. The acquisition of Stauffer Chemical's equipment not only enables Fansteel to lower the cost of production of refractory metals, but also signals the end of competition from Stauffer in the production of refractory metals and alloys. Taking over the Wesson Tool Corporation and making it a subsidiary of Vascoloy-Ramet gave Fansteel the advantage of having the most complete line of carbide cutting equipment on the market, which greatly reduced competitive pressures. Increased profitability will occur in future years because of this move when the operations of Wesson and Vascoloy-Ramet are completely merged, and the cost of running a second plant is eliminated.

The most recent Fansteel acquisition occurred on April 3, 1964, when it was announced that the company had purchased the B M W Manufacturing Corporation of Torrance, California, another industrial metals fabricator and machine-tool maker. This new acquisition will be operated as a subsidiary of Fansteel and should further strengthen the company's competitive position.

At the end of 1964 Fansteel acted on a long-considered decision to liquidate the major portion of its tantalum capacitor business, since the company is not sufficiently broadly based in the manufacture of electronic components to maintain a satisfactory competitive position. The manufacture of tantalum capacitor materials will continue, however, because of a growing emphasis on electronic materials. This withdrawal from capacitor manufacturing should advance its ability to sell to other capacitor producers.

Finally, Fansteel has made numerous changes in personnel in an effort to gain fresher and more dynamic leadership. A new president, Warren B. Hayes, was selected by the Board of Directors in February, 1963, and several of the officers have been replaced recently in the hopes of finding new men better equipped to deal with Fansteel's current problems and to achieve the long-range goals of management which are to expand the company's fields of activity and establish a new foundation for future growth.

FOR DISCUSSION

1. Explain the reasons for decline of profits at Fansteel.
2. Why has its Carbide Division been least affected?
3. How effective have been Fansteel's measures to overcome competitive pressures?
4. What are the objectives which Fansteel hopes to attain by changes in personnel?

SUGGESTED READING

"Cutting Tool Material Manufacturer Merger," *Steel*, September 2, 1963, p. 33.

"Fansteel Metallurgical Corporation," *Barron's National Business and Financial Weekly*, September 24, 1962, p. 20.

Sherman, Joseph V., "Beating the Heat-Refractory Metals are Playing a Vital Role in Space Age," *Barron's National Business and Financial Weekly*, July 10, 1961, p. 9.

CHAPTER 3

B. F. Goodrich Company

In 1870, THE EARLY PIONEERING DAYS of the rubber industry, the
B. F. Goodrich Company was founded as a small partnership by Dr. Benjamin F. Goodrich. Since those early days in Akron, Ohio, B. F. Goodrich
has grown into a sprawling industrial complex employing over 40,000
people and spanning both the rubber and chemical industries with the
most diversified product line of any company in the rubber-chemical
industry.

Incorporated in 1912 as a successor to the original company, B. F.
Goodrich has followed an expansion program of both internal growth
and outside acquisition to innovate and strengthen its product line. This
growth, originally spurred by the expanding automobile industry, has
branched off into the chemical and consumer products field since the
Second World War. This growth pattern can be easily followed by tracing the company's acquisitions and divisional growth.

In 1912 Goodrich acquired Diamond Rubber Company, also located
in Akron. After digesting this major competitor, Goodrich bought control of Ames-Holden Tire & Rubber Company, Limited (now B. F. Goodrich Company of Canada, Limited) and five years later (1928) bought
complete control of this subsidiary.

In 1926 Goodrich acquired full control over Philadelphia Rubber
Works Company and followed this by buying the entire capital stock of
Martha Mills of Silvertown, Georgia. The mill purchase supplied Goodrich with an internal source of rubber and tire fabrics.

A newly organized division, Hood Rubber Company, Incorporated,
acquired the total assets of the Hood Rubber Company of Watertown,
Massachusetts, thus adding a line of footwear and rain gear to Goodrich's
line of rubber goods.

Goodrich continued expansion in 1930 by acquiring Miller Rubber
Company, a manufacturer of industrial rubber products, and has since
operated it as a division of the company.

Weathering the Depression and building up steam during the war
years, Goodrich moved heavily into the chemical industry through the
creation of the B. F. Goodrich Chemical Company as a separate operating
division. The chemicals division's strength lies in the industrial chemicals,
plastics, and synthetic rubbers.

Chemical growth was strengthened by the 1950 acquisition of Harmon Color Works, which has since been operated as another division in the chemical operations of the company.

Goodrich's footwear lines were braced by acquiring I.T.S. Company, a major manufacturer of heels and soles for shoes. In this same year of 1953, Goodrich moved deeper into automotive accessories by acquiring the business of Walter Metzger, Incorporated, manufacturer and distributor of Koroseal upholstery to the transportation industry.

After a lengthy wait, Goodrich finally moved into the sponge and foamed products line in 1954 by the acquisition of the Sponge Rubber Products Company, now operating as a separate division.

In 1961 Goodrich sought to strengthen its competitive position in retail operations by the purchase of Rayco Manufacturing Company, with 140 automotive seat cover outlets. Further retail strength was added that year by the acquisition of the Vanderbilt Tire & Rubber Company, with 44 retail outlets and 8 department store car-care centers. Both of these retail acquisitions tend to have the majority of their outlets in shopping centers and department store locations.

In addition to a high growth rate, Goodrich has a number of notable firsts in both the rubber and chemical industries. The creativity of Goodrich scientists and engineers was noted even before the 1930's when they introduced high-carbon black in rubber to add toughness and abrasion resistance to tires. Goodrich's accelerators to speed vulcanization time plus antioxidants and age-resistors triggered broad technological advances throughout the entire rubber industry.

Goodrich has been a notable contributor to the synthetic rubber industry through many technological and design advances in the cold-rubber process used in synthetics. The self-sealing aviation gas tanks of the Second World War have evolved to the present puncture-sealing tubeless tires; again B. F. Goodrich holds the first and basic patent on these tires that shook the whole rubber industry.

All the creative technology for which Goodrich has been noted through the years has resulted in an enviable position in the plastic, synthetic, and industrial chemical lines.

Today, B. F. Goodrich has a product line spanning five divisions:

Tires: Tires of all types for all vehicles; automotive components and accessories; repair and retreading equipment.

Chemicals: Vinyl resins, compounds, and latices; acrylic elastimers and latices; antioxidents, water soluble resins; acids; polyurethane materials.

Industrial Products: Hose; belting; power transmission equipment; packing; extruded products; industrial clothing and thread; adhesives; rigid and soft plastics.

Aerospace and Defense: Solid propellants; rocket motors; pressure containers; electrical and pneumatic deicing systems; space suits and seals; fasteners; sonar.

Consumer: "Koroseal" products; vinyl, rubber, and asphalt flooring; wall coverings; fabrics and threads; foam rubber and foamed plastic products; surgical and hospital supplies; hose; raincoats and footwear; luggage.

Goodrich's diversification has unlimited potential. There is no barrier across lines, no cowardice toward exploration and exploitation of new and lucrative areas in either rubber or chemicals. B. F. Goodrich has the finest potential of any company in the rubber industry.

Potential, however, is no reflection of performance. Upon examining rubber industry figures, it is apparent that B .F. Goodrich is lagging behind and occupying fifth place of the Big Five in rubber. Goodyear, Firestone, U.S. Rubber, and General Tire all equaled or surpassed Goodrich's 7% increase in sales, while none of the others suffered half as much as Goodrich with a 15% decline in earnings. All of the Big Five suffered losses in earnings in 1962 and fared slightly better in 1963, but again Goodrich was comparatively poor in the showings. In 1964 Goodrich dropped from 62nd position to 64th in the top 500 industrials.

For the last several years Goodrich has suffered more than the others from an increasing profit squeeze. Goodrich's return on equity is a good indication of its place in industry (Figure 3.1). It is apparent that Goodrich has declined since 1956. Since Goodrich has been in a less favorable position than any of its competitors for approximately seven years, this decline becomes even more serious. Net income has steadily dropped from 6.04% in 1956 to 3.24% in 1962. There was a slight increase of 3.3% in 1963 and 3.9% in 1964.

If we isolate the chemical divisions and examine them for the reason for failure to offset declines in the rubber divisions, the answer is not heartening. Even the chemicals declined steadily and failed to bolster the rubber divisions, which is why Goodrich expanded and diversified its operations in the first place.

In summary, then, Goodrich has been plagued by rising expenses and declining income and has kept pace with increasing net sales. The return on equity has dropped more severely than anyone else's and steadily at that. What's behind this poor performance of a potentially fine competitor?

Price weakness, both in tires and in chemicals, has been a major factor in Goodrich's decline. Although the company was able to utilize economies of scale through unit volume and also utilize cost reduction programs, this was not enough to offset the vicious competition characterizing the tire industry and the falling prices in chemicals.

B. F. Goodrich is the major supplier to General Motors. To retain this account, Goodrich is forced to walk an ever-narrowing line as dictated from Detroit. The automobile industry is a direct factor in the manufac-

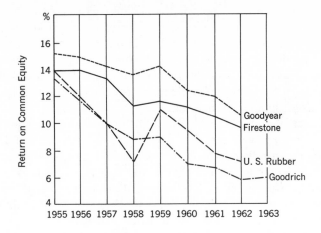

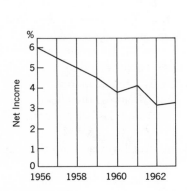

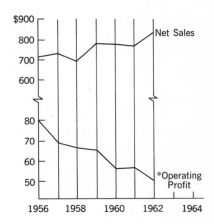

Figure 3.1
Profit Squeeze
Income Decline
Sales v Profits*
In Millions of Dollars

ture of tires and is scrutinized by Goodrich for both the original equipment and replacement outlets. General Motors is somewhat of a dictator as far as Goodrich is concerned; it must obey and conform with its ideas on prices or the account or a portion of it may be lost. The competition is far too stiff to slack off and fight with General Motors, so Goodrich will be forced to live with the ever-narrowing profit margins in the original equipment market.

In the replacement tire market competition is equally fierce not only with the Big Five, but also with a host of smaller manufacturers, private brands, and discounters eager for the slightest gap in a tire price which they might undercut. In addition, the replacement market is growing, being linked directly with disposable income and new car sales. When new car sales decline, people buy new tires and "make do" until things look better. Faced with an ever-growing number of aging cars and need for replacement tires, sharper competition for the replacement market and its larger profits loom for Goodrich.

However, Goodrich hasn't the retail organization or knowledge to really fight it out with retailing experts like Goodyear and Firestone. Sears is ever expanding its private brands, and most of the larger discounters have entered into the fight through car-care centers. This shift in distribution pattern, from smaller tire dealers into a small number of larger accounts, has forced price concessions in both private brands and brand name tires. When the chaotic price structure will settle down is unknown; the downward pressure on tires, both automobile and industrial, has continued for several years, although 1963 showed slight improvement all around.

The chemical situation isn't much better than that of tires. Although Goodrich holds a very strong competitive position in chemicals, profits have been dropping there also. Goodrich has a good research staff and is a very good competitor in almost all phases of the chemicals division. It has enjoyed this position since 1947, but now an increasing number of companies are in active competition and as a result many chemical prices have come tumbling down. An example of this is the drop in vinyl plastic, from $.38 per pound in 1954 to $.15 in 1962. All across the chemical lines there were general price shakeups, and competition has been fiercely contested. Often Goodrich cut prices to pass on cost savings and regain business only to trigger a price war it could not afford to wage and the whole cycle started anew.

Goodrich made cost savings of over $25 million in the rubber and chemicals division in 1962, only to have it disappear into a chasm of price cuts and concessions. If prices would hold steady, it would be "the first chance we have had to make those savings count in our earnings," said Goodrich's President Keener.

Goodrich is also dependent upon rubber price fluctuations since it was only in 1956 that they acquired any extensive crude-rubber holdings, and they won't appreciate the savings from those trees until 1964-1965. Previously, buying all their crude rubber placed them at the mercy of a shifting and arbitrary world price which again ate into the profits. Normally rubber is divided into approximately 35% crude and 35% synthetic, the remaining 30% being dependent upon the price of the crude. If crude is low, crude will be used for the balance; if it is high, synthetic will be used. By furnishing its own, Goodrich hopes to avoid much of the variance and speculation involved in crude-rubber prices.

Also contributing to the profit squeeze are the 40,000 workers in Goodrich's organization. The rubber workers have been relatively quiet lately, but the union's leadership is under fire from some members for not keeping up wage demands through the years. Even if wage demands and productivity are kept aligned, any price cuts or concessions will probably overshadow any increased production and economies of scale through a higher unit volume. In addition, if bargaining is drawn out, causing strikes and lost time, the effect could be a direct and lasting drag on the economy, especially disposable income. Also, remember that any strikes or lost time at General Motors, would have an adverse effect on Goodrich through the original equipment market.

Another major problem with Goodrich is decentralization. The rigid adherence to decentralization has created a real headache as far as marketing efforts for the diversified lines so prized by Goodrich. There has been little or no coordination of marketing efforts at the divisional level while new product planning has been hit or miss, at best. With the fierce competition confronting Goodrich in both rubber or chemicals, this failure to recognize a major marketing weakness is a direct reflection on management. This competition calls for some degree of initial centralization until the planning stages are complete and coordinated. There are tremendous savings available through centralization of isolated and repetitive functions across a company. Goodrich should investigate the waste opportunities in decentralization of all corporate functions.

Goodrich's purchase of Rayco and Vanderbilt has strengthened its retail operations immensely. Further efforts to establish a name in the mind of the public should pay off. The replacement market will continue to grow, and any efforts now to make inroads upon competition are going to be much less expensive than waiting until the competition is well entrenched in Goodrich's market. This places 200 outlets into a relatively untouched (by Goodrich anyway) market where the profits are larger than any other section of the tire industry, besides furnishing outlets for other accessories and upholstery items.

There must be some effort toward corporate centralization. Whether or not Goodrich has the management talent at divisional levels to practice complete decentralization in the face of ever-increasing competition is questionable. Some market planning is essential for any control over these diversified areas. Only recently has Goodrich centralized credit and warehousing operations, each previously performed at division level.

Goodrich should expand its rubber holdings in order to make it completely independent of the world rubber price which fluctuates for political and environmental reasons. This would allow considerable savings on raw material costs plus assuring Goodrich of a steady supply. The selection of its holdings appears to be excellent; Liberia has a certain degree of stability and political maturity that is lacking in Malaysia and Indonesia.

lthough tires make up 40% of Goodrich sales, this price competi-
tires could be disastrous unless it is coordinated centrally with
ontrol and strategy employed to advantageously compete with discounters and private brands. Tires can make or break Goodrich; chemicals
are not that strong yet to completely compensate for losses in the tire
markets. However, strong marketing action through retail outlets and
perhaps its own discount and car-care centers could divert some of the
competition.

Wages are an unknown factor. Any strike or major wage increase
could really cripple Goodrich. Pressure applied politically to insure that
the wage-productivity guidelines are followed generally, especially in the
basic industries, such as steel, auto, and construction, could be an answer.

Goodrich's problems center around competitive pricing, crude-rubber pricing, marketing efforts through retail outlets, decentralization, and
rising wage rates; however, the future may see solutions to these problems,
allowing Goodrich to realize its full potential.

FOR DISCUSSION

1. What is the major policy weakness in Goodrich's problem of decentralization? Could you suggest any solutions?
2. Evaluate the worth and deficiencies of the company's retail operations.
3. Which problem would you say is most pressing to Goodrich at the present
   time? Is the solution to this dependent more on internal factors than external
   factors?
4. Which problem would you say is of least importance?
5. How would you evaluate the company's performance in relation to its potential?

SUGGESTED READING

Clark, C. A., "B. F. Goodrich," *Barron's National Business and Financial
Weekly*, January 23, 1956, pp. 17-20.
Storch, H. B., "What Chance Have Rubber Producers For Gains in 1963,"
Magazine of Wall Street, May 4, 1963, pp. 198-218.
"The Weak Link," *Forbes*, June 1, 1963, p. 26.

A. O. Smith Corporation

THE A. O. SMITH CORPORATION, a diversified company producing
automotive chassis frames, pipe for the oil and gas industries, and a long
line of miscellaneous items, was formed in 1904 and became incorporated

in 1916. The home office is in Milwaukee, Wisconsin, and the company has 22 United States and international manufacturing locations.

The company traces its beginnings back to 1874, when an English machinist, Charles Jeremiah Smith, established a small machine shop in Milwaukee. Smith and Sons then began producing parts for baby carriages and bicycles, eventually becoming the largest United States manufacturer of bicycle parts. In 1902 the company began production of automobile chassis frames for the Peerless Motor Company. Prior to this time, all frames had been constructed of wood or structural steel, both heavy and quite rigid. Smith solved these problems of weight and flexibility by producing frames from processed steel, a process which revolutionized the industry. Under the guidance of A. O. Smith (eldest son of C. J. Smith), the process-steel method of frame production came to the attention of the automobile industry. Henry Ford, on the verge of mass producing his car, liked the new Smith process and contracted Smith to produce 10,000 frames in a period of four months. Such a strenuous demand (since average frame production in 1906 was only 12 per day) led to further technological developments and refinements in frame production which further added to the prestige of the Smith frame. Following the successful completion of the Ford project, Smith also became a frame producer for other automobile companies—Pope-Toledo, Cadillac, Packard, Elmore, Locomobile, and eventually the whole line of General Motors products.

Upon A. O. Smith's death in 1913, his son, Lloyd Raymond Smith, took over the company, led it into incorporation, and spearheaded its growth for the next 23 years. Under L. R. Smith's guidance the company created the first automatic frame plant in the industry. When completed in 1921, the line automatically turned out one frame every eight seconds, a production rate which enabled the company to produce millions of frames per year at lower and lower costs. This line, incidentally, stayed in continuous production for 37 years. During this period the company became General Motors' principal outside supplier of frames. The company also expanded its tubular products' production during this period (1913-1936), and it also commenced work in the process industries. Based on the development of perfected electric-flash welding methods, Smith became a producer of pressure vessels, primarily those used in the oil refining industry.

William C. Heath became president in 1936, as the company undertook an expansion and diversification program. This program led to the acquisition of meter production facilities (for measuring petroleum), the patenting of a new process of rust prevention for water heaters (a process which revolutionized the water heater industry), and the production and marketing of welding equipment and specially designed electric motors. During the Second World War the company shifted its facilities to war production and produced propeller blades, aircraft landing equipment, and five million bomb casings—roughly 80% of the United States' requirements.

In 1951 Lloyd B. Smith, grandson of A. O. Smith, became president of the corporation. During the past decade, Smith has increased its operations in the automotive, tubular, and consumer-products divisions while also undertaking a diversification program. The company had acquired the Burkay Company (water heaters), Whirlaway Motors (electric motors), Glascote Products (glass-lined equipment), Erie Meter Systems, Clark Controller (control equipment), and Ionia (fiber glass automobile body producer). Furthermore, the company has expanded by creating various subsidiaries (Harvestore—glass-lined farm storage silos) and by acquiring half-ownership in A. O. Smith Corporation of Texas (welded line pipe); DowSmith, Incorporated (reinforced glass fiber pipe); and Bisset-Berman Corporation (military intelligence systems).

A. O. Smith was ranked 178th in *Fortune*'s 1960 industrial rating. At the end of 1964 its rank slipped to 201st. The company produces a wide variety of products, but its leading products are automobile frames, tubular products, and consumer products, specifically water heaters. The Automotive Division generates 40% of sales, Tubular Division 20%, Consumer Products 20%, and all other products 20% (Table 3.1).

The company produces roughly 25% of the nation's automobile frames and 45% of the truck frames in the country. Until 1964 Smith produced 40% of General Motors' frame requirements; but with General Motors' decision not to produce its own Chevrolet frames in the future, the additional 300,000 to 400,000 frames should give Smith 50% plus of General Motors' frame requirements. The Automotive Division is operating in a rather select industry with only four major chassis producers outside of the automobile producers themselves. Smith and Budd Manufacturing Company are the two largest producers in the frame industry.

Tubular Products Division is in an industry presently faced with overcapacity. Smith continues to produce special piping needs which keep it on top of the industry in the area of glass-lined pipe products. In other areas of the industry its position is not as established; reasons for this situation will be discussed later. Water heaters (Consumer Products Division) are also in an industry which faces overcapacity. However, Smith technology, which led to the production of the first glass-lined water heater, has kept the company in a leading position in the industry. Presently, Smith is the largest manufacturer in the world of commercial and domestic water heaters.

Perhaps the major problem Smith faces today is that it is subject to fluctuations in motor vehicle output. When 40% of sales come from one industry, a company is definitely placed in an unpleasantly vulnerable position, a fact Smith clearly recognizes. A perfect example of this situation was the automotive decline in the mild recession of 1961. With car

Table 3.1

A. O. SMITH FIVE-YEAR HIGHLIGHTS, 1959-1963

	Net Sales	Net Earnings	Net Earnings Per Share	Dividends Declared Per Share	Long Term Debt	Stockholders Equity	Ratio of Current Assets to Current Liabilities
1959	$283,650,469	$11,482,044	$5.35	$1.53	$28,000,000	$94,299,146	4.9
1960	265,177,979	6,456,675	3.01	1.95	27,000,000	96,582,862	5.0
1961	221,952,033	869,831d	.41d	1.60	26,000,000	92,297,797	5.1
1962	249,053,000	5,675,165	2.65	1.00	25,000,000	96,893,362	4.5
1963	281,819,087	6,065,035	2.83	1.00	32,570,000	96,920,523	4.4
1963*	112,584,781	2,742,626	1.28	.25	32,570,000	99,126,819	4.4
1964	229,851,679	1,893,298	.88	1.00	32,440,000	97,684,958	2.5

* In 1963 changed its fiscal year from July 31 to December 31. Data shown is for the short period August 1, 1963, to December 31, 1963.

d = indicates deficit

SOURCE: Company Annual Reports 1962 and 1963.

sales down in 1961, Smith lost nearly $40 million in sales from the previous year. The result was a net deficit for the year, and the situation would have been much worse if it had not been for other divisions turning in profitable years. This dependence, then, on the automobile industry is clearly one of Smith's major problems.

Another problem which faced the Automotive Division, and one which the company is apparently overcoming, was that of "unitized construction." For the past few years the automobile producers were generally in favor of a unitized body—frame and body to be made as a single rather than separate unit. In this method there were supposed safety and cost advantages; in other words, no individual frame would be produced. The idea was tried and had some success in the various compact cars. If such a move had been continued and successfully carried to the bigger models, frame producers would have found themselves holding many empty warehouses, which were formerly production facilities. Faced with this situation, Smith and the other frame manufacturers undertook a full scale engineering research program to convince the automobile producers to maintain the standard frame. Apparently the program was successful because General Motors has returned to the use of chassis frames rather than unitized bodies with the 1964 models of four of its compact cars; however, if once again the tide should turn back to unitized construction, Smith would once again find itself in a most vulnerable position.

The Tubular Division, like the Automotive Division, has been one of the strongest divisions throughout company history. In 1927, with the invention and perfection of a new welding process for piping, Smith virtually revolutionized the industry. Furthermore, initial industry demand for piping was very great. With all the transcontinental natural gas and oil lines and oil exploration, Smith along with the other pipe producers found a ready market, both domestic and international in scope; however, by 1964, many of these conditions no longer existed. The foreign market had been virtually eliminated. Foreign pipe mills, freight charges, and lower prices of foreign steel destroyed the existence of a foreign market for tubular products; nevertheless, in the face of this depletion in foreign markets, pipe making capacity has increased. In the face of this rising capacity, with most transcontinental lines completed, the market for large diameter pipe has been static. Smith has recognized this problem and is presently attempting new means of retaining what percentage of the market it previously had. Demand for high strength pipe and casing has been rising; and in search of this market, Smith has installed larger presses and has expanded its research and development in this area.

Yet, the company still faces another problem with its Tubular Division. A. O. Smith is the only producer of large diameter pipe that is not an integrated operation. All other large producers of pipe are steel companies; the pipe producing facilities are a division of the entire operation.

For Smith, this could, if it has not already, result in higher costs for raw steel, which could result in higher prices and thus fewer customers or lower profits. President L. B. Smith in his 1963 report stated the future of A. O. Smith in tubular products by saying: "A. O. Smith's participation in the entire tubular goods market is not expected to change but we must expect more limited returns from the operations of the Tubular Products Division."

A. O. Smith is the world's largest manufacturer of commercial and domestic water heaters. Smith has become known as a pioneer in the industry through its research and development program. It was this program which developed "Permaglas," a process of glass-lining steel to prevent rust and chipping, yet still permitting the steel to be flexible enough for further operations. With this breakthrough in the production process, sales and earnings in the Consumer Products Division reached all time record highs in the middle 1950's.

However, when the patents on the Permaglas process expired, other producers quickly copied the process and began producing equivalent products; furthermore, with all the additional private residential construction in the past decade, the market for water heaters was very great. This new market and the relative ease of producing the product drew in producers from all over. Capacity increased, the market was flooded with products, and prices dropped. These "fly-by-night" producers and low prices still are creating major problems for Smith. The company has taken steps to counter the situation, mainly through cost reductions in the Consumer Products Division and through increased volume. In 1950 Smith opened production facilities on the West Coast, and it is now also producing water heaters under a nationally-known brand name of a large nationwide retail establishment, Sears & Roebuck. Also, the company has increased its total number of dealers to over 20,000 throughout the country.

Another problem which the company was faced with was that of the Process Equipment Division. This division produced various pressure vessels for petroleum refining and for atomic energy uses. The division, however, was faced with extremely high costs for tooling, specialized engineering abilities, and production skills; yet, in the face of all these rising expenses, demand was relatively poor. Based on these factors, Smith decided, in 1963, to withdraw from the manufacture of pressure vessels, heat exchangers, and related equipment.

Diversification was a cure for some of Smith's major problems. The company increased its number of products from 23 in 1946-1947 to 50 in 1964. The purposes of the diversification have been twofold: security and agility. The security element of the diversification policy paid off in 1961, when losses due to a poor year in the Automotive Division were held to under one-half of one percent of sales as a result of a good year in the other divisions. The agility element is being used as a means of gaining broad knowledge and experience, which will prepare the company to act decisively when markets are threatened or new opportunities appear.

Diversification at Smith has then been primarily aimed at the Automotive and Tubular Divisions to relieve some of the sales pressure from these areas; however, besides solving problems, diversification also creates problems. One of the first problems found in undertaking a diversification program is to locate acceptable ventures to acquire. Relatively profitable operations are usually not up for sale and the acquiring firm does not want to be burdened down by too many heavy losers, those firms most likely to be up for sale. Another problem is where to obtain the necessary capital to acquire these new interests. Third, Smith must decide how long to hold these acquisitions, how much to invest in them, and when to sell them if they prove continually unprofitable. All of these are problems which Smith has faced, is presently facing, and will continue to face if it is to continue its diversification strategy.

In summary, the problems facing the A. O. Smith Corporation include those problems in the Automotive Division, centered primarily around the extreme dependence of sales and earnings on motor vehicle output and also on the additional use of unitized bodies as opposed to chassis frames; and those in the Tubular Division, where Smith faces problems of overcapacity, a demand situation that will probably never be restored to old levels, and a highly competitive cost situation with the other tube producers, all of which are integrated operations. Consumer products, also plagued by overcapacity and low price levels, and problems related to the activation of its diversification program are also areas of concern, which will demand constant attention from Smith management.

FOR DISCUSSION

1. On what industry is Smith largely dependent for sales?
2. What was the problem associated with unitized construction? How did Smith solve this? Would you say that the problem was completely remedied by this solution? Can you suggest any other method?
3. In what does the strength of the company lie?
4. What problems does Smith face with its Tubular Division?
5. Do you appreciate Smith's solution to its major problems?

SUGGESTED READING

Annual Report 1964.
Rolland, L. J., "A. O. Smith Profile," *Financial World*, July 27, 1960, p. 22.
"Solid Demand, Firm Tabs Aid A. O. Smith Recovery," *Barron's National Business and Financial Weekly*, July 1, 1963, p. 22.

American Motors Corporation

AMERICAN MOTORS CORPORATION is a progressive company in two of the nation's largest and most highly competitive industries. Its compact Rambler cars sparked something of a modern revolution in the automotive industry, and its Kelvinator trademark is one of the oldest names in the electric appliance industry. The company ranks among the top fifty of the nation's largest and sells its products in every state and more than 140 foreign countries.

The story of American Motors actually begins with the merger of the ailing Hudson Motor Car Company and the Nash-Kelvinator Corporation on May 1, 1954. The immediate results of this merger could hardly be termed successful: the 1954 level of car production was less than half of the combined production of the two companies before the merger. Together, in 1953, Nash-Kelvinator and Hudson had 3.56% of the industry sales. In 1954 this dropped to 2.14% and in 1955, a year of record sales for the rest of the automobile industry, it reached a low of 1.91%.

To put the story in perspective, however, we need some background on the companies involved. Thomas B. Jeffery began production of the Rambler automobile in 1902 at Kenosha, Wisconsin., Jeffery was one of the first automobile producers to use the assembly line. After his death in 1910, his son Charles took over the leadership of the growing company.

During this year the other company which eventually became part of American Motors had begun its first year of production. The Hudson Motor Car Company was founded in 1909 by Joseph L. Hudson, and by the end of its first production year in 1910 it hit seventeenth place among automobile manufacturers.

Charles W. Nash, in 1916, purchased the Thomas B. Jeffery Company and changed the company's name to Nash Motors Company. In 1936 Nash, then 72, began to look for a successor. His search led to George W. Mason, then president of the Kelvinator Corporation, manufacturers of electrical appliances. Mason was unwilling to leave the Kelvinator Company, so the companies merged on January 4, 1937, as the Nash-Kelvinator Corporation. Mason became president of the new corporation, while Nash was elected chairman of the board.

Mason, as president of Nash-Kelvinator, put Nash engineers to work on a new, economical, light-weight car. In 1940 Nash brought out the Nash "600," the first mass-produced American auto of the single unit or unitized construction principle. The auto was so successful that it brought Nash from fourth place to second place among the independents in sales.

Following the Second World War, in which both Nash-Kelvinator and Hudson were actively engaged in the nation's defense effort, sales began to dwindle for the independents. Hudson's president, A. E. Barit, successor to Roy D. Chapin, sought a merger with another independent. The consolidation with Nash-Kelvinator in 1954 to form American Motors Corporation was the largest in the history of the industry. Mason became president, chairman, and general manager, with George Romney as executive vice-president.

Less than six months after the merger, Mason died and Romney was elected to the presidency. He inherited one of the greatest corporation muddles in history. The first year American Motors realized a loss of $24 million. The industry's banner year for total sales, 1955, brought losses of $7 million to American Motors. By the end of the first four years the company showed a total loss of more than $49 million.

Within a few months after his promotion Romney delivered his controversial "Dinosaur in the Driveway" speech, in which he blamed the other auto producers for "building gas-guzzling dinosaurs that overflow garages and parking spaces" and made known his cardinal philosophy that American consumers hungered for more useful and more economical smaller cars. Romney firmly believed in the future of the compact car. When, in 1950, Nash revived the Rambler name for its new compact, which was based on the design principle of the 1940 Nash "600," Romney predicted to his father that before long, the Big Three would be offering small cars. Few at that time would have believed him.

The big car concept which had begun before the Second World War gained fresh impetus after the war, expressing itself in the form of even larger, gaudier, and more costly cars. The industry capitalized on the fact that cars could be glamorized and merchandised as status symbols for their owners. The buyer had little choice. He could buy a big car or a bigger car. His alternative was one of the cramped foreign makes, which were beginning to invade the market. *Time* captured the situation in a 1959 article:

In 1955, Detroit sniffed the first faint signs of dissatisfaction; a ripple of interest in imported cars. At first, Detroit wrote it off as reverse big-car snobbery and the desire to have something different. When imports rose .8% of the market in 1955, to 8% in 1958, it became clear that more than snobbery was at work.

During this time Romney had been hard at work trying to spark some life into the company. His first moves were to sell surplus plants and liquidate costly duplicate leases. Next, he reorganized top management by retiring old executives and bringing in new hustlers. One such person brought in was Roy Abernathy, whose job as vice-president of sales was to overhaul and rebuild American's selling organization.

According to Abernathy:

Field personnel had grown rusty and apathetic; the dealer bodies were weak and ineffective and with few exceptions unable to step up to the competition of a tough buyer's market . . . the company had no hope of the future without an effective dealer organization.

Even though sales were falling, Abernathy and his assistants went from dealer to dealer, weeding out the weak and ineffective. Abernathy washed out 1,000 weak distributors in 1954-1956, then brought the dealer organization back to a fighting strength of 2,700.

Rigid expense control enabled American Motors to bring its breakeven point down to about 120,000 cars a year in 1957. With production potential doubled in 1959 to that of 1957, the breakeven point only increased to 130,000 cars a year. Four times as many cars were made in 1959 as in 1954, but with 40% fewer salaried employees and only 12% more hourly employees.

The gravest problem for the company was yet to be solved—selling the public. As stated earlier, the auto industry was already forcing the issue; all that was needed was someone to take advantage of it. Beginning with the 1958 model year, American Motors stopped making big cars and dropped the Nash and Hudson names. The company decided to put all its eggs in one basket and stake its automotive future on the Rambler. This was a calculated move to outflank competition, rather than to continue trying to meet them head-on. Romney then launched an aggressive information program to tell the product story to the public and to gain corporate identity. He assailed big cars as never before and attacked the false concept of car value based on size, flash, and power. Before long, insurance companies, cartoonists, newspaper writers, and even songwriters joined in lamblasting the big cars. The company attracted the attention of the public by selling Rambler's economy and compact size.

Finally, the public accepted the Rambler late in 1957; 1958 saw American Motors for the first time nudge into the black. This was even more remarkable since 1958 was a recession year, and General Motors was the only other auto manufacturer making a profit. American Motors was the only company in the industry to increase sales over 1957 (Table 3.2).

The Big Three, seldom caught napping, suddenly woke up and realized that American Motors had done the near impossible. In 1960 the Big Three, finally realizing the market potential, brought out their compact cars. Much to everyone's surprise, American Motors not only held its

Table 3.2
HOW THEY SOLD

	1955	1956	1957	1958	1959	1960	1961	1962	1963*
GENERAL MOTORS	3,639,120	3,024,286	2,683,365	2,157,443	2,543,089	2,869,799	2,724,009	3,599,473	3,810,000
FORD	1,908,736	1,694,108	1,818,169	1,230,394	1,698,814	1,749,302	1,670,459	1,824,864	1,880,000
CHRYSLER	1,206,195	922,043	1,096,359	647,932	682,791	921,337	631,762	666,900	926,000
AMERICAN	136,753	115,105	117,330	186,373	363,372	422,273	370,685	423,104	426,000
STUDEBAKER	147,864	104,798	67,754	47,798	133,382	106,244	72,155	77,877	65,000
Total U.S. Cars	7,111,443	5,857,061	5,775,515	4,275,997	5,427,144	6,077,865	5,476,125	6,599,703	7,120,000
VOLKSWAGEN	28,907	50,011	64,242	78,225	119,899	159,995	177,308	192,570	233,000
RENAULT	—	2,425	22,586	48,050	90,536	62,772	44,122	29,763	22,500
TRIUMPH	—	2,347	6,366	16,225	22,922	17,720	11,683	15,967	20,200
VOLVO	—	1,605	6,907	14,000	18,468	13,926	12,787	13,157	14,100
MERCEDES-BENZ	—	3,021	3,446	8,300	13,739	14,435	12,903	11,075	9,800
Total Imports	58,465	98,187	206,827	378,517	614,131	498,785	378,622	339,160	380,000
Total Car Sales	7,169,908	5,955,248	5,982,342	4,654,514	6,041,275	6,576,650	5,854,747	6,938,863	7,500,000

* Estimated new-car registrations.
SOURCE: *Time*, January 17, 1964, p. 81. Courtesy *Time*; copyright Time Inc. 1964.

share of the market, but increased it from 7.17% in 1959 to 7.25% in 1960.

George Romney resigned from American Motors in 1962 to make his successful bid for the governorship of Michigan. Roy Abernathy became president and chief executive officer.

The problems of American Motors now are not so obvious as the ones faced by the company in the 1950's. For the most part, these problems are either an economic or financial paradox or an extension of many of those already presented. In 1962 *Business Week* stated: "The company has reached a sales level that dictates some major changes in operation—in capital spending, in manufacturing, and in management—lest AMC slide back down and lose gains of the past seven years." These operations have changed little since the company first started showing a profit in 1958; however, the company has changed. The fight for survival has now changed to one of continued growth. The operating philosophies that helped build the company may now be holding it back by digging into the profits. It is a well-known fact that once a company's breakeven point has been reached and surpassed, profits should mushroom.

The paradox is that American Motors Corporation sales are increasing as a whole, while profits are tending to decrease. Table 3.2 shows sales have increased from 372,000 automobiles in 1959 to 455,000 in 1963. During this time, dollar sales increased from $869.8 million to $1.13 billion while net income dropped from $60 million to $37.8 million. Net income before taxes as a percentage of sales dropped from 12.12% to 6.6%. One reason for this decrease in profits is the cost of retooling, which has been needed to hold American's share of the market. Another reason is the added cost of offering expensive extras such as standard equipment, also needed to hold the market. These extras include such things as ceramic life-time guaranteed exhaust systems, curved glass windows all around, reclining seats, and others.

All auto companies manufacture essentials such as engines, car bodies, fenders, and suspensions. Almost all buy such basic items as steel, tires, and cloth. It is the big middle ground of parts—electrical components, instruments, transmissions, and spark plugs—that can be bought or made. This is the sensitive profit area. American Motors was forced to be an assembler of purchased parts in the 1950's in order to survive. The company still buys most of these middle-ground components; in fact, American Motors Corporation even buys industrial engineering to plan and execute its model changeovers.

Another important area is overburdened facilities. Much of the increase in production has been accomplished by expensive overtime and the addition of a third working shift. This third shift tends to wear out production tools faster and causes higher maintenance costs.

Thus far, the company has been extremely cautious in its investments in new buildings and equipment. This is, no doubt, due to the company's near tragedy in the mid-1950's. All investments have been from retained earnings and have, for the most part, been stop-gap investments with seemingly little long-range planning; for example, the Kenosha Lake Shore plant, used for body production, is an old, hastily outfitted furniture factory. The plant is inefficient even by American Motor's standards, which are outmoded and lack the competitive spirit that characterizes the rest of the industry.

Another problem area for American Motors is in sales and distribution. It has been unable to capture the market of younger car buyers in the 18 to 25 age group. This group cannot be ignored: first, because it amounts to approximately 10% of the market and is growing yearly due to the baby boom of the Second World War; second, because a young, satisfied Rambler owner today is a potential buyer for years to come. The company is trying to sell this group on its new line of hardtops and convertibles and their sporty new body styles.

There are many points around the country where there are no Rambler dealers, particularly across the South from Georgia to Texas and across the Great Lakes area. Undoubtedly one of the reasons Abernathy, as sales vice-president, succeeded Romney as president, rather than Roy D. Chapin, Jr., executive vice-president and general manager, was that Abernathy was more familiar with the important problems of sales and distribution. The Board of Directors must have felt this was an important area for future Rambler growth.

Another possible problem is the progress-sharing plan for hourly workers which was initiated in September, 1961. This plan, a milestone in union contracts, seeks to share the "fruits of progress" among workers and owners. The point to be made is that unless there are profits and substantial gains for the workers, there is a possibility of trouble. The progress-sharing plan could mean loss-sharing, too. Workers might be called on to give up a few pennies on annual raises to meet higher fringe costs if these cannot be met from the progress-sharing fund. According to *Business Week:*

In its second year of operation . . . AMC announced that its fiscal year profits were up 10.4%, but that the pie to be shared by production workers had shrunk 5% . . . Tony Russo, president of UAW Local #12 at Kenosha concedes that some of the men want to get rid of the program . . . What soured them was the discovery that their cut was $500,000 less than last year, though the company's net after taxes was $3.6 million more.

The final area to be discussed is the fickle and unpredictable buying public and American Motors putting all of its eggs in one basket. The fickleness of the buying public is evidenced by the decrease in the percentage of the market held by all compacts in the past few years. Total car sales in 1962, including imports, reached 7.2 million, with compacts making up 38% of this market. Sales reached an all-time high in 1963 of 7.7 million, but the share taken by compacts had shrunk to 33%. Though its sales (in 1963) set a company record, American Motors dropped from 6.2% to 5.5% of the market. Due to an expanding economy with its larger paychecks and the extra stimulus of a Federal tax-cut, there has been an interest in increased luxury. Undoubtedly, sales will pick up should the economy start to contract. Another and more important reason for the loss is that many of the Big Three's so-called "compacts" have increased in size so that they are no longer classified as compacts. With only smaller-sized autos to sell, it missed out on the upswing in large car sales. The company, however, has corrected the situation by adding about ten inches to the wheel base of its 1965 Ambassador line. For the first time since the company has started showing profits, American Motors has taken one of its models out of the compact line. At the end of the first quarter of the 1965 fiscal year, sales of Rambler's luxury Ambassador series were more than double the previous year's comparable figure. This could, however, hurt the sales in the compact line because the company is no longer in the position to lampoon the "gas-guzzling dinosaurs" of the Big Three. On the other hand, American Motors cannot afford to lose out on the big car market.

In 1963 the company was in its most solid financial position since it was formed, with a working capital of $188,867,000 as of September 30, 1963. However, at the end of fiscal 1964 its working capital decreased to $94,653,625. The decline in earnings from $37,807,205 in 1963 to $26,226,-735 in 1964 was primarily due to the dip in Rambler domestic sales volume and a lower proportion of sales in higher priced models during the fiscal year.

American Motors should achieve higher volume in the coming year because of the strong economy and its most effective array of new car models. Since the company is operating in the best sales period in automotive history, management should be able to effectively cope with its long-term problems of profit, sales, and distribution.

FOR DISCUSSION

1. Explain the contradiction of increasing sales and decreasing profits.
2. What decision was made by the Board of Directors to bring about the growth of Rambler? On what was this decision based?
3. What are the objectives of the progress-sharing plan? Is the plan adequate to produce the results and achieve the objectives it seeks?
4. Do you think American Motors is proceeding in a proper manner toward

solution of its problems of profit, sales, and distribution? Are there any procedures that you would change?

SUGGESTED READING

"American Motors comes to Fork in Road," *Business Week*, July 14, 1962, pp. 130-134.

"Another Run for the Record," *Time*, January 17, 1964, p. 81.

"Bigger Melon, Smaller Slices," *Business Week*, November 23, 1963, p. 32.

"Dinosaur Hunter," *Time*, April 6, 1959, pp. 84-89.

"Important Test for Profit Sharing," *Business Week*, November 18, 1961, p. 139.

Smith, R. A., "Will Success Spoil American Motors," *Fortune*, January, 1959, pp. 97-100.

General Motors Corporation

THE FORMATION OF GENERAL MOTORS OF NEW JERSEY, the world's largest private company, dates back to September 16, 1908. The company initially included Buick, Oldsmobile, and Oakland. William Durant organized General Motors with three main patterns in mind: variety of models, diversification, vertical integration. Durant accomplished his goal of variety of models by offering five completely different cars by the mid-twenties. Diversification was carried out by the addition of 25 companies during the first two years of operations. With a personal check for a little over $56,000, Durant purchased Frigidaire, which has since become one of the most important of the non-car divisions. Vertical integration was accomplished by buying nearly all of the productive capacity necessary to produce automobiles.

One of the most important reasons for the early success of General Motors was the high quality of the men in the organization. There was the master mechanic Walter Chrysler, who was in charge of Buick Division before he left to form his own auto company. The one-time president of General Motors, Nash, later formed Nash Motors. The most important influence came from Du Pont. In the early days Du Pont contributed money, advice, and confidence to put the company on solid ground. It is true that Durant founded General Motors, but it was A. P. Sloan that made it great.

In the early twenties General Motors expansion ran head-on with a declining business cycle. Durant was ousted and A. P. Sloan took his place. Thus began the Sloan leadership that lasted until the mid-1950's. Under the guidance of Sloan, the company became more systematic, cost conscious, and more conservative than it had been under the more colorful Durant.

Sloan continued the practice of vertical integration and diversification by the addition of many new companies. General Motors Acceptance Corporation was set up to provide credit to its many dealers. In 1926 Fisher Body was acquired to supply bodies for all its products. In the late 1930's General Motors went international by purchasing auto companies in Canada, Australia, England, and Germany. Electromotive was purchased in the early 1930's, later providing an extremely profitable division. In 1953 it purchased Euclid Road Machinery Company; Ethyl Oil Company represented an attempt to integrate into the oil industry. These are only a few examples of Sloan's influence in expanding General Motors into many new areas.

Sloan beat Ford in the 1920's by offering a large variety of models and colors to a consuming public that wanted something different. Sloan offered a yearly model change and installment buying through a good system of dealers. During the 1920's Sloan transformed a group of inefficient producers into a team that could top anyone, including Henry Ford. In 1927 Ford shut down for a six-month changeover to the Model A and began to copy the General Motors model change idea. The conservative policies of Sloan allowed the company to slip through the depression without the anxious moments that other producers faced. After the depression Sloan started a drive to retool and to add new features to the line, such as automatic transmission.

Other dynamic men have been added to the General Motors' line-up in more recent history; such a man was S. E. Knudsen. Knudsen's father was the one-time head of Chevrolet, so Knudsen was born into the business. In 1956 Knudsen took over the sagging Pontiac Division and has since built it into a best seller. He removed the excess chrome and gave it a more streamlined look. He destroyed the bad customer image that had developed around the Pontiac.

A very similar situation took place at Buick. Edward D. Rollert took over the Buick Division in 1959. Since then he has tried to create a new Buick image. In 1955 Buick was third in the market with 755,861 cars; then the Buick world fell apart and in 1961 Buick ranked eighth. The primary reasons were bad styling, mechanical trouble, and a poor customer image. Rollert added the Wildcat, the Special, the Skylark, and the Riviera. These additions, combined with more strict quality control, have improved the Buick position.

The most important asset of General Motors is its fine organization and the high quality of the men who run it (Figure 3.2). The top men are drawn from all sources. Mr. Goodman started out as an assembly-line worker without a college education and rose to a top executive position;

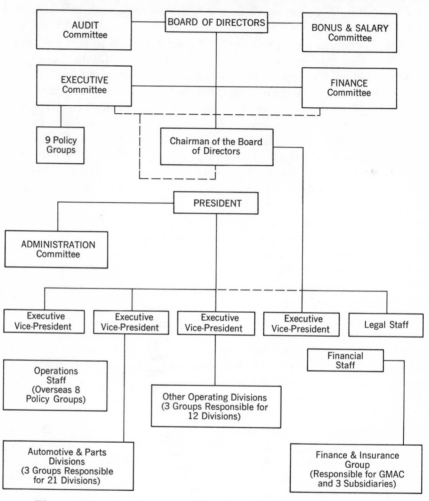

Figure 3.2
Lifelines of General Motors

however, most of the top management are college men. One of the methods the company uses to hold and attract top men is that of high salaries. Donner was the highest paid executive in the U.S. during 1962 with $791,475. The bulk of this pay was in the form of stock bonuses; $135 million of G.M. stock is owned by 350 top executives. This plan prevents some of the turnover among executives because if a man leaves before the end of the year, he loses his stock bonus.

The success of the company at present and in the future cannot be confined to this country. The Opel plants in West Germany have experienced a fast rate of growth and penetration into the European Market. The next main target of Opel is Volkswagen which can be beaten by the

new Opel Kadett. The Kadett has already cut deeply into the Volkswagen market, shrinking its European share from 34% to 28% in the 1962
model year. The Opel Company has also come out with two new models
designed to strike at the Mercedes. It appears that the foreign market may
offer many new opportunities in the future.

Chevrolet has passed Ford in recent years by a number of skillful
moves that Ford has not been able to counter. In the period 1959-1962
Ford has varied between 1.5 and 1.3 million units, but Chevrolet has
climbed from 1.4 to more than 2.1 million in the same time period. This
victory by Chevrolet was accomplished by the addition of Corvair, a
totally new type of car. Chevrolet designers were careful to design a small
car that would penetrate the foreign market without cutting into the
standard Chevrolet market. Ford did not exercise this same caution, and
the small Ford cut deeply into the standard Ford. Now that the trend is
away from the smaller cars, Ford has been left with a portion of its former
market.

These and other factors have combined to make General Motors the
largest and the most profitable of all private companies in the entire
world. In 1964 it strengthened its position as president of the "$ Billion
Sales Club" with a boost of $503 million in sales to $16,997,044,000 from
$16,494,818,184 in 1963, which was a boost of $2 billion from 1962. Some
perspective of the massive size of General Motors is also given in its total
assets of $11,245,299,000, average employment of 660,997 in 1964, and a
net profit in 1964 of $1,734,782,000. These figures show the unbelievable
scope of its operations. Gross sales have risen rather steadily from 9.8 billion in 1954 to the 1964 high.

General Motors has maintained better than half of the U.S. auto market for the past few years (Figure 3.3), and will probably maintain its
relative position because of large declines in American Motors and the
loss of Studebaker. The Chevrolet has been General Motors' number one
weapon in its deep penetration of the market (Figure 3.4).

This company has a tremendous impact on the U.S. economy. Ten
percent of all domestic steel is consumed at General Motors. By 1966 it
will have increased its car capacity by 20% and have created 50,000 new
jobs with a new plant investment of nearly $2 billion. It is obvious that
a company of such mammoth size as this holds tremendous economic
power. Such figures as these also point to the problem of long-range
planning. However, one of G.M.'s chief advantages has been its ability to
predict the market and to plan production. Its estimates of the 1962 market were laughed at by others in the industry, but the estimate was one
of the closest ever made.

General Motors has often been criticized because of the tremendous
economic power that it possesses. Many attempts have been made by the
government to curb its power, but most of them have centered around
the noncar areas. However, since 1955 the various automotive activities of

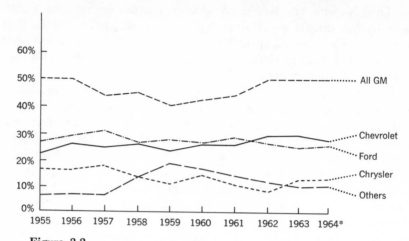

Figure 3.3
How GM has Shared in the Market Since 1955

NOTE: ° '64 estimated on production as of March 27, 1964.

the company have been investigated. It was in 1955 that General Motors first passed the 50% of the market point. Of all cars registered in the U.S., 51.9% were made by General Motors. These figures have led government

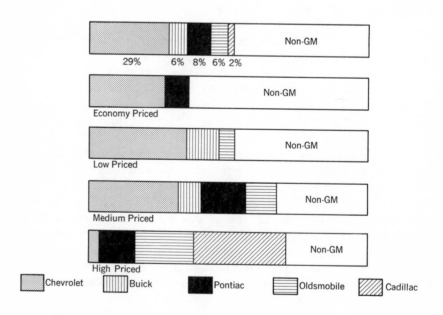

Figure 3.4
Code 1: How the Various Divisions Shared in the 1962 Market
Code 2: International Competition in 1962

agencies to set up a massive probe of General Motors for possible anti-trust violations.

Another area of General Motors that has recently come under investigation is that of stock ownership. In the spring of 1962 Du Pont was ordered to divest itself of its G.M. holdings. At that time Du Pont owned 63,000,000 shares of stock or 3.4 billion dollars worth. Du Pont was given ten years to get rid of the stock, which contributed one-third of the Du Pont profit in the form of dividends. Du Pont paid $130 million for this stock and received $2 billion in dividends in addition to the capital gain. The stockholders complained bitterly, so the government passed a tax bill allowing the Du Pont stockholders to pay only 25% on the General Motors' stock distributed to them as a dividend.

The company has been accused of using its influence as the nation's biggest rail shipper to force the use of General Motors' locomotives on all railroads. Eighty percent of all locomotives in present use were produced by General Motors. Another action seeks to nullify the 1953 acquisition of the Euclid Road Machinery Company, which is dominant in the manufacture of certain types of road equipment. It has also been accused of attempting to monopolize in many of these noncar areas. The attitude of General Motors is that it has done no wrong and that each charge must be met as it arises. So far, it has been fairly successful in defending its activities.

The results of the various investigations and disclosures are hard to pinpoint; but it appears that if General Motors continues to grow, the government may act against it. One such action might be the possible divesture of Chevrolet, but of course this is only speculation. General Motors appears to be a well-behaved giant since auto prices have remained constant over the past few years. Most experts will agree that it has the power to influence the market, but one can find very little evidence of the exertion of this power, except in the noncar areas.

General Motors also faces problems in distribution. Recently, there has been a clamor for wholesale handling of Chevrolet but the company has resisted the trend. The present system is one of franchises handled through General Motors Acceptance Corporation. Recently, this issue came up before the courts and G.M. was acquitted; however, the courts did require vast amounts of records for further study. Among those required were records of cost, price, profit, pricing systems, capital, advertising, and agreements between Buick, Oldsmobile, and Pontiac. General Motors objected to this probe on the grounds that it would be very expensive to gather such a vast amount of information.

Racing has been a traditional method of promoting new models since Henry Ford employed Barney Olfield to race his latest models. However, the General Motors' management has decreased the emphasis on racing to the point where its cars no longer hold most of the speed records as they once did. Only time will tell if this policy will be helpful to sales.

There is also much internal competition in the company that keeps it from becoming soft. Because many of its models overlap, there is a great amount of fierce competition among the various divisions.

The vast number of models made available today has caused vast logistic and production problems. General Motors now produces 138 different models. Optional equipment has added to this tremendous problem. Chevrolet offers four engines with three different carburetors in standard-sized Chevrolets. The other optional equipment brings the total number of varieties of power plants to 106 for standard Chevrolet alone. G.M. has met this problem of logistics with the use of high-speed computers and its elaborate queuing system, which provides the needed logistics for its mammoth operations.

Labor has also been a problem, just as with any large company. These problems have not been too serious in recent years, but there are many indications of a real battle coming up in negotiations. Since profits have been at record levels, Walter Reuther, the head of the United Auto Workers, has asked for the greatest wage boost ever. In 1964 Reuther requested a 10% raise in wages for all auto workers. The government has warned that this would be inflationary because the average increase in productivity was only 3.2%. Reuther points to the 4.9% increase in productivity in the auto industry, but he does not recognize productivity increases as a factor. He also maintains that General Motors could cut car prices, improve workers' pay and benefits, and still earn a satisfactory return on investment. Both sides are hoping to negotiate without government interference. The articles of the old contracts are already the most liberal in all of industry.

The company has been pressured by the N.A.A.C.P. to hire more Negro white-collar workers immediately. The policy has been started to hire whites only when no colored applicants can be found. This process of reverse discrimination is being used to correct the racial imbalance. It is possible that this program could lead to a general disruption in the G.M.s' employee development program. As men are hired and promoted because of race rather than ability, the human resources of General Motors will be endangered.

Government, distribution, labor—these are the main areas of concern for the company. If this leader is to maintain its record position, it must be alert to short- and long-range solutions to these problems.

FOR DISCUSSION

1. How has the calibre of men in the history of General Motors contributed to the success of the company?

2. What combined factors have made General Motors the largest and most profitable private company in the world?
3. What problem accompanies the tremendous economic power of the company? How has General Motors handled this?
4. Do you agree with General Motors' policy on racing? Can you suggest any modifications or alternatives?

SUGGESTED READING

"Antitrusters Try to Pin Monopoly Tag on G.M.," *Business Week*, December 1, 1962, p. 27.

"Attack on G.M. Worries Detroit," *Business Week*, October 21, 1961, p. 32.

Brooks, T. R., "What Makes G.M. Go," *Duns Review and Modern Industry*, September, 1963, p. 30.

"Cry Against G.M.A.C.," *Time*, November 23, 1962, p. 75.

"Flexible World of G.M.'s Planning," *Business Week*, October 5, 1963, pp. 136-138.

"G.M. vs. Everybody," *Time*, March 13, 1964, p. 98.

"How G.M. Did It," *Fortune*, June, 1963, pp. 96-111.

"$1,459,000,000 for G.M," *Newsweek*, February 11, 1963, pp. 68 plus.

"63 Million Shares to Go," *Time*, March 9, 1962, p. 87.

Sloan, A. P., "My Years With G.M.," *Fortune*, September, 1963, pp. 135-42.

"Strategist of Success," *Time*, January 24, 1964, pp. 62-64.

Pittsburgh Plate Glass Company

In 1883 PITTSBURGH PLATE GLASS COMPANY, one of the largest companies in the U.S., began operations in Creighton, a little town near Pittsburgh, Pennsylvania. This first plant was the beginning of a continuing course of expansion and diversification. The company became America's first commercially successful plate glass producer.

In 1896 Pittsburgh Plate Glass established the first units of its distribution system, known today as the Merchandising Division. Originally intended to distribute plate glass, the branches added facilities to handle the growing line of the company's products. Today, the Merchandising Division consists of over 300 units, including district headquarters, distribution branches, and paint stores. Through these establishments glass, paint, brushes, fiber glass, and other products are distributed to independent dealers, jobbers, distributors, and other customers.

Around the turn of the century Pittsburgh Plate Glass began to make its own paint and brushes, thus entering a product area long felt by the company to have great potential. Today, the company is a major producer of protective, decorative, and chemical coatings, as well as a leading plastics manufacturer and brushmaker. Its Paint and Brush Division operates 16 plants located from coast to coast.

In 1900 the Chemical Division was established when a soda ash plant was established at Barbeton, Ohio. Today, the Chemical Division operates 10 plants in the U.S. and Canada. The division offers 68 out of the more than 150 principal products available to the trade.

Newest of the operating units is the Fiber Glass Division, formed in 1952. Because of the company's long-time experience with flat glass production, the step to making fiber glass was a natural one. Today, the Fiber Glass Division is operating two plants; and Pittsburgh Plate Glass is indeed an important factor in the expanding fiber glass industry, which has solid market potential.

In 1958 the company formed Pittsburgh Plate Glass International S.A., to conduct its interests in trade and business abroad. In addition to this, it has two wholly owned subsidiaries in Canada. One is Canadian Pittsburgh Industries Limited, which makes and sells paint products; and the other is Standard Chemical Limited, a chemical producer and distributor. In addition to these, the company has a substantial interest in Southern Minerals Corporation, producers and transporters of crude oil and natural gas; Duplate Canada Limited, principally a fabricator of automotive glass; Pittsburgh Corning Corporation, manufacturing of glass blocks and Foamglas insulation; and Koppers Pittsburgh Company, maker of chemicals for paints, plastics, and related products.

As can be seen, the Pittsburgh Plate Glass Company story is one of integrated diversification. Mirrored in the company's operations are reflections of many industries—glass, paints, chemicals, fiber glass, plastics, brushes, and others—yet all had a common beginning in glass.

Pittsburgh Plate Glass is a well-diversified manufacturing enterprise. It derives approximately 40% of its sales from flat glass; 20% from paint; 20% from chemicals; 10% from metal storefronts, curtain walls, glazing, erection, etc.; 5% from fiber glass; and the remaining 5% from installed auto glass, jobbed glass, paint brushes, and resale items. Glass division product uses are about 40% automotive, 45% building, and 15% mirrors and furniture.

Although it is an extremely well-diversified company, there is no doubt that glass is still its biggest concern and its biggest volume business. The company's top competitor in the glass market is Libbey-Owens-Ford. At the present time this company leads Pittsburgh Plate Glass by about 37% to 27% in its share of the plate glass market, but falls into second place by a similar amount in sheet glass. However, when it comes to profitability Libbey-Owens-Ford has been the undisputed leader, consistently netting over 20% return on sales to Pittsburgh Plate Glass' 7 to 10%. This rate of return problem is one of great concern to company officials and one they greatly want to improve. Automotive glass has long been a big part of the company's production, and at the present time some 40% of its glass output goes to the auto industry. In recent years two of its biggest customers have started making their own (Ford and Chrysler); however, the slack caused by their departure has been taken up by American Motors, Studebaker-Packard, and in larger part by the ability of Pittsburgh Plate Glass to break Libbey-Owens-Ford's 30 year grip on General Motor's glass business. At present, it looks at though the company will continue to be a major producer of automobile glass, although the whole area is shaky ground for everyone concerned (as will be discussed later).

In chemicals Pittsburgh Plate Glass is the largest merchant producer of chlorine and in total production it is exceeded only by Dow Chemical. The trouble is that nobody makes much money selling bulk chemicals and to date its chemical division is just beginning to develop the more sophisticated chemical products that produce the big profits.

Paint accounts for only about 20% of the company's sales, and (like the major paint producers Sherwin-Williams and Glidden) it has felt the rugged price competition resulting from over 1700 producers scrambling for a share of the market. Industrial finishes make up 60 to 65% of its paint sales and its position in this market has remained steady over the past few years. The company has just recently developed a new method for the primer coating of automobiles through a joint effort with the Ford Motor Company. This new method should add many years to the life of an automobile and in turn provide a boost for the paint division.

Fiber glass is a rather new and growing industry in which Pittsburgh Plate Glass plays an important role. It is a field that provides plenty of opportunity for expansion and has great market potential. The company's Carolina plant is the largest plant in the world producing fiber glass yarn. The potential for new fiber glass products is almost unlimited and at present Pittsburgh Plate Glass continues to be a market leader in this area.

Sales for 1963 were better than $775 million, compared to $657 million in 1962. Part of this sharp gain can be attributed to an acquisition of the Houston Chemical Company in February, 1963, and the consolidation of certain majority owned subsidiaries for the first time. Earnings per share also made a sharp gain to $4.30 as compared to $4.05 in 1962. The sales performance of 1964 is a further indication of the benefits derived from the investment program of the past several years. The company's sales in 1964 increased by 6% to establish a new record of $827,600,000. Earnings equivalent to $4.61 per share were higher than for any year since 1957. Moreover, sales for the first quarter of 1965 were the highest in the company's history. While the company's president David G. Hill attributes this improvement to the strong national economy and a high level of demand for the company's products, the most important factor is the contribution of new investments of the last two years. These investments are beginning to contribute their proportionate share to the corporate income.

Generally, the outlook seems good. The recent high level of automobile production should be maintained, and many people are optimistically viewing it not as an unusual occurrence, but rather as a level which can now be taken for granted. Also, if present forecasts come true, outlets for construction should reach new highs; it also looks as if sales of paint, chemicals, and fiber glass stand a good chance of rising.

Hill was even more optimistic when he stated that they could probably reach $1 billion in sales around 1966. All this is credited to a change in the company's attitude from that of an ultra-conservative organization that carried caution too far, to that of a company that isn't about to let any good chances to expand go by. To see how this "new attitude" has affected the company, all one has to do is to look at its capital spending. In 1963 it spent $130 million in capital programs, a record investment, about twice as much as the company has ever spent before and almost as much as it spent in the previous four years combined. To this was added $57,300,000 in 1964 to help complete the largest modernization, expansion, and diversification program in the company's history. Among other things, the company has recently entered the antifreeze and gasoline additives business and the fertilizer business, and has built a new plant to produce glass by a revolutionary new "float process." In the past Pittsburgh Plate Glass has let a lot of good opportunities go by; now it seems determined to make up for lost time. Of course, a change like this cannot be made overnight and the company still faces rugged competition. On the other hand, it does have the money to invest and for the first time in a long time it seems determined to put that money to good use.

One of Pittsburgh Plate Glass' greatest problems of recent years seems solved for the time being anyway. Some 40% of the company's glass output goes to the auto industry, thus making it one of its most important items. The problem erupted a few years ago when two of its biggest customers, Ford and Chrysler, began making their own glass. In the past year and a half Ford has stepped up its own production to the point where it not only satisfies its own needs, but sells replacement parts as well. As for Chrysler, only a small percentage of its glass requirements are now supplied by Pittsburgh Plate Glass.

The slack caused by Ford and Chrysler has now been countered by increased output to American Motors and Studebaker-Packard, and, even more important, to General Motors. Libbey-Owens-Ford had a 30 year exclusive business supplying General Motors auto glass and only by breaking this stronghold has Pittsburgh Plate Glass been able to offset the shrinkage in other accounts. At the present time and in the near future the auto glass market looks good for the company; its General Motors contracts and the outlook for a continuous trend of high automobile production seemed to have temporarily solved this problem.

For the future, though, there is still a big problem facing this company and the rest of the glass industry in regard to auto glass: Just how long will it be before General Motors and the rest of the automotive industry find it more economical and beneficial to produce their own auto glass, as Ford has already done? To be sure this conclusion may never be reached; however, it still remains a distinct possibility. The answer to the problem seems as cloudy as the problem itself. The only answer seems to be diversification, and this presents problems in and of itself.

The most perplexing problem, the one of greatest concern to company officials, has been her shrinking profits. As President Hill stated, "We haven't had a really good year since 1955." In that year the company had an operating income on sales of 25.6%, operating income of $148.97 million, a net income of $61.43 million, and earnings per share of $6.26. Between 1955 and 1961 sales grew hardly at all and profits were in a steady decline: $6.26 a share in 1955; $4.36 in 1959; $4.05 in 1962. There was a slight increase to $4.30 in 1963 and $4.61 in 1964. Although the reason for these faltering profit margins can be attributed to many things (such as the cost-price squeeze and foreign competition), at least part of it can be found in problems of diversification.

While diversification has indeed safeguarded the company's future and opened up great potential in many areas, the company has also found that diversification causes problems as well as solves them.

Pittsburgh Plate Glass diversified itself into three main areas—paint, chemicals, and, more recently, fiber glass. Although they are three good businesses, they are three businesses the company has not been able to derive substantial profits from.

Until recently it has, for the most part, produced "bulk chemicals," products that provide very little profit margin, and has missed the boat in plastics, synthetic fibers, antifreeze, gasoline additives, and fertilizer. Its chemical division has only recently begun to produce the products that account for good profits.

When Pittsburgh Plate Glass expanded into paint, it entered one of the roughest markets imaginable. There are some 1,700 producers scrambling for a share of the market, and even the major producers have had a hard time pushing their returns on equity much over 10%. The answer here seems to be in research and development to get profits from products no one else has.

Fiber glass offers areas of great growth potential. It is such a new area that much has been spent on research and development in an ever-changing market. This division has great, but latent, profit-yielding possibilities which because of its newness have not yet been realized.

The relatively small profits of Pittsburgh Plate Glass' divisions that have resulted from diversification have indeed been a problem in the past and remain so today. The trend, however, seems to be favorable. The many years spent developing these divisions and their products seem to be paying off since the company is now placing on the market the more sophisticated products from which good profits can be reaped. Couple this with the "changing attitude" of top management and it would seem that this problem is on the way to being solved.

Foreign competition has been a big problem to many industries; the glass industry is no exception. Up to 75% of the cost of producing some pressed and blown glass items can be attributed directly to labor and in these areas foreign competition can be a serious problem. The lower wages paid in other countries make the importing of such items quite feasible.

In sheet glass, low price imports from Belgium and Japan have put considerable pressure on U.S. prices. At the present time imported glass now captures about one-fourth of the U.S. market. Some of these foreign products are able to undercut U.S. prices by 10 to 15% and some by as much as 30%. Tariffs as high as 60% have been imposed as a deterrent to imports, but most of the high tariffs have been on less important items. On the whole, the tariffs have been rather ineffective as far as glass producers are concerned, and an increase of about 5% on tariffs in the summer of 1962 alleviated the pressure only slightly.

To combat the problem, Pittsburgh Plate Glass has, like other glass producers, stressed other things rather than price—better products and technology, newer products, more immediate delivery, etc. However, it has recently done something else in order to compete more favorably with foreign producers and with producers here in the states. It has built a plant to produce glass by means of a new, less expensive process. This process takes us to the next problem facing the company.

Pittsburgh Plate Glass has constructed a new plant in Cumberland, Maryland, to produce glass by a new process called the "float process." This is the first facility that has been built in North America for producing glass by this process. Although no major problems have yet been encountered with this new plant and process, it remains a matter of great concern. Much money has been put into this plant, and if successful it could make the company the largest and most profitable producer of glass in the world. The problem is simply that Pittsburgh Plate Glass wants no problems; it wishes nothing to prevent the success of this new plant.

This float process produces glass combining the desirable characteristics of both plate glass and sheet glass. The ribbon of glass is formed on the surface of molten metal in an exactingly controlled environment. Both glass surfaces emerge smooth and flat without grinding or polishing. "Float" glass is said to be comparable to plate glass in quality, but can be produced at a 30% lower cost. The new plant layout has been designed so that the glass has a continuous straight-line-process flow from raw material to finished product; it is designed for an annual production of nearly 50 million square feet of glass.

The construction of this new plant to produce glass by the float process could indeed be the most profitable innovation that the company has ever adopted. As yet no problems have come up. It is Pittsburgh Plate Glass' problem to see that none do.

Its reputation for carrying caution too far, the result of years of tight control and conservative action (or inaction) by the founding Pitcairn family, is a trait that was visible in the company's unwillingness to gamble on anything short of a sure bet. As has already been pointed out, the company would not expand into new and profitable fields in its chemical division; it even took them 11 years before they would consider making glass by the float process.

Just recently, the company has seemed to recognize its problem and is doing something about it. As was mentioned earlier, there seems to be a new attitude and a determination not to let anything good get by these days. Each year brings the company closer toward fulfillment of long-range objectives, which include introduction of new products, broadening markets for existing products, development and implementation of more efficient manufacturing processes, and the creation of a marketing and distribution system which will provide maximum product availability and service.

President Hill has tried to liven up the company's management. In the last 7 years he has gone from being the youngest man at the top management level to the oldest (61), and he has reduced the ages of top management from 55-80 to 45-61.

Although Pittsburgh Plate Glass is definitely on the right track to a more dynamic and fruitful management, it must stay on this track if its former level of productivity is to be achieved. With its long tradition of conservative management this will not be easy to obtain and certainly cannot be accomplished overnight. This is perhaps the company's greatest liability for its other problems are in part caused by this overconservatism. Until the company rids itself of this attitude, these problems cannot be solved.

FOR DISCUSSION

1. What is Pittsburgh Plate Glass' biggest concern? What is the company's competitive position in this area?
2. What problem faces the glass industry in regards to automobile production? In what does the answer to this problem lie?
3. What problems have resulted from diversification?
4. What types of management decisions are needed to solve its problems?

SUGGESTED READING

"On the Move," *Forbes*, April 1, 1964, pp. 16-17.
"Spreading the Problems," *Forbes*, March 15, 1963, pp. 14-16.

CHAPTER 4

Armour and Company

ARMOUR AND COMPANY, a highly diversified food and nonfood enterprise, was originally incorporated in Illinois during April, 1900, succeeding the co-partnership of Armour, which was established in 1863. In December, 1922, Armour and Company of Delaware was incorporated and acquired from the parent company of Illinois certain property rights and assets for financing new acquisitions. These acquisitions were composed mainly of packing houses, cold storage plants, fertilizer works, and various foreign subsidiaries. This new organization thus comprised an important element of the total Armour enterprise. From 1926 through 1932 this company also made acquisitions in the areas of leather, outside packing companies and branch houses, railroad tank cars, chemical and food specialty companies, and produce packing plants throughout the United States.

In 1920, faced with the pressures of pending antitrust action, Armour and the other leading packers signed a consent decree, agreeing to refrain from retailing and limiting their marketing of food products to those foods related to meat or meat production. This consent decree was petitioned for modification, but in 1932 the United States Supreme Court reversed a district court decision which stated that the decree could be modified. During 1932 Armour disposed of all produce packing plants as a result of this decision.

September, 1943, brought the Illinois Company to an approved merger with its principal subsidiary, Armour and Company of Delaware, which has been operating on a dual basis with the Illinois firm. Armour of Illinois thus assumed all liabilities of the merged subsidiary. Four years later this company was incorporated as Armour and Company of Delaware.

During 1958 Armour sold all of its foreign food operations, including six packing plants in South America, to International Packers Limited for 885,000 shares of that company's stock. Other foreign operations in chemicals and pharmaceuticals, located in Western Europe, Mexico, and England, were retained. The present name was adopted in October, 1960, after the merger of Armour and Company with two subsidiaries.

By far the most impressive and progressive period of Armour's development has occurred since the reorganization in 1957, headed by newly-appointed president William Wood Prince. This reorganization has led to extensive product diversification and development, cost reduction programs, and modernization of operations.

The diversification and product development at Armour and Company has resulted in a broad base of operations and products. The company is divided into two major divisions, food and nonfood. These divisions are further broken down into seven autonomous companies: foods, grocery products, industrial chemicals, agricultural chemicals, pharmaceuticals, leather, and abrasives. Outside the operations of the individual companies, Armour has developed a central research center which is constantly working toward the future development of Armour and the betterment of mankind. Research in the fields of liquid protein, enriched foods, and cancer are a few of these test areas.

Although approximately 80% of Armour's $1,887,000,000 in 1964 sales originate from the food division, less than 50% of the net income comes from this area. The smaller percentage of sales coming from the nonfood divisions actually accounts for most of Armour's profit.

As far as Armour's position in the meat packing industry is concerned, in volume of sales it is surpassed only by Swift and Company. Total sales for the top five packers in the country indicate that in 1962 Swift and Company had sales of $2.5 billion; Armour and Company, $1.8 billion; Wilson and Company, $711 million; and John Morrell and Company, $571 million (Table 4.1). The meat packing industry certainly is not a small business, with dollar sales falling between auto sales and steel manufacturing. However, through the years it has been known as a low margin business with the packers' profits in 1963 reaching only .6 of $.01 on each dollar of sales. This is the worst showing of any major United States industry.

Speculation in the meat market has been a chronic sore spot for a long time and no end appears in sight. Changing levels of the unpredictable meat supply drives prices of meat to packers up and down; and because the packers have no influence on the comparatively steady prices of retail meat, they find themselves in a profit squeeze. Substitutes for meat in poultry, fish, and cheese keep the retail prices steady; therefore, packers' profits show great leverage, for small changes in margins can mean larger increases in profit return.

Competition in the meat industry is keen as there are close to 3,000 firms in one or more phases of meat packing, and the number of these regional packers continues to grow. During the 1950's, 65% of the meat packing was handled by the top ten packers while only 40% was handled by these packers in 1963.

Because of the low profit margins and the unpredictable fluctuations in meat market prices, the packers are now increasing their efforts in areas of brand name processed meats that have higher margins and also have been diversifying into other fields.

Table 4.1

LEADING MEATPACKERS COMPARATIVE EARNINGS

Company	Net Sales (In Million) $	Net Earn Share $	Net Profit Margin %	Cash Div. Per Share $	Div. Yield %
Year 1958					
ARMOUR AND CO.	1,850	1.08	.3	——	3.3
SWIFT AND CO.	2,645	1.70	.3	2.00	3.5
WILSON AND CO.	685	3.10	1.1	1.00	3.3
MORRELL, JOHN AND CO.	402	2.80	.5	.30	1.5
HYGRADE FOOD PROD.	411	2.39	.3	1.00	3.0
Year 1960					
ARMOUR AND CO.	1,736	3.10	.9	1.40	2.9
SWIFT AND CO.	2,443	3.10	.7	1.85	4.6
WILSON AND CO.	585	.53	.3	1.60	5.1
MORRELL, JOHN AND CO.	512	3.17	.6	.80	2.5
HYGRADE FOOD PROD.	417	3.54	.6	1.00	3.7
Year 1963					
ARMOUR AND CO.	1,811	2.97	.7	1.40	3.1
SWIFT AND CO.	2,473	2.85	.7	1.60	3.6
WILSON AND CO.	NA	2.81	NA	1.60	3.6
MORRELL, JOHN AND CO.	613	2.05	4.0	.80	3.3
HYGRADE FOOD PROD.	425	.76	.10	1.00	5.8

Source: *Magazine of Wall Street,* 1958, January 2, 1960; 1960, July 15, 1961; 1963, January 11, 1964.

Armour is the leader in this drive toward diversification, emphasizing strides in pharmaceutical research as a result of its experiments with the by-products of meat processing and in the development of chemical products. Armour was the first to introduce the revolutionary line of freeze dried foods where 90% of the moisture is removed from food before it is packaged, thus enabling the food to remain fresh, without refrigeration, from one to two years.

Dial soap of the Grocery Products Division continues to be the leader of the $250 million toilet soap market with a 13.5% share.

In the field of industrial chemicals, Armour continues to be a leader of fatty-acid research and development, a field which Armour owned alone until it recently entered into competitive agreements with two other companies.

Vertagreen and other Armour fertilizer products are leaders in a large competitive field, but only Armour will very shortly be able to boast of having a basic position in the production of the three fundamental elements—nitrogen, potassium, and phosphorus—used in the manufacturing of fertilizers.

In the pharmaceutical field, Armour realizes that it is, and will always be, only a middle-sized drug firm; thus it has adjusted its research to concentrate on products made from animal glands while staying clear of antibiotics and similar drugs.

Swift and Company, the giant in the industry, is concentrating its diversification in the fields of poultry (where it is a leader), dairy products, and pet foods. Wilson and Company is maintaining a somewhat different pattern of product mix with its top subsidiary, Wilson Sporting Goods, being the largest manufacturer of athletic equipment.

In their efforts to modernize operations and plants, Armour and Wilson appear to have left Swift and Company behind in the early 1960's, primarily due to Swift's tremendous size. However, Swift is now making its move and can be expected to challenge any advantages in efficiency of operations picked up by Wilson and Armour.

Armour's position, in relation to Swift, has continued to improve during the 1960's so that for the first time in the history of the company its earnings (net) per share have overtaken the leader, $2.97 to $2.85.

Although one of the major factors of Armour and Company's extremely low margins is the fluctuating supplies and prices of meat supplies, it has also been plagued with several problem areas. The public continues to demand meat regardless of the cost to the packer; because packers are unable to influence retail prices, margins fluctuate. Unable to build up inventories when stock prices are down, and caught by labor guarantees of 36 hours a week, packers find it necessary to purchase stock regardless of the price at any given time.

Much of Armour's packing has operated from several large slaughterhouses built many years ago to handle peak supplies of hogs during certain periods of the year; but because the farrowing of hogs is now evened out throughout the year, large portions of the.huge plants stand idle. Armour only operated at approximately 70% capacity in the late 1950's. During this same period the costs of the plants were tremendously high.

Elaborate systems of branch houses, previously used for railroad distribution of meat to small butchers and grocers, were also being maintained even though 80% of Armour's meat was being transported by truck to large chains. These chain stores put even tighter squeezes on profits through their demands for better bargains and were better informed as to alternatives in the meat markets; therefore, in the late 1950's, Armour undertook a reorganization in an attempt to stem the squeeze on profits and to spread out into different fields, thus combating the increased competition squeeze by the smaller packing houses. Most of the corrective actions taken in the late 1950's and early 1960's are still in operation, while newer methods are constantly being introduced.

The first program which William Prince, president, undertook was the decentralization of the top-heavy organization hierarchy, located in Chicago, breaking it down into manageable divisions. Previously ignored communications systems were utilized, and the morale of the managers indicated general improvements. Local managers developed cost accounting systems and for the first time in Armour's history, branches were aware of valuable cost data. Data processing systems replaced older ledger systems and a private teletype was installed between the southwestern plants, linking them with an instantaneous communications system.

Volume is no longer the factor emphasized at Armour and earlier goals of overtaking Swift and Company sales at all costs have been abandoned. Units which no longer make profit, but merely add to net sales, are being closed. Since 1960 the number of branch houses in operation have dropped from 155 to 133, and eventually all branches will be replaced by 50 modern sales and distribution centers. Old cavernous slaughterhouses with high overhead costs in the large cities (Los Angeles, Chicago, San Francisco, Baltimore), have been abandoned in favor of more efficient plants operated at near capacity.

Technical developments in operations are also a main target in the planning to cut costs and strive for efficiency. Old plants are being equipped with new assembly lines; automatic slicers; weighers; packagers; infrared cookers, which enable the ham treatment to be finished in 3 minutes rather than 18 hours; injection pickling; and conveyor systems.

Even though the older plants are being equipped for more efficient operations, Armour feels that its future lies in specialized operations plants built near the source of supply, rather than the old integrated slaughterhouses. New plants, now being built, separate the hog and beef operations—beef abattoirs being located near feed lots in the western ranch country while hog slaughtering will be done in the corn belt. These plants, equipped with the latest equipment, are constructed with removable sides so they can be enlarged or reshaped quickly and cheaply. Through these strategically located plants loss of animal weight will be eliminated, costly transportation will be decreased, and meat will be prepared according to regional preference.

The extensive modernization within Armour has also created the problem of unemployment for several thousand workers. Armour employment has dropped from 60,000 in 1954 to 40,000 in 1959 to 33,500 in 1964; but Armour has been a leader in attempting to aid displaced workers from plant closings and modernization.

In 1959 Armour, with the consent of the two meatpacking unions, Amalgamated Meat Cutters and Butcher Workmen, and the United Packinghouse Workers, established a tripartite automation committee to study possible solutions, training programs, transfers, and other methods to aid the displaced. This committee consists of nine members—four from management, four from the unions, and an impartial chairman—and is financed by the company at $.01 per hundred pounds of meat shipped. The committee, permitting the use of experts or professionals deemed necessary has had to chart its way through unknown territory with the eyes of government, labor, and management watching very closely. Although labor has generally supported the work of the committee, Armour's two largest competitors, Swift and Company and Wilson and Company, have refused such a plan in favor of higher wages.

One of the accomplishments of the committee thus far has been a three year contract in 1961, guaranteeing displaced workers up to one year's wages. Although the unions hail this guarantee as a major breakthrough in job security, the scope of the displacement problem remains extensive; and the automation committee recognizes that the job must be attacked, not by a single company, but by the whole nation.

With the growth of large chains, demands for uniform and high quality grade meat are increasing. Since no amount of experience or training can insure this uniform quality in the inspection of animals, Armour is attempting to introduce factory methods into the development of its basic raw material—meat.

Characteristics that determine qualities of meat are hereditary; therefore, Armour has established the Beef Cattle Improvement Program, which today is coordinating (through several universities) planned mating, intensive records of heredity, and histories of cows and calves. In this manner Armour is attempting to take the element of chance out of the quality of meat and to make meat more like manufacturing than commodity handling.

With the de-emphasis on volume, Armour recognized that many of its accounts were ordering on a small basis—100 pound to 200 pound orders. Surveys of their territories showed that order costs of handling these smaller orders ranged from $2.12 to $19.78 per 100 pounds, depending upon the size of the order and area of delivery. Costs on orders over 300 pounds were in the small-order category; margins were being eaten up by high-order costs.

Late in 1960 Armour announced that only orders above a set minimum would be accepted, with the minimum varying between market areas and types of products. By 1963 all Armour plants had some form of minimum-order standard, which has resulted in lower selling costs and fewer sales personnel, with no long-run effects on total sales.

Even Armour's program of diversification and product expansion has hit certain snags. The courts continue to maintain pressure on the company, restricting the marketing of foods to those related in some degree with meat and prohibiting them from any retail activity. This restriction

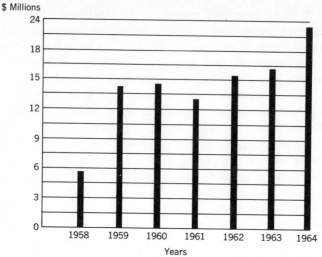

Figure 4.1
Armour Earnings (Net) From Annual Report 1964

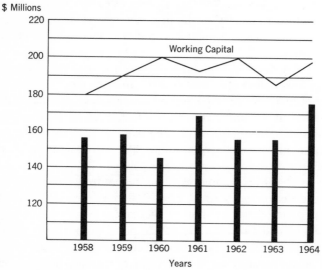

Figure 4.2
Working Capital Long-Term Debt From Annual Report 1964

has limited the extent of Armour's diversification, even though Armour has petitioned for modification of the 1920 consent decree several times.

Although Armour has been in the fertilizer field for many years, increased competition from several smaller companies has given this larger company something to think about. Armour has countered by developing vertical integration of its inorganic raw material supplies. This can be evidenced by the company's $60 million expansion of phosphate and nitrogen production, started in 1960.

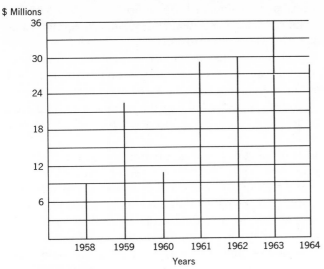

Figure 4.3
Armour Capital Expenditures From Annual Report 1964

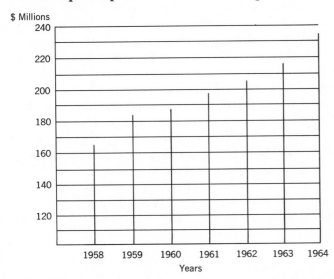

Figure 4.4
Stockholder's Equity From Annual Report 1964

Along with greater pressure to market increasing numbers of products, Armour has also found that manufacturing controls are necessary in their large-scale operations. Managers have embarked upon improved methods in order to meet required qualities, quantities, and cost ranges for the multitude of materials required. Production control must recognize alternative sources of materials, proper lead times, and routing to insure that production schedules are maintained. Inventories must be controlled so that the total investment is kept at a minimum while protecting against shortages, which will magnify the already glaring profit squeeze.

The pharmaceutical division has developed difficulties pertaining to diversification primarily because it has concentrated too heavily upon bulk products such as insulin and vitamin B-12, both selling in highly competitive markets. Lack of ideas has been holding the company back. Recent experimentation in unexplored areas has led to new drugs which Armour now considers its own.

Within the leather division poor earnings continue to plague the company, although several techniques are being developed to help increase leather profits. Tanning techniques have stood relatively still while fighting a losing battle with cheaper mass-produced leather substitutes. Even though Armour continues to be a leading supplier of shoe leather, the 30 to 60 day period for tanning has taken the profits out of the business. Experimentation with new solvent methods of tanning are now being undertaken to attempt to complete this operation in approximately 24 hours.

Concerning its financial standing, dividends were resumed in 1960 after an 11 year lapse, and these dividends will be supplemented from time to time with the distribution of the remaining 757,594 shares of stock of the International Packers Limited. This stock must be distributed between 1964-1967. Cash dividends have held at $1.40 from 1961 to 1964 with 5,493,582 shares outstanding. In 1965 this increased to $1.60. In November, 1963, there were 20,590 shareholders compared to 18,682 in 1959. Although working capital dropped from $198 million in 1962 to $191 million in 1964, this can be primarily attributed to the extensive modernization and expansion program; however, the 1963 ratio reflected a healthy 3.61 (Figures 4.1, 4.2, 4.3, 4.4), and the 1964 ratio was 3.26.

Although there was a slight increase in sales in 1964, the decrease in sales as of the fiscal year 1963 shows that much remains to be done, especially in the problem area of the meat market, if Armour is to realize the expected breakthrough.

FOR DISCUSSION

1. Do you agree with Armour's policy of abandoning efforts to overtake sales of Swift and Company at all costs? What are the benefits of this policy? Are there any disadvantages?
2. What factors are part of the problem of competition?
3. What problem area should be of primary concern to the company? What procedures has Armour followed to improve the situation? Can you suggest any additions or improvements?
4. What policy controls have been necessary due to the company's large-scale operations?
5. What major decisions would you say must be made to increase sales?

SUGGESTED READING

"Armour's Shift Brings Better Profit Status," *Financial World,* January 18, 1961, pp. 14-26.

"Armour's Star," *Time,* March 3, 1961, p. 84.

"Armour Widens Horizons, Bolsters Earning Power," *Barrows Magazine,* August 6, 1962, pp. 20-25.

Strout, C. K., " '64 Prospects for Meat Packers," *The Magazine of Wall Street,* January 11, 1964, pp. 423-431.

The Kroger Company

THE KROGER COMPANY was established in 1882 by B. H. Kroger, a twenty-two year old from Cincinnati, Ohio. With only a few years of experience as a grocery clerk, he decided to open a grocery store. He called it the Great Western Tea Company. In the very first year of operation it made a profit, and soon after this a second store was opened. The combined profits made a third store possible. The rate of expansion after this was slow, but by 1891 the Great Western Tea Company had 7 stores and by 1902 there were 36. In 1902 the Great Western Tea Company changed its name to the Kroger Grocery and Baking Company. Soon after the name change, growth became more rapid. As the chart below indicates, at one time the Kroger Company had over 5,000 food chain stores. (One basic reason expressed for the decline in the number of stores is the trend toward larger stores.)

	1920	1925	1930	1949	1964
KROGER	799	2,559	5,000	2,204	1,431

Over the years the Kroger Company has grown not only because of the construction of new stores but also through acquisitions. Some recent acquisitions show a continuation of this trend by the Kroger Company; for example, in the 1950's Kroger acquired control of 26 Henke and Pillot Stores of Houston, Texas, and the 25 unit Krunbo Food Stores, Incorporated, of Wisconsin. Whereas Henke and Pillot Stores were in an entirely new marketing area, the other acquisition put Krunbo and Kroger in direct competition with each other for more intensive market coverage. In 1958 Kroger acquired the 44 Wyatt and Evans Food Stores in Texas. On April 6, 1959, however, the Federal Trade Commission charged the Kroger Company with illegally acquiring, since 1927, more than forty corporations and its 1,900 stores. The commission charged that the acquisitions violated the antimerger laws in that they could result in a substantial lessening of competition or a tendency toward monopoly in the processing, manufacturing, purchasing, and distributing of grocery products and in the sale of merchandise in retail grocery stores. Kroger, however, continued its acquisitions and in 1963 the 56 stores of the Market Basket chain in Southern California were purchased. This was the first time Kroger had ventured into the Far West.

Since the 1920's Kroger has been second or third in total number of stores in the food chain industry. Kroger was second behind Great Atlantic and Pacific Tea Company until just recently, when Safeway Stores became second in total number of stores.

	1920	1925	1930	1949
A & P	4544	4034	5737	4600
KROGER	799	2559	5302	2204
SAFEWAY	191	1050	2675	2177
NATIONAL TEA	163	761	1600	655

According to the 1964 annual reports of the three leading companies, Great Atlantic and Pacific had 4,585 stores, Safeway 2,099 stores, and Kroger 1,431 stores.

The average annual sales per store for Kroger and the industry has improved greatly since 1930. This increase, as shown by the table below, is a good indication that the size of all stores in the industry has increased. The average sales per store in 1930 and 1950 were:

	1930	1950
A & P	$67,726	$680,000
SAFEWAY	82,144	568,000
NATIONAL TEA	53,279	497,100
COLONIAL	35,274	488,637
KROGER	50,376	419,300

° 1930 refers to predecessor companies.

As the chart indicates, in 1950 Kroger ranked fifth in average sales per store; but in 1963 Kroger ranked first. Kroger had average sales per store of $1,541,100; Safeway had $1,286,000; and the leader in 1950, Great Atlantic and Pacific, is now third at $1,218,200. In 1964 Kroger had average sales of $1,582,359.

In total sales in 1964 A & P led the industry with $5,079,564,213. Safeway ranked second in total sales with a total of $2,817,568,934. Kroger was third with $2,327,563,209. This rank order has existed since the mid-1950's as indicated by the chart below.

(In Millions of Dollars)

	1954	1956	1958	1960	1962	1964
A & P	4,140.0	4,481.9	5,094.7	5,246.6	5,310.5	5,079.5
SAFEWAY	1,813.5	1,989.3	2,225.4	2,469.0	2,509.6	2,817
KROGER	1,108.7	1,492.6	1,776.2	1,870.3	1,947.6	2,327

According to Standard and Poor's stock reports, in 1964 A & P was the largest company in the food chain store industry, when comparing net worth (the total assets minus the total liabilities). A & P's net worth was $290,998,000. The second largest food chain store according to net worth was Safeway, which had a net worth of $272,351,600. Kroger was the third largest food chain store, having a net worth of $235,238,796.

Thus we can see that Kroger is ranked as one of the top food chain stores in the United States. More specifically, it was in 1964:

1. Third in total stores with 1431 stores.
2. First in average sales per store, which is $1,582,359.
3. Third in total sales with sales of $2,327,563,209.
4. Third in actual value according to net worth, which was $235,238,796.

The Kroger Company, even though it is relatively a strong company in the food chain store industry, is not free of problems. Three such problems that the Kroger Company faces are the decrease of the ratio of income to total sales, the increase of competition, and stores that are too small to meet today's needs.

During the 1950's there was an increase in total sales in both the entire industry and in the Kroger Company, but even with the increase in sales the net income before taxes or net operating profit ratio declined. Wilbur B. England, in a 1959 study printed in the *Harvard Business School Bulletin*, number 156, showed this decline in a table (excerpts from table shown below).

FUNCTIONAL EXPENSE ANALYSIS OF SELECTED FOOD CHAINS AS A PERCENTAGE OF SALES

	1950	1952	1954	1956	1958
GROSS MARGIN	18.51	17.97	18.87	19.08	19.51
EXPENSES					
Store	10.85	11.01	11.83	12.85	13.58
Warehouse	1.17	1.14	1.17	1.15	1.12
Transportation	1.07	1.03	1.01	.95	.91
General and overhead	2.02	1.99	2.07	2.01	1.85
Total	15.11	15.17	16.08	16.96	17.46
NET OPERATING PROFIT	3.40	2.80	2.79	2.12	2.05

Unable to find what was not omitted from the net operating profit; we will assume that only taxes have not been omitted.

As one can see, the major reason for the decline in the net operating profit is the increase in store costs. Mr. England broke down these store costs even further than the table indicates. He said that the largest store costs are payroll (6.86% of total sales), advertising (2.3%), and real estate (1.27%).

In the annual report of 1963, comparing the net income before taxes with the net operating profit in the table above, Kroger, in 1958, had a ratio of 2.5% (net income before taxes divided by the total sales). In 1962 this ratio fell to 2.27% and again in 1963 to 2.14%. This would indicate that Kroger is typical of the industry trend—a decrease in the ratio of net income before taxes to total sales.

The Kroger Company has taken several steps in an effort to better its net income before tax ratio to total sales. It has recently acquired a very efficient food chain in Southern California called Market Basket. As stated earlier, this is an area of the United States that Kroger has never ventured into before and perhaps this will bring about a more favorable ratio.

Even though acquisition can be very favorable to Kroger, there is always a fear of causing a monopoly which would possibly mean government intervention; so Kroger is now expanding into another field, namely the drug industry. By 1964 Kroger had a total of 146 drug stores. Depending upon the area of location, these drug stores are called Superex, Gasen, and Sav-On. Most of the stores are adjacent to Kroger food stores for convenience; however, some of the drug stores are located away from the food stores. In 1963 the drug division did not show any profit due to the vigorous growth program. In 1964 it made a modest contribution to profits and it is expected that 1965 profits will be substantially greater.

Kroger has taken another step to increase the ratio of net income before taxes to total sales. It has ventured into the manufacturing of its own products under the Kroger label. These products amount to 10% of Kroger's entire sales. Selling its own products usually means a greater profit than selling brand names.

Competition has always been a problem to Kroger as well as to the other food chain store companies. Since Kroger is basically located in the Middle West and in the South, its greatest competitors in the industry are the Jewel Tea Company, The Great Atlantic and Pacific Tea Company, and the National Tea Company. When Kroger competes with fellow companies in this industry, it is competing with stores that also offer low prices because of a large volume of merchandise. Many times Kroger has to sell products at cost or even below cost in an effort to get customers into its stores. Kroger hopes that once the customer is in the store, he will buy products that will show a profit. To offer low prices to customers as well as make a profit, Kroger, as mentioned previously, has gone into the manufacturing of its own products. Since this only amounts to 10% of total sales for the company, brand names still seem to be what customers want to purchase. Kroger also offers Top Value stamps in an effort to lure customers into its stores, but actually trading stamps have little value in accomplishing this since almost all food chain stores offer them.

Kroger also faces competition from discount houses. Presently there are not too many in existence, but they are located in areas that are largely populated. At the present time they account for 2% of all sales of food. Some food chain store companies operate these discount houses, but Kroger has not ventured into this field.

There is an idea in the minds of many people that the small, independent stores are almost out of existence. This is not true; in fact, small stores are stronger now than they have been in years. In many communities small grocery stores have organized to compete with the low prices of Kroger. Kroger can sell at low prices because it purchases brand name foods in quantity, thus for a cheaper price. The low prices can be passed on to the customer. Independent grocers are now organizing so they can buy in quantity, thus at a cheaper price. The best example of independent grocers organizing in an effort to compete with Kroger and other food chain stores is the Independent Grocers Alliance of America.

Although there still is some concern about its owning too many small stores, the Kroger Company has made great progress in eliminating this problem. The reason for having large stores is to have more products available to the customer, and thus to have one store shopping. Kroger has, in the new larger stores, even made certain hardware goods available to the customer. This is in addition to large, modern, and attractive bakery and meat departments. According to the 1963 annual report, in 1954 the average store was 6,738 square feet; but in 1963 the average store was 15,468 square feet. New stores opened in 1964 averaged 14,871 square feet. Kroger has increased its store size both through the construction of new stores and through the remodeling of older stores. Even though Kroger has solved, to a large extent, its problem concerning small stores, it still has stores that are too small for today's needs; but when Kroger builds a new store or remodels an old store, now more than ever, it must carefully consider the costs involved. In the 1920's if a store was built and it proved to be unsuccessful, the loss was not as great as it would be today. Today, when Kroger constructs a large supermarket type store and it is not profitable, causing Kroger to close it, it can lose as much as one million dollars.

Through the years the Kroger Company has been one of the leading food chain store operators. The decisions the company makes in the future can strengthen or weaken the standing of Kroger in the industry.

FOR DISCUSSION

1. Why has there been a decline in the number of stores since 1920?
2. What decisions will determine increase or decrease in Kroger's position in the industry?
3. What is Kroger's major problem? Do you think Kroger has made the right decisions concerning this problem?

SUGGESTED READING

Barnett, H. R., *Man Management in Chain Stores*, New York, Harper & Row, 1931.

Beckman, T. N., and Nolen, H. C., *The Chain Store Problem*, New York, McGraw-Hill, 1938.

"Prospects Mixed For Food Processors and Grocery Chains," *The Magazine of Wall Street*, March 7, 1964, p. 618.

Jewel Tea Company, Incorporated

IN 1899 Frank V. Skiff went into business with a horse, wagon, and $700. He set up a route for customers who regularly bought coffee from him. He also carried spices, tea, and other staple groceries. Two years later he was joined by his brother-in-law, Frank Rose, who became a partner with him in forming the Jewel Tea Company.

In 1932 Jewel started its chain store operation by acquiring 77 Loblaw Stores in Chicago and 4 in the Midwest, and by 1936 it had 100 stores. By 1952 its products included frozen foods and meats and it had introduced self-service.

The D. M. Jacobsen Company, a produce agency, and the Eisner Grocery Company, with 41 stores in central Illinois, were absorbed by Jewel in 1957. The company extended its chain to Europe by joining Grand Bazaar of Antwerp, the leading department store, to develop a chain of supermarkets in Belgium in 1960.

Jewel's firmly established reputation with the consumer for quality and value has put the company in a strong competitive position. In 1935 Jewel's management realized that other merchants in Chicago had a competitive advantage because of their larger size and ability to buy in larger quantities. Jewel was making daily deliveries of fresh fruits and vegetables in small quantities. As a result it decided to become expert in the field of merchandising perishables—fruits, vegetables, meats, poultry, and fish.

It familiarized itself with various chain store problems of distribution and experimented with new practices and policies. By 1936 the foundation for its new practices and policies was built. In 1937 Jewel found that where a meat market was added to a store, its grocery sales showed a 21% increase and a total sales increase of 50%.

In 1956 George Clements, president of Jewel Tea Company, stated that its competitive position was affected by an increase in demand for food products due to upward surge in population, rise in income, improvement in products, higher standard of living, and automobiles. During the 1950's Jewel Tea was pressing A & P for the top share of the Chicago market, displacing National Tea, whose share declined.

The following market ratings compare 1952 with 1956 results. According to the consumer panel, A & P in 1956 had the largest share of the market, 17.1%, compared with 12.3% in 1952. Jewel went up from 8.6% to about 14%, and up to 15.5% in 1957. On the other hand, National, which had 10.1% in 1952, slipped to 9% in 1956. Other chains were Kroger, which went down from 4.2% to 3.6%, and High-Low, which declined from 4.4% to 3.4% (1952-1956). According to Chicago consumers, Jewel had a young and progressive image and clean, white stores; on the other hand, National was closing many of its stores.

By the early 1960's Jewel's competitive position was strong. Jewel is a well-managed, strongly financed, regional chain, operating 324 markets (1964), centered in the Chicago metropolitan area and covering a territory extending into parts of Wisconsin, Indiana, and Michigan. Jewel also has a home-route business accounting for about 15% of sales.

In 1963 Jewel showed a relatively small increase (6% change) in sales. However, its total sales were well above the other chains (except for Food Fair in Philadelphia). In earnings Jewel showed a negative change (8%), but its total earnings were well above other competitors.

A study of grocery dollars spent in Chicago during a two-week test period in 1962 showed that Jewel rang up 43.1% of all grocery dollars spent during this period (National Tea had 40.8%, A & P had 33.9%, and Kroger had 28.3%).

Relative volume of sales in 1963 among representative national food chains show Jewel comparatively lower in total sales than A & P, Safeway, Kroger, Winn-Dixie, and Grand Union.

Sales trends for Jewel showed a steady rising trend in sales from 1950 to 1962; however, in 1963 sales slipped somewhat. The 1964 sales show a slight increase over 1963, but this sales figure includes the Star Market Company's sales. Total sales increased from $751 million in 1963 to $782 million in 1964, and net earnings increased 15.7% to $13 million compared with $11 million in 1963.

Jewel faced many problems in the past, and some of those problems are closely related to current ones. Before and around 1932, ordinances in various cities prohibited salesmen from soliciting at homes. This was disastrous for Jewel, since its primary business was home routes. Jewel counteracted these ordinances by buying a pilot group of chain stores (The Loblaw Stores). This marked the beginning of the chain store operation of Jewel.

In 1934 Jewel became interested in demand factors. It decided to conduct a survey to discover what the housewives wanted in a food store. Jewel interviewed 18,000 women. They determined what women wanted most: a clean white store, freshness, honesty, friendliness, and a guarantee of quality. The Jewel Ten Commandments were eventually drafted from these findings.

Further, in 1934, Jewel needed to determine a basic policy in regard to perishables and canned goods. It solved this problem by developing a code for the purpose of rebuilding customer confidence that had been lagging. This code included: constantly inspecting canned goods to insure satisfactory quality and to avoid disappointing customers on substandard merchandise; maintaining a high level of quality on butter, eggs, and bakery goods; developing fruit and vegetable departments, stressing freshness.

Around 1939 Jewel did not have a clear sales policy, with each store maintaining its own standards of operation. Management then pronounced its Ten Commandments: (1) clean and white stores; (2) friendliness; (3) self-service; (4) true quality; (5) fresh produce; (6) low prices; (7) reliable weights; (8) variety of foods; (9) uniform pricing; and (10) Jewel growth.

During the war (1942-1946), a major problem was the meat shortage. People had money and red ration points, but no meat. From 50 to 300 persons lined up at some markets; therefore, Jewel developed its Fair Share policy. This policy involved first-come-first-served; only one kind of fresh meat to a customer; no tie-in sales; retail sales only; and all sales as per OPA requirements. This program created a favorable customer impression and showed that Jewel managers were avoiding the questionable practices of others. Further, during the war the food restrictions created other problems, in personnel and in food products. Jewel eased the situation by replacing men with women. In addition, 251 restricted items were added. A final war-time problem was the supply shortage. Items in short supply were allocated to stores as soon as they were received in the warehouse. Stores generally received small insufficient amounts at a time. To solve this crisis, Jewel's merchandising policy was revised. All supplies were held back at the warehouse until there was an adequate supply for all.

During 1949 Jewel customers were complaining about the lack of frozen foods available (new home freezers were becoming more common); thus, Jewel added many new frozen products to accommodate the home freezers.

A new type of problem developed in 1950. Jewel began experimenting with the effects of an air-conditioned store on sales. After such a unit was installed, Jewel showed a 7.9% increase in sales for a hot and humid four week period compared with the same period the year before. Also, in 1950, Jewel noticed that previous pricing policy caused difficulty with respect to the change of price of items already on the shelves. Consequently, a new fair price policy was established. If a can or package has been marked with a price and placed on the shelves, this price would not be affected by a rise in prices. If, however, the wholesale price declines, then the retail price would also decline.

During the mid-1950's Jewel found that a basic philosophy in the conduct of its business should be formulated. Up until then there was still a problem in pin-pointing a definite and concrete philosophy. G. L. Clements, president, said:

Regardless of whether a man is at the top or bottom of the business ladder, he is first of all a human being, subject to the same frustrations, fears, and personal needs common to all; after that he is president, vice-president, department head, supervisor, and foreman. In Jewel we meet this opportunity by eliminating the concept of management by edict—by issuing orders—the Ivory Tower complex. Each one of our executives is asked to consider that he works as the first assistant to the next person in line below him. He begins by developing an understanding within himself that he does not run the business, but assists others who do. He tries to forget he is boss and tries to remember that any prestige he might have comes from what he can accomplish for others, rather than from symbols of his office. Responsibility has been delegated to the department heads assigned to various functions and activities for the business. Each spends his time helping subordinates in their decisions, advancing helpful suggestions, keeping them informed, etc.

Toward the late 1950's Jewel had to decide how to handle the problem of running out of merchandise on faster selling items due to lack of space. Jewel decided to spread out the housewares section over a 12-foot area on two shelves rather than on six. Further, it cut down on shoe polish, small glass jars, and other items from two layers to one. Also, adjustable shelves were installed for customer convenience.

In 1958 Jewel faced the difficulty of attracting suitable and qualified personnel. It developed a program consisting of the following points: good pay; satisfactory employee atmosphere; good opportunities for individual advancement; peace of mind; planned future; insurance program (hospitalization, medical, surgical, and group life); retirement fund (15% of net income); and scholarships.

As 1959 was ending, Jewel was faced with the problem of how to keep its sales volume up during a strike in the Hammond-Gary area. This difficulty was solved by means of credit, which was offered through Jewel's 12 area supermarkets in the strike territory. The above program was only applicable to persons who were not working as a result of the strike.

The 1960's presented Jewel with many problems which were encountered previously, but it also had to solve problems of a new and different nature. In 1961 the Jewel store in Joliet had a parking lot which was 200 feet away from the store. As a result, the customers were greatly inconvenienced. Jewel decided to develop a warehouse chain conveyor system which was adapted to shopping carts. Bagged groceries were placed in a cart and the customer was given a number. A tow then pulled the cart via an underground tunnel to a parcel-pickup room in the parking lot. Empty carts were returned to the store on a return run.

Another problem situation, which Jewel had to develop a program and policy for, concerns the opening up of a new competing store next door. At Jewel, preparations for such an occurrence begin many months before the competing store opens. First, staff meetings are called to decide on policies; then increased customer service and friendliness are stressed and sales promotions are often instituted. Finally, participation in community activities is stressed.

In 1961 Jewel found that four stores in the Chicago area and one store in Peking, Illinois, were too far from their primary territory, making the cost of supply too great. The solution was to shift these stores to the super-value-store system in Minneapolis (no change in personnel).

Concerning its competitive position, in 1962-1963 management evolved a sound strategy for meeting the challenge of the chain retailing environment and capitalizing on it for future growth. Through mergers with a promotional drug chain (Osco Drug) and a discount operation (Turnstyle), management gathered considerable competitive merchandising knowhow. Jewel management now considers itself not as an operator of supermarkets, but as a general retailer, specializing in merchandise which can be handled under self-service and mass-merchandising methods and which can be offered with the convenience of one-stop shopping. Management can offer the competitive, flexible strategy of Jewel-Osco combinations, both small and large, and large Family Center operations combining food, drug, variety, and general merchandise lines. Further, Jewel stresses quality and value and strives for a position of permanence in the community. The Family Center concept offers Jewel the opportunity to move into new areas with a merchandising strategy obsoleting existing competition.

To compete, Jewel must offer to the customer convenient, one-stop shopping, around a centrally located parking lot in stores selling by means of self-service. In addition, in an effort to meet competition, Jewel has formed its own discount companies to control their costs and to gain greater margins (Food Fair, Stop & Shop, Jewel, Giant Food, Thriftmart, and Lucky Stores now own their own discount companies).

Jewel's diversified retail stores meet competition in the following ways:

1. Having the ability to handle perishable foods, particularly fresh meats; cleanliness of stores and friendly atmosphere; and the ability to respond with innovations to satisfy the ever-changing demands of customers and to keep prices and costs down.
2. Concentrating on food values without stamps, based on experience derived from observing the use of stamps by two other major competitors in Chicago in 1962. Jewel withstood this competitive challenge from trading stamps in providing better values, and pleasant shopping experiences.
3. Requiring the manager to maintain efficient low-cost operations by requiring him to keep a careful watch on expenses for each of the fresh produce, dairy products, shelf-stocking, and cashier-checkout service. A watch is especially kept on operating costs and related factors such as dollar sales and pounds handled per man hours.
4. Meeting the demand for convenient one-stop shopping, resulting from the growth in automobile ownership.
5. Meeting the demand for items and services contributing to a higher standard of living, and for reduced work at home resulting from the rise in the income level of customers.
6. Providing extra features such as specially cut meats, frozen fresh pastries, etc.
7. Lowering production and handling costs through new methods.
8. Improving scheduling, use of pallets, and use of improved delivery equipment of greater capacity.
9. Establishing stores having the ability to adapt themselves successfully to new competition, notably from discount houses.
10. Extending supermarket concept to include drug items, beauty aids, etc.

A problem faced every year is the seasonal slowdown of the meat business during Lent. For a while Jewel had advertised other items quite heavily; but in 1962 Jewel decided to try an all-out effort on advertising meat during the Lenten period, and an increase was experienced in the sale of meat. Consequently, Jewel's policy was revised. Another meat problem involved customer irritation in regard to the purchase of meats. If a customer wanted a rib roast, he had to buy short ribs with it at rib roast prices. Jewel then adopted the policy of giving "extra value trim," by separating cuts (excess fat was removed before weighing).

A final food problem concerns why other companies dated their foods and Jewel did not. It appears that Jewel does not have a definite policy on dating foods because dating, or time as such, has little bearing on freshness, wholesomeness, or quality of most food products. Temperature is the important idea in the preservation of perishable foods. In each store Jewel has a Dairy Code Book, which shows how to take care of foods.

Further, Jewel has been working on the task of assuring quality control. The following are procedures instituted by Jewel:

1. *Baking Mixes:* raw materials are checked when received; samples of each batch are baked in test kitchens before packaging; and a sample is baked after packaging.
2. *Wearing Apparel:* all washables are checked for shrinkage, color, and washability; children's wear is tested on children; men's pants and women's wear are also tested; incoming shipments are spot-checked for size, color, etc.; and periodic inspection trips are made to suppliers.
3. *Hard Goods:* appliances are tested and evaluated in the laboratory and in the test kitchen; shipments are spot-checked; outdoor furniture is drop-checked; and special pots and pans are use-tested.

Still another area of controversy is the trading stamp issue. Since A & P started to use Plaid Stamps, Jewel is the last holdout. Jewel fights the competitors' stamps by intensive advertising, price promotions, concentration of stores, lower advertising and transportation costs, and closer supervision. In order to counter A & P Plaid Stamp giveaway, Jewel inaugurated the Private Label Game in March, 1962. This provides for sampling of private label products. Top winners receive $100 for collecting facsimile coins numbered 1, 9, 6, and 3.

Lastly, Jewel has made attempts to solve the problem of morale, security, and teamwork by means of its profit-sharing program. This program has developed a Trust Fund which has swelled to $55 million at the end of 1961. This plan provides an incentive to save, and a reward for doing so, since the amount of distribution is affected by the amount of the employee contribution. Estimates up to $136,000 can be in a fund for a 65 year old retiree who has worked 45 years.

Although Jewel is in a good competitive position at this time, its problems are of a repetitive nature. Management is constantly aware of these problems and must continue to take the necessary steps to maintain the company's strong position.

FOR DISCUSSION

1. What policy decisions have been made at Jewel Tea and what were the objectives of these policies?
2. In what ways has Jewel shown its awareness of flexibility of policy; of ethics?
3. What strategy has management evolved concerning competition? What procedures has Jewel followed to meet it?

4. What are some of the decisions that Jewel has made and how effective have they been?
5. Give an overall evaluation of the Jewel Tea Company.

SUGGESTED READING

"Jewel Tea Plans Stores To Fit the Neighborhood," *Chain Store Age*, March, 1963, pp. 16-17.
"Reviving an Ailing Store," *Chain Store Age*, February, 1960, p. 26a.

CHAPTER 5

Shell Oil Company

WHEN SHELL ENTERED the petroleum industry in the United States and started oil production and marketing operations, the industry was already 53 years old. From this small beginning in 1912, as the American Gasoline Company, which was marketing on the Pacific Coast, and the Roxana Petroleum Company, which was producing oil in the Midwest, Shell grew rapidly into a major firm, today ranking in the top twenty industrial enterprises in the United States and in the top seven oil producing firms.

Much of Shell's progress came from its close association with the Royal/Dutch Shell Group, which at the present time owns about 69% of the United States Shell Oil Company. "The Group," by which Royal/Dutch Shell is known in the oil industry, offered advice and technical knowledge gathered from its world-wide experience in oil; so even as a newcomer Shell was able to pioneer many developments that have had a strong influence on the oil industry in the United States.

Therefore, much of the history of United States Shell is closely aligned with the history of the "Group," which is the world's second largest oil company—after Standard of New Jersey—and the third largest industrial organization in sales, surpassed only by Standard and General Motors Corporation. Royal/Dutch Shell is controlled in partnership by two companies; one Dutch (Royal Dutch Petroleum Company) and one British (Shell Transport and Trading Company, Limited). Royal/Dutch Shell is a "two-headed creature" that owns or partially owns 500 world-wide subsidiaries and produces 14% of the free world's oil.

The U.S. branch of the "Group," Shell Oil, is controlled by the "Group's" board of directors. Since the organization believes in independent management in its subsidiaries, the Shell Oil Company is much on its own. It has four separate companies: the Shell Oil Company, Shell Chemical Corporation, Shell Development Company, and the Shell Pipeline Corporation.

Shell Pipeline Corporation was incorporated in 1927, although Shell operation of pipelines in the United States stretches back to 1915. Both Shell Pipeline Corporation and the Pipeline Department of Shell Oil Company have been leaders in pipeline development over the years. They were responsible in 1927 for the first automatic main-line pipeline pumping station. In 1939 they began shipping natural gas dissolved in crude oil and in 1942 developed a portable pipeline for military use. By 1953 Shell was blending products in pipelines, thus eliminating the need for tank blending.

The Shell Development Company, formed in 1927, was a pioneer organization set up to do basic research and develop new products and processes. Since its beginning it has contributed research achievements in all of Shell's operations. It has made improvements in well drilling and oil explorations, which have revolutionized the oil industry. It has discovered many important oil-producing areas in the U.S. and is responsible for recent developments in offshore exploration and production.

The Chemical Corporation, originated in 1929, has pioneered the manufacture of new chemicals from petroleum, such as ammonia from natural gas, synthetic glycerine, rust inhibitors, soil fumegation, and most recently, airport asphalt and synthetic natural rubber.

Shell maintained rapid growth and during the Second World War produced 12% of the aviation fuel with 6% of the refinery capacity. After the war Shell made several important discoveries in many states, with the newest and most important in the four corner area of Utah, New Mexico, Colorado, and Arizona. In 1955 Shell's refinery capacity reached over half a million barrels per day. This type of rapid growth has made Shell large enough to join the ranks of the twenty largest business enterprises in the nation.

In 1960 the "Group" recognized the need for decentralization of its top management. The result was an organization that allows the managing directors of Royal/Dutch Shell to use their knowledge and judgment in the capacity of consultant whenever anything out of the ordinary comes up.

Shell Oil, a leading integrated oil company in the United States, ranks among the top seven in crude oil production, refinery runs, and product sales, employing close to 40,000 people. It is also the largest manufacturer and marketer of chemicals.

Net crude output in 1963 was 164,912,000 barrels compared with 123,121,000 in 1962 and 119,647,000 barrels in 1961. In 1962 the six Shell refineries in the U.S. had a daily average capacity of some 594,000 barrels. In addition, Shell holds interests in 35 wholly or partially owned natural gasoline plants. Net natural gas production in 1962 was 474,125,000 Mcf., substantially above the 412,005,000 Mcf. of 1961.

Shell products are marketed through 23,500 retail outlets with gasoline sales accounting for 49% of product volume. Refined products in 1962 were up to 242,326,000 barrels from a volume of 223,094,000 barrels in 1961. Like product volume, sales have increased through the years (Figure 5.1).

Cash dividends have been paid to stockholders since 1836. In the past five years through 1963, these dividends have averaged 44% of net. There

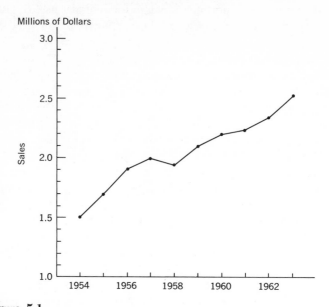

Figure 5.1
Total Revenue—Sales and Other Operating Revenue
Refined Products and Other Operating Revenue + Chemical Products + Crude Oil

1963 —	$2,562,680
1962 —	2,351,171
1961 —	2,238,639
1960 —	2,167,832
1959 —	2,129,958
1958 —	1,953,754
1957 —	2,047,068
1956 —	1,891,627
1955 —	1,717,048
1954 —	1,522,088

are 22,183 shareholders (as of 1963) with 60,547,568 shares of common stock (par $1) outstanding; 69.4% is owned by Shell Caribbean Petroleum, in turn 100% owned by Canadian Shell, Limited, which in turn is owned by the Royal/Dutch Shell Group (Figure 5.2).

There are five major problem areas which the Shell Oil Company is attempting to deal with at present. They are competition, labor, automation, modernization, and overcapacity in its chemical industry.

Competition is by far the most important and immediate problem facing Shell. The amount of crude oil available has increased to a large extent and this has drawn new "wildcat" firms into the industry. They are doing a great deal of exploration, developing new oil fields, and selling crude oil at lower prices. In order to keep its share of the market in crude oil and to meet the new lower prices, Shell has had to keep up with them in exploration and drilling.

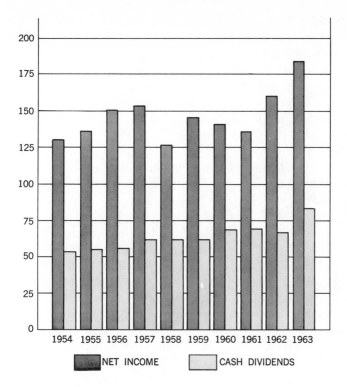

NET INCOME   CASH DIVIDENDS

Figure 5.2
Net Income and Cash Dividends
In Millions of Dollars

Shell also has had to meet competition increase in new sources of power, namely natural gas and atomic energy. At the present time, atomic energy is not an immediate threat but it will pose a competitive problem in the future. Natural gas is an important and immediate threat to the oil industry. Shell has tried to cope with this new power industry not by fighting it, but by joining in the production of natural gas. It has become a large producer of natural gas with an increasing capacity.

Another problem in this area of competition is the advent and increasing supply of politically priced Russian oil. This in recent years has been a major problem for all oil companies.

With this increase in competition has come several related problems: modernization and automation. In order to meet competition, costs must be reduced in order to have a reduction in price. This necessary increase in efficiency has made it impossible to operate without the modernization and automation of existing plants and equipment.

Of course, modernization, expansion, and automation call for additional spending. The major problem involved here is where the additional funds will come from; Shell has three ways of solving this problem.

One advantage Shell has over the other companies in the industry is that of writing off drilling and other intangible expenses as they occur and not over a period of years. This system allows any additional new income to be used for expansion, modernization, or automation.

The second means of obtaining additional funds is the standard method available to all companies; and that is to issue bonds, sell stock, and utilize any other means used by industrial firms to seek funds. Shell is in a good position to employ this method because of its high earnings over the years. They are solid and this attracts investors because the element of risk is smaller.

The third possibility of new funds comes from an increase in sales to its jobbers and increasing jobbers' sales to the consumer. Shell has been working with jobbers for more than 40 years. The Shell jobber system is now one of the biggest in the petroleum industry. The company helps jobbers by having local representatives assist them, not a remote home office; by providing expert advice on station location and layout; by giving its jobbers sound financial guidance; by awarding geographic jobber franchises whenever it is possible to do so.

With an increase of efficiency, modernization of plants, and adoption of automation, men are displaced. Shell has this labor problem. In 1963 Shell was the victim of a labor walkout in Houston. The issue was one of management rights versus job protection in an age of automation. Shell solved this problem but in the future there will be more of them to solve in this area; with labor costs already high there is is no telling what the outcome will be.

Another problem at present is an overcapacity in its chemical plants; this, however, will not be a major problem in the long run. With increasing demands for synthetic materials in the "space age" this overcapacity may be turned into an undercapacity if Shell does not keep a watchful eye on the industry.

Shell Oil Company has been increasing its share of the market every year and in time it may rank number one in oil production in the U.S. With this incentive it is trying hard to find the answers to the above problems and is counting on its top management and association with the Royal/Dutch Shell Group to help it succeed.

FOR DISCUSSION

1. What long-run problem does Shell have regarding labor?
2. What are the major considerations in Shell's most immediate problem of competition?

3. What major problem accompanies modernization and expansion and what has Shell done to solve it?
4. What general objective in oil production does Shell have? Is the company proceeding in the right manner to achieve this goal?

SUGGESTED READING

Burck, Gilbert, "The Bountiful World of Royal Dutch-Shell," *Fortune*, September, 1957, pp. 134-141; October, 1957, pp. 138-144 ff.

Enos, John L., "The Mighty Adversaries: Standard Oil Company (N.J.) and the Royal Dutch-Shell Group," *Exploration Entrepreneurial History*, April, 1958, pp. 140-149.

"Royal Dutch-Shell Group; Diplomats of Oil," *Time*, May 9, 1960, pp. 92-94 ff.

Standard Oil Company (Indiana)

STANDARD OF INDIANA was organized in 1889 by the Standard Oil Trust. The company has experienced a phenomenal growth because of its early establishment in the Middle West, where the greatest potential oil market in the world was located.

Standard was built in Whiting, Indiana, and the refinery there is one of the largest in the country and also one of the first oil refineries in the West. The principal function of the company at this time was to supply kerosene, lubricants, greases, and other petroleum products to the various Standard marketing companies across the nation.

With the coming of the automobile, an increased demand for gasoline and motor oils was foreseen by Standard's executives. This foresight prompted the company to build and operate company-owned service stations. This pioneer development met the expansion of the automobile market and made gasoline and motor oil easily attainable for motorists.

In 1911 the Supreme Court dissolved the Standard Oil Company (New Jersey) from the Standard Oil Trust. This action resulted in the Trust being broken; the thirty-four companies owned by the holding company became free, independent, and separate. Standard of Indiana was one of these thirty-four companies and it came out of the dissolution owning three large refineries and the marketing organization it had established in the Middle West; but, the company was left without any pipeline system to ship its crude oil to the refineries. This problem was not solved at first because the company remained a refining and marketing company. For the time, the crude oil was obtained from the Prairie Oil & Gas Company and other smaller organizations. The Prairie Company continued to ship the crude oil to the refineries as it had done before.

The rapid expansion of the gasoline market led to the crude oil shortage in 1916. Again, the perceptiveness of its executives enabled Standard to overcome this possible problem. In 1909 the officers realized the future demand for oil and told the company's chemists to come up with a way to get more gasoline from crude oil. The process set up by Burton to achieve this end involved cracking crude oil through the use of high temperature and pressure.

The Burton invention allowed Standard to produce two barrels of gasoline to every one that was produced before from crude oil. The invention also opened the eyes of other chemists in the oil industry to the fact that chemical changes could be obtained in crude oil. This awakening resulted in a new interest in research and many new products from crude oil.

The company owes most of its advances and market standing to the Burton process. The process left Standard with one of the industry's best research divisions, which it still maintains to this day. This research has kept its products high in quality and has resulted in many new products for its customers.

The increasing demand for gasoline and other oil by-products made the company start buying pipelines in 1921. The company again realized the potential market openings and began to build its own pipelines in 1938. In 1939 the first fully-owned and built pipeline was opened, going from Sugar Creek to Council Bluffs. The beginning of the 1950's showed Standard with a total of 16,180 miles of pipeline.

The most important event in Standard's history was the acquisition of the stock of the American Oil Company. American became wholly owned by Standard in 1954 and increased the number of states Standard markets in from the original 15 to 48.

As stated before, Standard has had a phenomenal growth since its start in 1889. Now, Standard of Indiana is the dominant refiner and marketer of petroleum products in 15 midwestern states under the Standard brand name. The growth may have been phenomenal but the oil industry as a whole is increasing at a terrific rate.

A comparison of Standard (New Jersey) and Indiana Standard brings to light many interesting points on Standard of Indiana's standing in the oil industry in the U.S. The size and volume of New Jersey Standard's business leaves it standing far in front of Indiana Standard. The Indiana company has total assets of over $3 billion and yet this is only about one-fourth of New Jersey's.

The sales volume of the two companies shows that Indiana is far from first place but it is ranked nineteenth in the top 500 industrial firms in the U.S. New Jersey has annual sales above $10 billion while Indiana is operating on sales of $2,147,761,000 a year. Part of New Jersey's large size and sales volume may be attributed to the large amount of earnings every year. New Jersey makes seven times as much as Indiana every year in net income. This also may be one reason for Indiana Standard's decline in market standing. Indiana and New Jersey are almost even in dividends paid per share each every year; New Jersey has many more shares outstanding. This means that even though Standard of New Jersey pays slightly higher dividends, it is retaining more money.

Standard is ranked ninth in the country for the amount of invested capital. However, its rate of return is only 6.8% and this pushes it down to 349th in this category.

Many of Standard's problems arise from the company's attempt to overcome this low rate of return. The company has a firm belief that increasing efficiency will enable it to increase its rate of return. One major step towards efficiency was the introduction of a project system in the research department. The project system was set up by an outside consultant named A. D. Little. The system consisted of a cut in the department budget of $1 million, a large manpower lay-off, and stringent bookkeeping.

The new system also resulted in the elimination of two levels of supervision between the bench chemists and the individual directors of each division. Because of this and the manpower lay-off, the system may or may not help increase the rate of return. The cut in levels of supervision will curtail the amount of communication within the industry. A cut like this one increases the span of control a supervisor has and means he has less time to spend with each employee. The lay-off may result in the employees feeling insecure in their jobs because of this decrease in communication; however, the company doesn't openly admit that this is one of its problems and there is no evidence that it is trying to overcome its lack of communication.

The cut in the budget of $1 million has reduced the amount of research the company can do. The company will need higher sales through new and better products and research is the only means to this end, but the company feels that it is justified in its cut because of the use of newly acquired computers.

The computers determine each day's run at the Whiting refinery. The efficiency of the company has been increased by the project system and the use of computers, but the number of employees has been highly decreased. In the seven years between 1956-1963 the total employment of Standard decreased by 14,000 employees. The Whiting refinery itself has decreased its employees from 8200 to 2800. Better communication seems to be the only solution to the problem of insecurity created by this large lay-off.

Another problem that Standard of Indiana is now confronted with is being faced by the oil industry as a whole. Crude oil is becoming scarcer as the years go by. One of Standard's mistakes in creating this problem was the selling of its overseas drilling rights to Standard of New Jersey. Many wells are being discovered overseas by Standard (Indiana), but the U.S. government has set a limit on the amount of oil that can be imported. This quota was set right after Indiana's sale to New Jersey and it was based on the number of oil wells owned by the company at that time.

Indiana Standard recognizes this problem and has taken great strides towards overcoming it. One step was the acquisition of the Indiana Oil Purchasing Company. This company has the job of purchasing crude oil for Standard from the wildcat drillers in the United States. Another step has been the increase in Standard's overseas operations. The operations have been extended by building new refineries overseas to handle the higher output of the oil wells so that the company can meet the expanding foreign market for oil and its by-products.

Price wars and intense competition are two road signs of the oil industry and are creating problems for many oil companies. Indiana Standard and many other oil companies make the biggest percentage of their profits from the gasoline sales. A price war could have disastrous effects on their plans; however, there are two major ways a company could avoid them. The company could diversify its product lines to lessen the reliance on gasoline sales, or the company could expand its sales operations so that a price war in one area would not affect its entire operation. Standard has taken the second alternative and is using the subsidiary American brand name to market its products outside the fifteen midwestern states. The only way Standard could meet the other alternative would be to increase its research. New products could be developed from increased research in oil.

The problem of intense competition ties in with the idea of new product lines and efficiency. The company is trying to meet this problem by putting four interrelated solutions together: (1) it is using automation to cut down the size of its labor force and labor costs so that lower prices can be charged for its products; (2) it is using more stringent accounting to rid itself of worthless projects; (3) it is improving the refinery processes through research and modernizing the equipment used; (4) it is trying to improve its domestic crude oil supply.

Standard is trying to overcome all these problems so that it can increase its rate of return. A year or two ago, the company put into operation a plan to increase the rate from its low of 6.8% to the 11% normal for the industry. This plan was to take ten years to complete. Recently, however, a restudy of the plan showed the rate would only be increased to approximately 8.5% with the present operations. Standard is at this time working on a revision of the plan.

According to M. J. Rathbone, chairman of Standard Oil Company of New Jersey, the free world will be consuming oil and gas at 2½ times the current rate by 1985. In view of this the company faces a promising future and will undoubtedly remain alert to its problems.

FOR DISCUSSION

1. What major problem underlies many of Standard Oil's other problems? What procedures has Standard Oil followed to overcome this?
2. What is the nature of the problem that Standard Oil shares with the oil industry?
3. How has Standard Oil met the problem of price wars? Do you feel that the company chose the best alternative?
4. Do you think that the decisions management has made regarding the problem of competition will provide the solution the company is hoping for?

SUGGESTED READING

Giddens, Paul H., *Standard Oil Company (Indiana): Oil Pioneer of the Middle West*, New York, Appleton-Century-Crofts, 1955.

"Standard Oil Company (Indiana)," *Chemical & Engineering News*, September 2, 1963, p. 70.

Union Tank Car Company

THE HISTORY OF UNION TANK CAR COMPANY dates back to 1873, when it became part of Standard Oil of New Jersey. Prior to this it was known as Star Tank Line and Pipeline Company, which was founded by J. J. Vandergrift. Standard acquired Mr. Vandergrift's company in exchange for stock in Standard Oil.

The number of tank cars in Standard grew rapidly during the next two decades. By 1891 Standard had incorporated several other tank lines, such as Green Land Line Company, into its oligopoly. Because of government pressure, both state and federal, the tank car division was made a separate company on July 14, 1891. It was chartered in New Jersey and called the Union Tank Line.

The darkest day in the long history of Union Tank Line was on May 15, 1911, when the Supreme Court ordered Standard Oil to dissolve for violation of the antitrust laws. The dissolution left the company in poor shape. There was only a handful of office employees, a small office, and hundreds of tank cars. Mr. Felton, Union Tank Line president, was the only one who foresaw a great future for the newly independent company. He realized that the Standard refiners needed the company as badly as it needed Standard since no oil could be shipped without the combination of the two.

On June 11, 1919, the company adopted a new name, Union Tank Car Company, which is its present title. The demand for tank cars was great during the First World War. Several thousand tank cars had been ordered during the war but delivery did not come until 1919. Mr. Felton had the large problem of where to store these cars. He managed to find storage areas and new consumer outlets to use the cars.

The Great Depression placed many thousands of firms in bankruptcy, but not so Union Tank. It managed to maintain a relatively strong financial position because of its long term leases and its ability to generate cash even in the lows of the depression.

The effect of the Second World War was tremendous. Even after the war, the company continued to show remarkable growth. The demand for cars of all types made expansion a necessity. Expansion was not limited to the car leasing industry, but rather the company diversified into other industries, such as construction, water purification, and international trade. This diversification was felt to be necessary in the mid-1950's in order to continue the rapid growth the company had already experienced.

Over the years Union Tank has grown from a small, insecure company in 1911 to one of multi-million dollar size. All of this has been possible because of excellent leadership and being born into a ready-made market which needed the services the company had to offer.

The railroad car leasing industry is one of few firms with large capital investments. The entire industry consists of only four firms: Union Tank Car Company, General American Transport Company, ACF Industries Incorporated, North American Car Corporation. The only other competition stems from refineries which have invested in their own tankers.

The car leasing industry is large and covers the leasing of every type car from the ordinary freight car to special purpose and flat cars. In this vast industry Union Tank stands out as the world's largest lessor of tank cars—the company presently owns some 50,193. These are predominantly used for the transportation of petroleum products and chemicals. The company has long-term lease contracts with most of the Standard Oil refineries. The nonpetroleum products carried account for only 25% of the lease revenue. The company also derives about 50% of its income outside of the car leasing industry.

Other firms are larger in size but lease other type rail transport vehicles. General American has the largest privately owned fleet of freight cars (66,000) and public tank storage terminal facilities in the U.S. In 1963 it had a gross revenue in excess of $187 million (which was better than twice that of Union Tank); of this, 46.2% was derived from car leasing and storage operations, and 53.8% from manufacturing.

ACF Industries is also larger than Union Tank in gross revenue by almost double, or $228.6 million. The company is a leading builder of railroad cars as well as a large lessor of tank and special purpose cars through its Shipper's Car Line Division; however, the leasing division is not as large as Union Tank when the total number of cars is compared. It only has 19,640 presently under lease.

North American is the fourth largest in the railroad car leasing industry in the U.S. At the end of 1963 the company owned and operated 18,425 cars. The company has a wide range and variety of cars, from tank cars to stock and flat cars.

A comparison of the four companies shows that although Union Tank is the largest tank car lessor in the world, it is not the largest car lessor. In gross revenue it is only third largest in the U.S. and ranks much lower on the world market; however, gross revenue alone does not indicate the size of the firm within the industry. In total number of cars owned, regardless of type, Union Tank is second only to General American. Diversification outside the industry also affects the relative size of the companies. Car leasing is not the primary income for all of these companies.

The railroad car leasing industry has shown remarkable advances in the past decade. The trend is always up, up, and up. Union Tank has also followed this same basic upward trend. From Figure 5.3 it can be seen

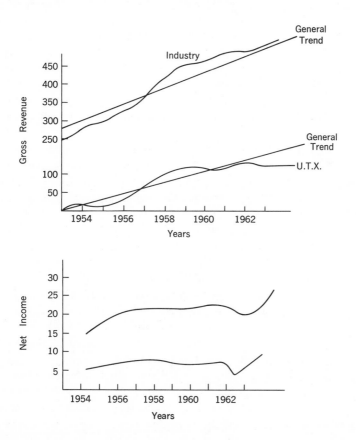

Figure 5.3
Comparison of U.T.X. to the Industry in Both Gross Revenue and Net Income

that the entire industry has experienced a vast growth in sales. In the percentage of the market Union Tank which was capturing only 6% of the industry in 1954 gained a high of 19% in 1963; however, net income has not increased proportionately to the rise in sales.

Union Tank has, in the past several years, been expanding into other areas of car leasing in an endeavor to increase its share of the market. In 1963, 1,021 new cars were added to the company. These new cars served a variety of different purposes:

Chemical	55%
Liquified Petroleum Gas	26%
Food	8%
Liquid Oxygen	2%
Hopper Cars	3%
Others	6%

This indicates that Union Tank is presently expanding within the industry, and in the future can be expected to hold a much larger share of the market than it presently does.

The short- and long-run prospects for Union Tank Car Company are good. Per-share earnings in 1963 raised to $2.31 and in 1964 to $3.41 from the $.11 per-share in 1962. The earnings are expected to continue to rise in the near future. Standard and Poor's states: "In view of the secular growth in the petroleum and chemical industries, as well as prospects for additional sales from new acquisitions and extension of leasing operations, revenues should expand over the long term."

Although there is a steady upward trend in company growth, certain points do stand out which indicate problems which the company is presently facing. The first problem is that increasing sales do not yield a relatively larger profit (Figure 5.3). In the past decade sales rose from $28.1 to $126.4 million in 1963 and $115.6 million in 1964, while net income rose from $5.1 to $8.2 million in 1963 and $12.1 million in 1964. Sales more than quadrupled in this period while net income did not even double. Normally, income (profit) is expected to rise at a corresponding rate to sales, but this did not occur in this case. The lack of correlation between the two indicates that the returns on increased sales are rising at a sharply declining rate. This falling profit percentage places the company in a poor financial position.

The declining profit percentage does not appear to be unique to Union Tank. Figure 5.3 indicates that the industry as a whole is having the same problem. The probable cause of this problem is increased competition and therefore a lower price.

A second problem is how can dividends be paid to stockholders with less money being earned. An expanding company must get capital funds from some place, and Union Tank is no exception to this rule. The increased funds must come either from long-term debt or from more shares of stock. Union Tank has financed predominantly through the issuance of more stock. In 1954 there were only 2.1 million shares outstanding and at the end of 1963 there were 3.5 million shares outstanding. At the same time the ratio of long-term debt to total assets declined, indicating that fewer long-term debts were outstanding.

Both of these first two problems find their source or cause in the third problem. Diversification of interest is a direct cause of the first two problems. Diversification was originally decided upon in 1956 by Mr. Locke, the president, because he foresaw a very poor forecast for the railroad industry. At the time, the production industries were expanding at a much more rapid rate than the car leasing or railroad industry in general, and therefore it was considered desirable to diversify into other fields. Since this time, diversification has proven to be the source of many problems for Union Tank. Outstanding is the loss the company took in 1962. In fact, the net income retained showed a $5.31 million loss. With the highest sales ever, the company managed to produce the lowest earning-per-share in ten years. How did this happen?

The low profit on earnings per share can be explained by the loss sustained by one of the subsidiaries of the company—Graver Tank. Union Tank integrated this company a few years ago in an endeavor to vertically integrate. In 1962 Graver attempted to expand its operations into missile base construction. However, this was a poor choice since the project netted an $11 million loss. The large sales figure in 1962 is also related to this project. The contract which caused the loss was also the one that pushed sales up that year.

Presently, Union Tank has a total of ten subsidiaries or divisions. This rising number of new subsidiaries has forced the company to slowly change its organization. This has been a slow evolution which has presented the company with many problems. Proper control is one of these problems. Certain reports are required, such as forecasts and financial statements from each division; but the larger the company, the harder it is to control. As a result, Union Tank has made each subsidiary a division; and, as a result, each division functions on its own and has its own top management. As a whole, the company has decentralized authority in which the division directors have almost full authority. If better control had been exerted by the main office over the Graver Company, the $11 million loss might have been avoided.

How has Union Tank financed the acquisition of these new companies? As was explained before, it was done through the issuance of stock. This is a problem because as stocks are issued to purchase another company, the stockholder finds his stock diluted by so much; that it, with each stock issue, the original stockholder owns a smaller percentage of the company. Therefore, the earnings of the new division must be as high or higher than the company or else the stockholder will lose money. If the new division doesn't attain the same level of earnings as the parent company, then the percentage earnings-per-share declines. This was the case in 1962 when Graver showed such a large loss that the earnings-per-share fell from $2.31 to only $.11.

The forecasts by Mr. Locke that the railroad industry was declining proved to be a false prediction. In the past few years the railroads have made vast gains and the future looks even more promising. This indicates another problem the company is facing: while diversifying into other industries, the company failed to recognize the potential offered in its own industry. According to Mr. Romans, assistant treasurer of Union Tank: "The company did not realize the tremendous growth opportunities available as soon as they should have." To illustrate this point, Mr. Romans pointed out that in the past three years the tank car division has shown the most rapid growth and highest profit of all the divisions. This shows a great oversight on the part of the company in its own industry. The problem now is whether or not the company can avoid these poor estimates in the future.

A general condition of inefficiency has existed within the company. Management has been attempting to remedy this; therefore, in 1963 earnings were reduced by an estimated $.24 per share for write-offs resulting from the closing of unprofitable activities in several divisions. These inefficient operations have now been eliminated. In general, the company has recognized the problem; now the big question is: What action will be taken in the future to prevent this?

How does the future of the company appear? According to Standard and Poor's Corporation, the company will be expected to have added growth in tank car leasing revenue and special equipment revenue. This will come from a greater demand for this type of car. Further improvements are looked for in operation of the company's diversified interests, particularly the Lindsay and Smith & Loveless divisions. Such measures must be taken if the company is to overcome its problems of finance and diversification.

FOR DISCUSSION

1. What factors were responsible for Union Tank's tremendous growth?
2. What problems surround Union Tank's diversification of interest?
3. What policies are a necessary outgrowth of the rising number of new subsidiaries which has forced the company to slowly change its organization? What are the factors necessitating these policies?
4. How has lack of insight hurt Union Tank?

SUGGESTED READING

Carr, Albert Z., *John D. Rockefeller's Secret Weapon*, McGraw-Hill, New York, 1963.

CHAPTER 6

Burroughs Corporation

THE BURROUGHS CORPORATION, since its inception in 1886, has grown from a one-shop operation to a world-wide organization with 38,000 employees, 37 manufacturing plants, and a marketing organization that includes 22 subsidiary corporations throughout the world. In 1904 the Burroughs Adding Machine Company, as it was called then, maintained its home offices and several manufacturing facilities in the Detroit area, the present corporate headquarters. Based there, in addition to corporate staff offices, are the offices of most major operating groups of the company. Burroughs Business Machines Limited of Canada is headquartered in Toronto, Ontario.

In 1946 Burroughs Corporation participated with the University of Pennsylvania in a study to determine the potential application of electronics to computational equipment. Burroughs Corporation has been the only other computer maker in the office machine industry to attempt a serious challenge to I.B.M., the leader. Since 1956, when Burroughs acquired the former Electro Data Corporation and took over marketing of that firm's 205 computer system, final testing, assembly, and central processor production for commercial computers has been assigned to the Electro Data Division in Pasadena, California.

Burroughs today provides employment directly for 36,000 persons throughout the free world. In the last few years Burroughs' research, manufacturing, and marketing facilities have responded to the changing and rapidly increasing need for better and more computational equipment. Electronic Data Processing (EDP) has put a severe short-run strain on the corporation, but as will be shown later it is a sound long-term investment. At present, Burroughs products are marketed in 125 countries. Through its 10,000 man International Division the company operates 25 foreign subsidiaries and 6 plants in 4 overseas countries and sells products through 50 distributors and 3,800 independent retail dealers abroad. Great emphasis is being placed on research and new product development because president Ray Eppert believes this is the only way for American corporations to compete in the world market. Over half of the products marketed today were still on the drawing boards five years ago.

Burroughs is a major manufacturer of office equipment and is aggressively pursuing the application of electronics and automation to office procedure. Burroughs has a major position in the fast-growing electronic data processing market and is particularly strong in the banking field.

Revenues for 1962 broke down as follows: business machines, 42%; office accessories and supplies, 6%; military products, 15%; business form, 7%. In recent years expanded research, development, and marketing expenses have greatly hampered earnings. This is reflected in the Forbes Yardsticks of Performance group rankings in which Burroughs has been slipping (Table 6.1). Electronic Data Processing has made this mark on the balance sheet. One reason is that President Ray Eppert, running a comparatively small company, has much less bread-and-butter income than I.B.M. to pay the bills. Another factor is defense business, a normally low profit proposition, which amounts to 25% of Burroughs' total volume, but seldom more than 1% of a company like National Cash Register. President Ray Eppert says:

Sure it's been a drain, but we're very glad we wrote this long-term insurance policy. In the future, the greatest success will be obtained by those companies not dependent on just computers or conventional business machines, but rather, it will be those companies . . . providing a fully integrated total processing system.

Burroughs' business machine line consists of more than 200 different models classified into the following groups: (1) adding, calculating, and cash registering machines; (2) accounting machines, tape perforating equipment, and magnetic ink recording equipment; (3) electronic data processing systems, including computers, high speed printers, card readers and punchers, magnetic tape readers, disc files, and other peripheral equipment. In 1962 approximately 45% of dollar value of the incoming orders for these products was on a lease basis.

In answer to the computer challenge by the industry leader, I.B.M., Burroughs in the mid-1950's set out on a crash program to manufacture a full line of computers. Spending some $30 million more than National Cash Register, Burroughs turned out everything from its 25,500 tiny E103 and its giant 35,000 computer selling for $2.1 million, to its big computer systems for the military, costing as much as $6 to $8 million. Not even Burroughs' healthy office equipment business could carry the load, and computers didn't help sell calculators; so Burroughs' earnings-per-share dropped from $1.42 in 1962 to $1.04 in 1963. In 1964 they declined 40%, the lowest earnings in the last decade. Significantly expanded research, development, and marketing expenses have greatly hampered earnings in recent years; but indications are that these costs will be less in future years. The 1963 lag in earnings was attributed primarily to less military business, but a decline in relatively low-margin defense business should have improved overall margins. Instead, Burroughs' net margins continued to shrink.

The Burroughs' stockholders have some comfort in that probably only

I.B.M. of the big computer manufacturers has turned the profit corner on its computers. Not only are research and development costs fantastically high but most computers are rented, not sold. It often takes five years before rental income and depreciation catch up with out-of-pocket capital costs. Sperry Rand Corporation, for example, is only now getting close to making money on its computers; and it was ahead of I.B.M. at the start.

The major problem of the Burroughs Corporation is the high cost of producing business machines. President Ray Eppert took a major step toward lowering these costs when he announced the initiation of a two-year plant consolidation and realignment program that will shift adding machine production overseas.

Higher volume and an enlarged base of rental revenues, are expected to aid margins, but the problem of high production costs still faces Burroughs. The step Burroughs has taken to lower production costs is to shift the production of adding machines from Detroit to plants in Scotland, France, and Brazil. The critical question is whether or not the shift of production facilities overseas will solve the problem of high production costs. Some time ago, Burroughs made a similar move, ending calculator production in the U.S. and importing the machines from a plant in Scotland. This move was successful, and there is reason to believe that the present program will also have favorable results. A company statement said:

High costs of manufacturing adding machines in the Detroit area make it impossible for Burroughs to market competitively and profitably in the U.S. However, increasing production of these machines abroad will enable the corporation to compete in the U.S. with products of foreign manufacturers and with foreign-built products of other U.S. firms.

What other companies shifted operations abroad? I.B.M. World Trade Corporation is a wholly-owned subsidiary, which carries on I.B.M.'s business through its subsidiaries outside the U.S. The Moore Corporation has just made its first significant move outside North America by acquiring an interest in Britain's Lamson Industries, the leading foreign producer of business forms. Said Moore's President, W. Herman Browne: "This gives us a toehold in the rest of the world." Not only are the costs of production lower, but also a company gains a competitive position in the world market.

In Shathleven, Scotland, Burroughs produced adding machines at a cost of production 40% below that of the Detroit plant. Justification of this parallel production was no longer possible, so Burroughs shifted production of adding machines overseas and it now supplies American customers from abroad. While the labor costs in Great Britain are lower, their fringe benefits amount to only 10% of total labor costs; whereas in the

Table 6.1
YARDSTICKS OF PERFORMANCE: Office Equipment

CORPORATE PROFILES

	Total Assets	Sales (millions)	Latest 12 Months Net Income
ADDRESSOGRAPH-MULTIGRAPH	$ 178	$ 249	$ 17
BURROUGHS	390	390	9
CONTROL DATA	133	136	6
I.B.M.	2,374	3,175	424
MOORE CORP.	124	204	17
NATIONAL CASH	463	642	22
SCM CORP.	92	131	3
XEROX	214	245	33

GROWTH[c]
(5-year compounded rate)

	Sales	Earnings	Group Ranking
CONTROL DATA	89.2%	77.4%	1
XEROX	43.6	62.9	2
I.B.M.	15.2	19.5	3
SCM CORP.	6.5	13.1	4
ADDRESSOGRAPH-MULTIGRAPH	12.0	5.1	5
MOORE CORP.	7.4	6.5	5
NATIONAL CASH	8.2	0.9	6
BURROUGHS	4.4	D	7
INDUSTRY MEDIAN	7.8	9.8	

PROFITABILITY[c]
(5-year average)

	Return on Equity	Cash Flow to Equity	Oper. Profit Margin	Group Ranking
Xerox	26.6%	63.6%	36.1%	1
I.B.M.	17.6	38.5	38.6	2
Control Data	8.6	24.7	21.1	3
Moore Corp.	16.8	20.5	18.8	3
Addressograph-Multigraph	13.8	18.3	17.1	4
National Cash	10.2	23.1	14.9	4
Burroughs	6.7	16.6	9.0	5
SCM Corp.	3.0	9.2	5.7	6
Industry Med.	12.0	21.8	18.0	

TREND[c]
(latest 12 months vs. 3-year average)

	Earnings	Net Profit Margin[a]	Group Ranking
Xerox	+128.2%	+2.3	1
I.B.M.	+ 36.9	+1.4	2
Control Data	+ 71.7	+0.4	3
Moore Corp.	+ 19.0	+0.5	4
SCM Corp.	+ 3.2	+0.1	5
Addressograph-Multigraph	+ 7.4	−0.1	6
Burroughs	− 12.3	[b]	7
National Cash	+ 2.8	−0.4	8
Industry Med.	+ 17.2	+0.3	

D–declined.
a Gain or loss in percentage points.
b No change.
c Companies are listed in each group in order of their performance.
SOURCE: *Forbes*, January 1, 1965.

U.S. fringes run to about 25% of the total. The United Auto Workers Union recently won a bargaining election in Burroughs' Detroit area plants. *The Wall Street Journal* hinted that this might precipitate the closing of the plant, but a company spokesman denied this. The point was made, however, that any company can control its labor costs much more easily in countries other than the U.S., where labor unions are mighty. Labor costs are rising faster abroad than in the U.S., and the time when labor costs will catch up with the U.S. seems far off. An increase in pay of only 3 to 3½% in the U.S. is equivalent to a pay increase of about 10% in many countries abroad; so, if our pay scales here continue to go up, even at a moderate rate, foreign wages can go up much faster without wiping out the difference in labor costs.

The long-range benefit of shifting operations overseas is that a company maintains a position in the world market. According to Ray Eppert the U.S. must secure a favorable position in the world market to insure future growth. Because foreign countries export mainly the older, more conventional products, we should stress the development of more advanced products. Our high cost of production makes it difficult to compete with foreign countries. Raising tariffs is not the solution because it merely invites foreign countries to do the same. Burroughs has secured a good position in the world market through its wholly-owned foreign subsidiaries.

Burroughs' solution to high production costs is a very good answer, but several aspects of the problem remain unsolved. Are foreign workers as skilled or as productive? Burroughs has made direct comparisons between plants in Michigan with those of France, Brazil, and Scotland. The results showed very little output per-man-hour in France and Scotland; and while Brazil was lower, their overall costs were small enough to make production very possible. In Scotland the Burroughs plant union has readily accepted and promoted the idea of individual incentive, a plan seldom used in the United States.

The rising problem of local antagonism or nationalism is being felt by Burroughs, but this problem has been met by Burroughs' employing few Americans abroad. Great Britain does not have any Americans in Burroughs' marketing or production; in fact, the total number of Americans Burroughs has abroad is 12 out of more than 10,000 employees in their foreign operations.

A most critical area of nationalistic sentiment directed at Burroughs is South America, specifically Brazil. Former president Joao Goulart's term was abruptly ended in March 29, 1964, by an anti-Communist revolt lead by General Humberto de Aleucar Castelo Branco, who was nominated on April 4, 1964, to serve out deposed Goulart's constitutional term. But if the revolt had failed and pro-Communist Goulart had remained president, the seizure of American property would have been an inherent risk of producing in that country. This is an omnipresent danger with most foreign operations.

The Revenue Act of 1962 put pressure on Burroughs to bring earnings back to the U.S.—the tax-deferral provision requiring American companies to pay U.S. taxes on earnings whether or not those earnings are brought back to this country. The law is aimed at the "tax havens," thus preventing American companies from avoiding taxes by piling up earnings abroad, and reducing the advantage of moving U.S. operations abroad. President Eppert's plan to encourage exporting consists of an incentive tax (a lower rate or a rebate on export business). This plan would act as a partial subsidy for our higher labor costs, insure maximum effort to export, and reduce the number of companies that shift operations abroad.

In summary, Burroughs' answer to rising cost of production is a good one and probably should have been initiated sooner; but I.B.M. is still the leader and will not be caught in the near future. *Forbes' Annual Report* of January 1, 1964, offered two basic truths about the office equipment industry: (1) If a company has to be second in any market, it is imperative that the market in question be a dynamic and growing one; (2) The greater truth is that in any market it is better to be first.

FOR DISCUSSION

1. What has made profitable marketing of business machines extremely difficult for Burroughs? How has Burroughs overcome this?
2. What is the general objective of overseas operations? What problems are associated with such operations and what has Burroughs done concerning them?
3. What is Burroughs' position in regard to competition?

SUGGESTED READING

"Burroughs Corporation Today," Burroughs Corporation, Detroit, Mich., 1962.
"From Adding Machines to Computers," Burroughs Corporation, Detroit, Mich., 1962.
"Why American Companies Are Going Abroad," *U.S. News & World Report*, February 10, 1964, p. 64.

International Business Machines Corporation

THE 1880 CENSUS took seven years to compile. There was concern that the 1890 census with millions of additional people would taken even longer and prevent a reallocation of seats in the Congress every ten years. This concern was dismissed, however, when Dr. Herman Hollerith, a statistician from Buffalo, developed a counting machine which utilized the punched card. His machine made it possible to take the 1890 census of 62 million in comparison to the 1880 census of 50 million in one-third of the time.

Slowly, Hollerith discovered commercial uses for the machine. With the beginning of the new century the machine was employed in a number of commercial applications. In 1911 the company which was formed to develop the Hollerith equipment was merged with two others to become the Computing-Tabulating-Recording Company. Four basic business machines were in operation by 1914. These machines were popular and were made to perform a number of functions.

Nevertheless, the company was in a poor financial condition. Total bonded indebtedness was three times its assets. Thomas J. Watson, Sr., previously sales manager for National Cash Register Company, became its president in 1914. His first act was to borrow $40,000, mostly on his own credit, and to place $25,000 of this loan in research and development—a most unusual expenditure at this time. By 1915 sales had risen considerably and the sales force was reorganized and strengthened.

In 1917 the company changed its name to International Business Machines Corporation. By 1930 the company was set to introduce a whole new series of machines for data handling. Machines were developed which could not only add and subtract figures but could also perform full-scale record keeping and accounting operations. In 1931 it introduced the I.B.M. 400, which could handle alphabetical information to process business accounts. By 1934 the I.B.M. 405, which was a follow-up to the 400, was introduced and became known as the "work horse" of the line. In 1949 the I.B.M. 407 was introduced and was able to type 18,000 characters per minute, over 10,000 characters per minute faster than any earlier machine. The 600 series, which was electronic (most machines up to this point were electro-mechanical), quickly gained wide customer acceptance.

At this point there was growing dissension between Watson, Sr., and

Watson, Jr., as to whether the company should plunge a great share of its capital into computer research. Watson, Sr., was against this move for in 1950 it was predicted that eight or ten large computers would satisfy the needs of the whole scientific community.

However, due mainly to the persistence of Watson, Jr., in the early 1950's when he became president, the company did decide to actively compete in the computer field. Since I.B.M. helped build and finance the electro-mechanical Mark I, the first stored-program machine in conjunction with Harvard University, it was able to compete with UNIVAC. These new computers were the 701 and the 702. The 704 and the 705 followed and quickly caught up and passed UNIVAC in numbers and units installed.

When Thomas Watson, Sr., stepped down and gave complete control to his son in 1956, the company was clearly out in front in computer sales. Watson, Jr., lost no time in exercising some of his newly acquired powers. Said Watson: "We had a superb sales organization, but lacked expert management in almost everything else." So he, along with Albert L. Williams, who is now president, and Louis H. LaMotte, who is now chairman of the executive and financial committee, redesigned the organization of the company between the spring and fall of 1956 (Figure 6.1 denotes I.B.M.'s present organization structure). The new organization, which deleted 110 executives in a new line and staff structured organization, was completely decentralized over the old organization. Division-profit responsibility and clear-cut lines of authority were developed in the new organization, and four small divisions and one large one were increased to eight divisions of approximately the same size. These are:

1. *Advanced Systems Development Division*—develops systems that will lead I.B.M. into commercial markets in which it is not presently engaged.
2. *Components Division*—manufactures and processes components used in data processing machines.
3. *Data Processing Division*—markets and services the complete line of I.B.M. punched card accounting machines and electronic data processing equipment; operates data centers in Chicago, Cleveland, Los Angeles, Philadelphia, and in the midtown and Wall Street areas of New York City.
4. *Data Systems Division*—handles the development and manufacture of large computers.
5. *Electric Typewriter Division*—develops and produces, markets and services a full line of electric typewriters, electronic typing calculators, dictating equipment, and related supplies. In 1961 this division introduced the I.B.M. electric typewriter, which replaces the conventional typewriter's metal type bars and moving paper carriage with a single sphere-shaped element covered with 88 raised characters.
6. *Federal Systems Division*—develops, makes, sells, and services systems for military purposes.

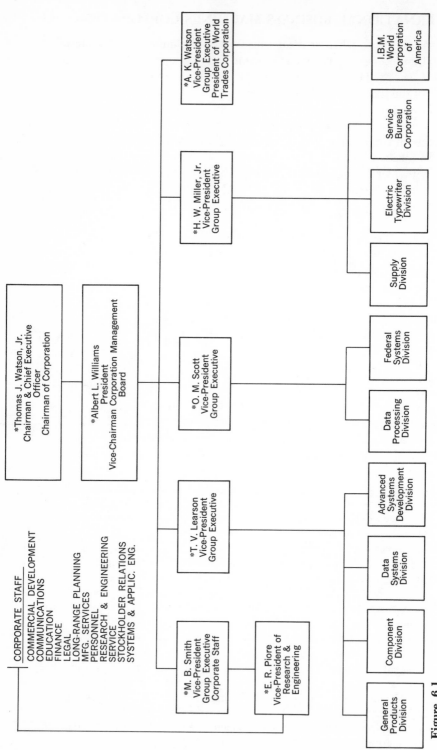

Figure 6.1

* Corporate Mgmt. Committee

7. *General Products Division*—handles development and manufacture of intermediate data processing systems and punched card accounting machines.
8. *Supplies Division*—makes punched cards, magnetic tapes, and other products for use with data processing machines.

This entire revamping of the company's organization took place simultaneously, and six months later when the smoke cleared, it was facing a few new problems.

Reorganization was fast and men were placed in jobs which they were not fully prepared to handle, for many had to make the switch from an operating job to a staff job. Also, quite a number of executives had to become experts in a hurry and for six months these men were put under great pressure; however, 80-85% of the choices made by Watson and Williams for the jobs turned out to be correct.

The business of I.B.M. underwent just about as large a change as I.B.M. itself. It meant the foundation of new goals and policies, a new sophistication in its products, and a new place for I.B.M. in the business picture.

In 1964 the company was ranked ninth among the twenty largest companies in American industry, representing a substantial rise from 18th position in 1963. Since Watson, Jr. took over in 1956, it has increased its rentals and sales by over 300% to $3.2 billion and profits by over 425% to $364.25 million in 1964. I.B.M. has grown faster than General Motors, United States Steel, and American Telephone and Telegraph; and if it continues at approximately the same rate, it will become one of the top three or four companies in the United States.

The company has installed more than three-fourths of all of the computers in the world—13,000 to 14,000—more than ten times the total of its nearest competitor. It has well over 19,000 data processing customers and is the undisputed leader in the office equipment and electronic-data processing fields.

Let us now take a look at the four basic segments of the digital computer market composed of desk-sized, small, medium and large machines respectively.

In the desk-sized units (selling for $50,000 or less and renting from $1,400 down to a few hundred dollars), I.B.M. has slightly more than 80% of the business when the 5,000 installations of the electronic computer, the 632, are included. Sperry Rand is coming up fast with its comparable 1004. In the strictest sense, however, neither machine is a computer, for both are externally programmed, which limits capacity and flexibility. "Thinking" computers of this size are manufactured by Litton's Monroe Division (Monorobot), General Precision, Burroughs, and Clary. Friden added its name to this list in June of 1963. These firms have installed well over 1,000 desk-sized machines.

The so-called small computers are in the arbitrary price range of $59,000 to $300,000 and correspond to rentals of from $1,500 to some $10,000; Sperry Rand may hold a slight edge over I.B.M.

As of the beginning of 1963 Sperry Rand had installed about 500 of its higher priced UNIVAC Solid-State 80 and 90 computers, compared to some 600 I.B.M.'s nontransistorized 650 and Ramac 305 and 1000 of its solid state 1620; however, Sperry Rand's sales of those computers totaled $140 million while I.B.M.'s sales for the above-mentioned computers were only $130 million. The remaining 20% of the market in the small computer classification was shared between Control Data, Radio Corporation of America, National Cash Register, Burroughs, General Precision, and an aggressive newcomer General Electric.

In the medium scale category (up to $1 million in price or $20,000 in monthly rent) I.B.M. is way out in front. Its 1400 series, mainly the 1401, accounted for almost 90% of all machines installed up to July of 1963 in this price or rent range. The major competitors for the remaining share of the market are Radio Corporation of America; Minneapolis-Honeywell Regulator; General Electric; National Cash Register; Addressograph-Multigraph; Advanced Scientific Instruments; Thompson Ramo Woolridge; Computer Control; Digital Equipment Corporation; and Burroughs, which has introduced its B5000, the most advanced machine in the entire group. Nearly 50% of all computers rented or sold fall in this price range and represent a combined approximate value of $1.5 billion.

The large machines range in price from $1 million to $4 million. I.B.M.'s 7000 series, particularly its 7070 for business use and 7090 for scientific use, accounts for about 95% of the 700-odd computers of this size in existence. However, Control Data and Minneapolis-Honeywell Regulator are proving to be increasingly tough competitors; International Telephone and Telegraph, Teleregister, and Philco remain in the running, while Sperry Rand is making a recognizable bid with its UNIVAC III, 490, and 1107. In the upper-price ranges of the large computer market Control Data and Sperry Rand appear to be in the lead in the field.

The financial story in the computer market competition is short and pointed. I.B.M. and Control Data have scored notable profits and profit growth in computers; no other company in the business has been able to break even (Table 6.2).

Radio Corporation of America, National Cash Register, and Sperry Rand recently announced that their data processing operations might break into the black by 1964. General Electric, Minneapolis-Honeywell Regulator, and Burroughs are not far behind the above-mentioned three in being close to recognizing profits in this ever-expanding market. One thing is certain. These six, along with Control Data, are in the business for good and have the potential to give I.B.M. its first real battle in a decade.

Many of these companies have announced new developments and

Table 6.2

I.B.M. PROFITS AND PROFIT GROWTH

Company	Domestic Sales, Service and Rental Revenue		Net Income		Earnings/Share of Company
	1963	1962	1963	1962	1963
INTERNATIONAL BUSINESS MACHINES	2,059,610,111	1,925,221,875	290,460,000	241,390,000	$10.45/share in 1963 up from $8.72 in 1962.
SPERRY RAND BUSINESS MACHINES EQUIPMENT AND SUPPLIES SEGMENT	?	368,000,000	Operated at loss in E.D.P. Segment	Operated at loss in E.D.P.* Segment	First nine months of 1963-64 earnings/share were $0.57 up from $0.38
RADIO CORPORATION OF AMERICA ELECTRONIC DATA PROCESSING SEGMENT	?	?	Operated at loss in E.D.P. Segment	Operated at loss in E.D.P. Segment	At $1.20/share up from $0.93/share in 1962.
NATIONAL CASH REGISTER ELECTRONIC DATA PROCESSING SEGMENT	237,040,000	?	Operated at loss in E.D.P. Segment	Operated at loss in E.D.P. Segment	$2.42/share in 1963 down from $2.47/share in 1962.
CONTROL DATA	63,110,000	41,030,000	3,060,000	1,540,000	Up in 1963 to $0.75/share from $0.39/share in 1962.
BURROUGHS CORPORATION BUSINESS MACHINES SEGMENT	?	177,660,000	Operated at loss in E.D.P. Segment	Operated at loss in E.D.P. Segment	$1.04/share in 1963 down from $1.42/share in 1962.
GENERAL ELECTRIC COMPUTER AND BUSINESS MACHINES SEGMENT	491,870,000	479,270,000	?	?	$3.00/share in 1963 up from $2.97/share in 1962.
MINNEAPOLIS-HONEYWELL REGULATOR COMPANY ELECTRONIC DATA PROCESSING SEGMENT	?	?	Operated at loss at E.D.P. Segment	Operated at loss at E.D.P. Segment	1963 earnings/share $4.83 and up from $3.72 in 1962.

* E.D.P. = Electronic Data Processing.

contracts in the electronic-data processing segment, substantiating their future growth potential. These orders and developments indicate that I.B.M. will be facing real competition in the future.

However, even with this additional competition, the company's future is a bright one. John Diebold Associates, which follows the computer industry as closely as Gallup follows public opinion, predicted that by 1965 rentals will reach $1.5 billion and that outright sales to the military alone will top $2 billion. This prediction would mean a four-year period, for in 1961 I.B.M.'s rentals brought in over $1 billion or 71.2% of its total income. Another estimate is that by the early 1970's electronic computers and industrial electronic controls will account for 20% of the durable goods sold—claiming a good share of all new plant and equipment spending. A future such as this is not comparable to that of many companies in any industry. However, even a company with as bright a future as I.B.M. cannot advance at its present pace without facing many gigantic problems.

Even though the company was revamped in 1956 under Watson's modern, reasonably decentralized organization, the company's continual growth presents problems of sheer size; yet I.B.M. still practices some policies of small business. With 127,468 (as of January 1, 1964) employees separated from the top office by nine levels of management from the production line and eight from the salesmen, T. Watson, Jr., maintains an "open door policy," which allows any employee to bring grievances directly to his office.

Watson believes that one of the company's biggest problems is the complacency of employees in a large corporation that dominates its field, for they become too relaxed and overconfident. I.B.M. never dismisses an employee to combat this complacency, however. Instead, if employees do not meet the high standards that have been set, they are demoted and dropped in salary. While some have resigned, a surprising number have buckled down and made a good comeback. Another impetus used to fight this complacency is high salaries and commissions. If a man meets the standards, he soon can afford luxuries.

The company also faces a problem of software. Software is the programming which adapts a computer to the specific needs of a company; it is the key to increasing the applications of computers. This situation, which will demand of I.B.M. that it have men who are experts in almost every kind of business in the world, arises because of the special relation that exists between a computer maker and his customer.

Very unique demands are put on the person who sets up computers. Computers are just a tangle of wire and circuits until they are educated to solve the specific needs of a firm. When a computer is bought or rented, it is a general purpose machine. By additional programming it is made a special purpose calculator, educated for specific needs. To educate a computer, however, the programmer has to know not only the technical procedures but also the business needs the computer was hired to answer.

The reason that software is such a serious problem is that a tremendous number of computers are out with customers who are now renting or have purchased them. Some customers have as much as $3 million tied up in computer programs. As T. Watson, Jr., put it:

We would like to be able to take the programming from a machine like the 705 and put it into some other machine like the 709 or 7080. Our customers have often been disappointed in this way.

They've spent several million dollars on one of our computers, then we've come up with something much more rapid and had to ask them to spend several million dollars more. We are hard at work on this problem and so far have had mixed success.

Another problem in software was brought out by a mangement consultant firm, McKinsey and Company. This company studied the results of twenty-seven companies that had extensive experience in the use of computers. The report revealed that only nine of these twenty-seven top computer users were using their computers really efficiently and had recovered their original investment; so I.B.M., which has always had a long history of educating its customers, took on the job of educating its computers too. At present, it is more limited in the educating of the computer than in the actual functioning of the computer itself.

Facing this problem squarely, the company is shifting much of its effort in breaking down these limitations. A large share of its $60 million a year educational expense goes for educating its programmers and systems men, and some $26 to $28 million is budgeted for educating its customers.

This $60 million-a-year business runs schools in 38 U.S. cities and 52 countries. It trains or retrains 100,000 of its employees and about the same number of customers complete courses at its training schools each year.

The company does not only instruct its customers in technology; for it realizes that if the top executives have not learned how the company should utilize its computer, the results would be disastrous. The McKinsey study highlighted this problem by its findings: "None of the eighteen large companies whose computers were not paying off were technically inept; they had simply fallen down on their managerial approach." Therefore, across the country I.B.M. runs executive education classes, which include many varied facets of management training.

Another method being used to combat its software problem is the development of such programming systems as Fortran and Cobol. Through these systems a computer, in part, can program itself. The company has also been able to distribute programming packages, which can be used in certain industrial functions which are somewhat standardized, such as payroll, to partly solve the software problem.

The "building block" concept in computers is another approach being employed to solve this problem. Instead of customers purchasing new machines and doing away with their old ones as new and faster computers are developed, a customer will simply add a computer of the same model to the one he has rather than replace it with a bigger, costlier unit.

The company's World Trade Corporation has even a brighter future than I.B.M. at home and yet it faces big problems also. From a 1950 figure of $51 million its World Trade Corporation increased its gross earnings by 629% to $372 million by 1960. By 1960-1962 it had increased its gross earnings another 76% to $653 million. However, the serious shortage of qualified personnel presents a major problem overseas. In Europe there is a great supply of skilled technicians but elsewhere they are in very small supply. Therefore, outside of Europe there are two main problems, lack of computer skills and lack of business training; so the company has set up schools in conjunction with universities where people will be trained in accounting, advanced arithmetic, economics, and some administrative procedures. These students will then seek employment in either government or industry where they will work for I.B.M. or its future customers.

Between 1952 and 1956 there was another outside force irritating the company—the Department of Justice. An antitrust action was brought against I.B.M. for dominating the punch-card industry. A consent decree was handed down instructing the company to divest itself in this market to only 50% of industry capacity and to license competitors under its patents at reasonable royalties by 1963. Father and son disagreed on how this decree should be handled. Watson, Sr., felt that accepting the decree was admitting guilt. He was ready to fight it all the way through the court system. Younger Watson, however, felt that this decree was handed down in the public interest and that it was a method of correcting imbalance. This was a tactful way of handling the situation since the company didn't want to create a poor public image. Watson, Jr. let it be known that he had no argument with the government.

The one dark cloud which shades any feelings of optimism for future growth is further antitrust regulation. I.B.M. presently dominates 70-80% of the computer market. The company met with trouble for dominating the punch-card market. Will this occur again?

I.B.M. has continued to capture far more than the 60-65% of the share of the market; this is the ratio which is often used in determining whether or not the Sherman Antitrust Act is being violated. Its competitors are fully aware of this and are doing everything possible to drive this fact home in Washington. One circular distributed in Washington openly points out that the company today has approximately 80% of all the government's EAM (punched-card machines) and EDP business. UNIVAC is determined to fight this monopoly.

A congressional committee, whose chairman is Representative Olsen of the House Subcommittee on Government Statistics, is concerned about raising federal outlays for data processing. Congressmen on this committee discovered that 96% of rentals paid last year went to I.B.M. At present the government has found that gigantic savings can be realized through purchase instead of lease. Some change may be enacted in the future.

Early in 1963 the Justice Department found it necessary to prod the company. A U.S. District Court ordered it to comply at once with the 1956 ruling; the company replied that to the best of its knowledge its card press capacity "is now within 2% of the target." It promised to get rid of the excess by September 1. It also consented to cut itself down to 50% of the industry capacity in "feature cards"—an important innovation since 1956; these are mainly punched utility bills and merchandise coupons.

I.B.M. also faces another problem: it possesses about 80% of the computer market. Chairman Watson doesn't expect to have the company take a bigger share of the market. He stated:

I would think that you would not see our percentage of the industry increase. If it moves in any direction at all, it would probably be somewhat downward. After all, we have some fairly formidable competitors in such companies as Radio Corporation of America and General Electric.

In other words, the company is not going to concentrate its efforts on increasing its share of the market as much as increasing the market itself; and it is through its educational drive that it plans to increase this market. In addition to postponing any antitrust action, this emphasis on education will also aid in alleviating its other major problems of software and overseas shortage of qualified personnel.

FOR DISCUSSION

1. What is I.B.M.'s competitive situation? What are the factors that have contributed to it?
2. What policies has I.B.M. formulated relative to employee complacency? How effective have they been?
3. What is the problem connected with software?
4. What is the major objective of I.B.M.? What is the nature of the decisions the company is making relative to this?

SUGGESTED READING

"Can I.B.M. Keep Up The Pace?" *Business Week*, February 2, 1963, pp. 92-98.
Elliot, Jr., J. R., "Something to Think About; I.B.M. is Finally Facing Real Competition in Computers." *Barron's National Business and Financial Weekly*, July 1 and July 8, 1963, pp. 3 ff.
"I.B.M.'s Growth Power," *Dun's Review and Modern Industry*, July, 1963, pp. 33-35.

CHAPTER 7

Eastman Kodak Company

RATED AMONG THE BEST MANAGED COMPANIES in the world, Eastman Kodak is dedicated to the mass low-cost manufacture of quality products, world-wide distribution, extensive advertising, intensive research and development, continuous modernization, and expansion via reinvestment of earnings and generous employee benefits.

Originally, photographic supplies were Eastman Kodak's only products. George Eastman, founder of Eastman Kodak, began making and selling "dry plates" in 1880 for the then cumbersome photographic process. In 1884 he organized the Eastman Dry Plate and Film Company to manufacture his transparent film on a larger scale. In 1888 the young company developed and began selling the No. 1 Kodak Camera and a flexible roll film—the first major steps toward simplifying and popularizing photography.

By 1927 Eastman had a virtual monopoly of the photographic industry in the United States. Yet Kodak is certainly not a monopoly in either the orthodox legal or economic sense of the word. It owes its market dominance to no shrewd mergers. It has not bought out its competition, nor does it hold a patent position that would guarantee its preeminence; but Kodak's big customers and distributors agree, almost without exception, that its products are of good quality and carry a fair price.

As time passed, Kodak became more and more integrated. Now, once it takes delivery of the basic cellulose pulp and the metallic silver, which is the base for recording the photographic image, Kodak does not have to go outside the company for any of the important elements involved in the packaged film that eventually arrives on the shelves.

Kodak has diversified greatly, too. In recent years 20% of Kodak sales has been of products that did not exist five years previously; in fact, for the photographic equipment field alone Kodak has announced a new or improved product on the average of one every five working days. Not counting different sizes of the same product, Kodak makes about 180 kinds of color and black-and-white films; more than 300 kinds of photographic plates for amateur, professional, medical, dental, graphic arts, and other uses of photography.

Excluding chemical and fiber divisions, the primary manufacturing plants are in Rochester, New York. The Kodak Park Works, the largest Kodak manufacturing complex, covers more than 1,000 acres and employs about 20,000 people. In the more than 140 major buildings located there, materials of high purity become finished photographic films, papers, and chemicals.

Other divisions at Rochester manufacture photographic chemicals, camera lenses and filters, special photographic and electronic products for military projects, and various photocopying and microfilming devices. Kodak has spread world-wide, opening manufacturing plants in England, Canada, France, Germany, and Australia. These foreign operations manufacture almost exclusively cameras and photographic films and paper.

While two-thirds of Kodak's billion dollar sales come from photography, the remainder is derived from expanding product lines in plastics, man-made fibers, chemicals, vitamin concentrates, and other items (Figure 7.1).

Financially, Eastman Kodak is in excellent shape. With sales of over a billion a year, Kodak turns in net earnings of around 13.5% of sales. 1964 marked the eleventh consecutive year of sales advances, thirteenth straight year of improved earnings, and seventeenth year in a row that dividends were increased. In the decade through 1962 domestic earnings expanded 182% while sales increased 67%, accomplishing an annual growth rate twice that of the U.S. Gross National Product. Dividend payments during this period climbed 190% (Figures 7.2, 7.3).

Eastman Kodak has no long-term debt and in 1962 retired the few remaining shares of callable preferred stock it had outstanding. The firm is internally financed, with large cash reserves as the source for all capital expenditures. Expansion of capital facilities are made on a strict "pay-as-we-go" basis.

Because of Eastman Kodak's early start in the field of amateur photography, it has completely dominated the photographic field for many years. Kodak's forbidding command of most of the amateur film market has been so strong that many of the best-managed companies in the world have hesitated to try to compete with it. This trend is changing, however, and here is where its problems lie—in competition.

Dupont, for example, has long had a respectable industrial film business and could easily have made consumer film. DuPont held back for years, however, and it finally decided to go ahead and make amateur color film only last year. It manufactures the film under the DuPont-Bell & Howell label, leaving all marketing headaches to the Bell & Howell Company.

Minnesota Mining and Manufacturing is also technically expert in photochemistry and has felt in the past that to break Kodak's grip would cost more than the job was worth. Very recently, however, Minnesota Mining acquired the Dynacolor Corporation; this will mean more competition for Kodak in this important area. Dynacolor was originated to compete directly with Kodak's amateur color film. Technicolor Corpo-

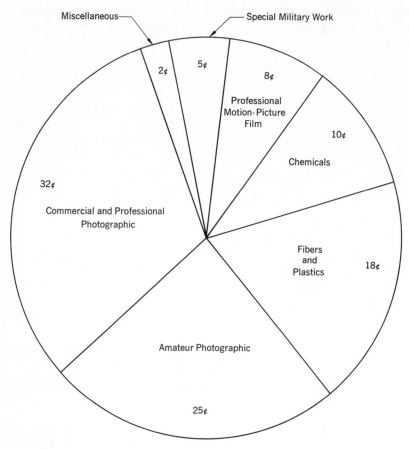

Figure 7.1
Kodak's Sales Dollar by Product Group

32% Commercial and Professional Photographic: films, papers, plates, and equipment for medicine, industry, commerce, photofinishing, etc.
25% Amateur Photography: films, cameras, projectors, photo aids.
18% Fibers and Plastics: man-made fibers, plastics, plastic sheeting
10% Chemicals: photographic developers and fixers, industrial and organic chemicals
8% Professional Motion-Picture Film: negative and positive film
5% Special Military work: missile parts, research and development
2% Miscellaneous: vitamin concentrate, monoglycerides, etc.

ration of America plunged into 8 mm color film in 1961 for the same reason. Both of these firms package their film in yellow boxes, attempting to capitalize on the omnipresent yellow box which Kodak has made a trademark for photography. Figure 7.4 and Table 7.1 show the comparative chemical positions of these firms.

"Although the Kodak name is a tremendous asset," says Kodak president William S. Vaughn, "it won't carry a product indefinitely. We

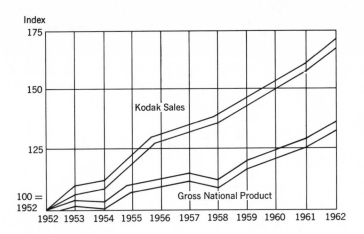

Figure 7.2
Kodak Sales Versus U.S. GNP

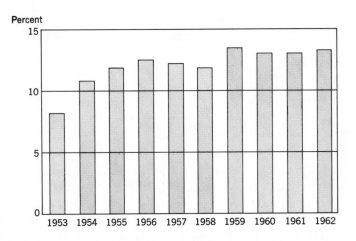

Figure 7.3
Net Earnings as a Percent of Sales

could only trade on our name for a while." In other words, if the other fellow comes up with something Kodak doesn't have, neither price nor entrenched marketing position can keep the newcomer out. Polaroid is living proof!

Dr. Edwin Land offered his Polaroid camera to Eastman Kodak after the Second World War. Kodak turned down the scientist's Polaroid invention, claiming it was "too busy." This is one of the biggest breakdowns of corporate sensitivity that Kodak has had to account for. Only recently has Kodak begun to make up for its failure. Under a contract with the

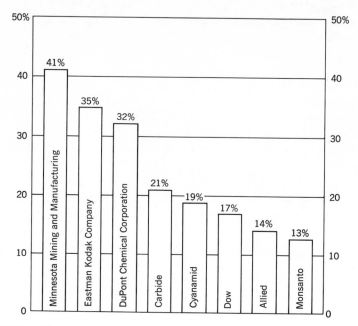

Figure 7.4
Return on Total Capital
Before Federal Income Taxes
Five-Year Average

NOTE: Although Eastman Kodak Company is not really a chemical company, it is with the big chemical companies that Kodak is usually compared.
SOURCE: *Forbes,* April, 1963, p. 24.

Polaroid Corporation, Kodak shared in the development of the negative component of the new color film, Polacolor, and worked out the manufacturing techniques. Kodak is now also a supplier of the color negative material to Polaroid and continues to furnish some of the black-and-white negative material and lenses for the Land cameras.

An even more recent "goof" occurred when Kodak allowed Revere Camera to make a major breakthrough with its "zoom" lens for movie cameras. In the case of the zoom lens Kodak's greatest strength also proved to be its weakness. With its eye trained on the mass market, Kodak usually tends to think of the economic value of bringing out low-cost items. It thereby encourages more people to take up snapshooting and consequently boosts sales of Kodak film.

Kodak's technicians hadn't neglected the zoom lens' potential, however. "We had often wondered who would buy an amateur movie camera for over $200," says Vaughn. When Revere brought out a $210 zoom-lens camera in 1959, Kodak got the answer: thousands! Belatedly, Kodak introduced a zoom-lens movie camera at the end of that year.

It is clear that Kodak must not neglect market research as a technique for tuning in more closely on the wants, needs, and desires of the consumer market. In the case of the Polaroid camera and the zoom lens, Kodak might have discovered that the demand was there if they had gone out to the public and asked.

Often, however, Kodak does ask the people what they want and what problems need to be solved. One such problem that Kodak has long been trying to solve is the commonly clumsy business of loading a camera. Many people find this task a difficult and often exasperating one.

Kodak has recently come up with a partial solution to the problem. A prepackaged film, Kodapack, in a plastic cartridge that needs only to be dropped into the new Kodak Instamatic camera has been brought onto the market during the past year. This cartridge eliminates fiddling with or winding the spool. When the film roll is exposed, the amateur photographer need only lift the cartridge out and insert another one. There are no seals to break, and there is no threading of paper into slots. Kodak expects that eventually 50% of its still-camera sales in the United States will incorporate this device. Kodak has made even greater application of Kodapack. In the spring of 1965 the film cartridge idea was further adapted in its Instamatic movie cameras and projectors.

The company has also answered consumer demands for a home developing kit for color film. In addition, it has improved on its color film. Where Kodak color film previously tended to the "reds," and exaggerated brilliant colors, its new Kodachrome produces more realistic results than in the past. With greater competition forthcoming in the amateur color film market, Kodak must continue such research to maintain its reputation.

Kodak is facing heavier competition in another area, too—photocopying devices. In the area of industrial products Kodak is not able to count on the kind of marketing dominance it achieved in the retail trade area. Thus, when Kodak fails to produce the "right" product in this line, it takes a heavy beating. Such a product is the Verifax photocopier. Sales of this machine have not kept up with industry's fast pace, and Kodak lags a long way behind leading Minnesota Mining Thermofax. The principal trouble with Kodak's copier is that it produces wet copies, which are harder to make and messier to handle.

To fight competition, Kodak has unveiled two new copiers: the Verifax Cavalcade, with some automatic features and built-in paper storage; and the Kodak Readyprint Copier, which is able to reproduce any type of document in 25 seconds. To meet competition, Kodak should probably attempt to enter the dry copier field; but as of now it remains hesitant about cashing in on the burgeoning demand for dry copiers. A Kodak spokesman has said, "Verifax has held its market position in the face of increasing competition and we have new equipment and materials coming along that should lend additional strength."

Table 7.1

YARDSTICKS OF PERFORMANCE: Chemicals

CORPORATE PROFILES

	Total Assets	Sales	Net Income
		Latest 12 Months (millions)	
INTEGRATED MAJORS			
ALLIED CHEMICAL	$1,069	$1,031	$ 79
AMER. CYANAMID	739	761	77
DOW CHEMICAL	1,069	1,047	92
DU PONT	2,970	2,738	490
MONSANTO	1,416	1,318	110
UNION CARBIDE	1,832	1,789	173
SPECIALISTS			
AIR REDUCTION	349	329	18
CELANESE	551	435	40
DIAMOND ALKALI	182	172	13
EASTMAN KODAK	1,171	1,193	171
W. R. GRACE	723	732	37
HERCULES POWDER	346	501	36
HOOKER	217	210	19
INT. MIN. & CHEM.	255	235	17
KOPPERS	224	320	9
MINN. MINING	653	861	99
NATIONAL LEAD	442	670	55
ROHM & HAAS	249	315	33
STAUFFER	238	270	23

GROWTH[c] (5-year compounded rate)

	Sales	Earnings	Group Ranking
INTEGRATED MAJORS			
MONSANTO	12.4%	8.5%	1
AMER. CYANAMID	5.4	5.9	2
ALLIED CHEMICAL	5.3	5.7	3
DOW CHEMICAL	7.2	4.9	3
DU PONT	5.3	4.1	4
UNION CARBIDE	3.4	1.6	5
SPECIALISTS			
INT. MIN. & CHEM.	14.6	14.6	1
CELANESE	9.4	14.4	2
MINN. MINING & MFG.	12.9	12.5	3
W. R. GRACE	5.4	11.8	4
HERCULES POWDER	13.3	8.3	4
ROHM & HAAS	7.6	8.8	5
EASTMAN KODAK	5.4	6.1	6
DIAMOND ALKALI	5.1	2.8	7
HOOKER	4.5	3.1	7
STAUFFER	3.0	1.5	8
AIR REDUCTION	4.9	D	9
KOPPERS	1.2	0.6	9
NATIONAL LEAD	4.0	b	9
INDUSTRY MEDIAN	5.4	5.7	

PROFITABILITY
(5-year average)

	Return on Equity	Cash Flow to Equity	Oper. Profit Margin	Group Ranking
Du Pont	17.5%	24.6%	31.6%	1
Union Carbide	15.3	28.9	26.8	1
Dow Chemical	11.2	25.2	25.3	2
Monsanto	10.8	23.4	23.7	3
Amer. Cyanamid	11.9	21.2	22.4	4
Allied Chemical	10.8	21.5	21.0	5
Minn. Mining	21.5	28.3	28.0	1
Eastman Kodak	17.3	23.3	29.2	2
Rohm & Haas	13.9	25.1	26.7	3
Diamond Alkali	12.2	26.0	22.4	4
Hercules Powder	13.9	25.2	21.4	5
Hooker	12.4	20.9	23.5	6
Celanese	10.8	21.6	23.1	7
National Lead	16.8	21.4	18.6	7
Stauffer	11.7	21.6	22.2	8
Air Reduction	9.1	16.3	18.6	9
W. R. Grace	7.0	16.5	13.1	10
Int. Min. & Chem.	8.6	15.9	13.7	10
Koppers	4.5	13.5	8.9	11
Industry Med.	11.9	21.6	22.4	

TREND[c]
(latest 12 months vs. 3-year average)

	Earnings	Net Profit Margin[a]	Group Ranking
Monsanto	+38.6%	+1.1	1
Amer. Cyanamid	+29.3	+1.1	2
Dow Chemical	+27.2	+1.0	3
Allied Chemical	+25.1	+0.5	4
Union Carbide	+15.1	+0.4	5
Du Pont	+10.0	+0.2	6
Int. Min. & Chem.	+36.1	+1.2	1
Rohm & Haas	+33.8	+1.3	1
W. R. Grace	+36.7	+1.0	2
Koppers	+36.9	+0.4	3
Celanese	+36.4	+0.8	3
Eastman Kodak	+19.9	+1.1	4
Stauffer	+24.2	+0.8	4
Hooker	+23.6	+0.5	5
Diamond Alkali	+18.7	+0.4	6
Hercules Powder	+16.5	−0.2	7
Minn. Mining & Mfg.	+17.6	−0.5	8
Air Reduction	+9.8	−0.2	9
National Lead	+13.0	−0.4	9
Industry Med.	+24.2	+0.5	

D—declined.
a Gain or loss in percentage points.
b No change.
c Companies are listed in each group in order of their performance.
SOURCE: *Forbes*, January 1, 1965.

Another field in which Kodak lacks a built-in advantage is chemicals. It makes a normal profit on its chemical production, but it doesn't lead the chemical industry either in profitability or major research breakthroughs. Overall, however, Kodak holds a strong position against the major chemical companies (Figure 7.4). Although it has no unique position in any of its many cellulose plastics and fibers, polyolefins, or industrial chemicals, Kodak is trying hard to improve its position in this area, and has been recently investing millions of dollars in its polyester fiber Kodel in an attempt to take on DuPont's mighty Dacron. So far the operation has run in the red for two years, but added improvements and greater selling efforts are expected to bring sales to a profitable level. Kodak is also trying to take on Minnesota Mining in the magnetic recording tape field, even though the latter has successfully dominated the field for 15 years. To be successful in these areas, Kodak is going to have to trim considerably its production costs in order to make a better showing.

Aside from direct production costs, Kodak has been plagued with other sources of higher costs. A basic factor has been the rising cost of silver. Kodak is one of the largest users of silver, which is required in the manufacture of the film base. To date, Kodak has been unable to find a replacement for silver in the film base. To offset this, Eastman Kodak has recently had to raise the retail prices on its film products by 9%. This raise in consumer prices should help future results, since higher prices for silver penalized 1963 profits by approximately $.05 per share.

Labor costs have been steadily rising also. This problem is not different from any other company's labor problem except that none of the Kodak workforce is unionized. Nevertheless, Kodak pays above-union wages and has a bonus plan that usually results in a cash bonus of ten weeks' salary for the employee—from janitor to president—who has worked for Eastman at least five years.

Other factors of higher cost are the heavy promotional expenditures for the new Instamatic camera and film cartridge, and the cost of Kodak's participation in the World's Fair exhibit. The latter amounted to roughly $.06 per share ($5 million) in 1963. These two areas of expense should net great returns in the future, however.

The World's Fair presented an excellent opportunity for stimulating both amateur and professional photographic sales. Of the millions who went to the fair, most took pictures (and hopefully used Kodak film!), and many perhaps took along a new Instamatic, purchased especially for the occasion.

In general, then, the outlook for the future is very encouraging for Kodak. Public reception of the new Instamatic group of cameras and film has been favorable, but sales have been limited by the need to stock the channels of supply throughout the world. These will be readily available from now on, however, and should easily make up for the expected decline in sales of conventional cameras.

With further emphasis on the development of new products, Kodak should be able to maintain its dominant position in the photographic industry; however, tougher competition in the film manufacturing area and photocopying field can be expected. The management of Kodak must continue efforts to improve product lines and to maintain a high quality product if it is to remain the leader in the photographic industry.

FOR DISCUSSION

1. What is Kodak's basic problem?
2. What specific decisions proved to be costly to Kodak? What was lacking in these decisions?
3. Evaluate Kodak's decisions relating to competition. Which would you say were the most effective? Why?
4. What areas need concentration if Kodak is to remain a leader in its industry? Can you suggest any procedures?

SUGGESTED READING

"Competition for Xerox," *Barron's National Business and Financial Weekly*, January 21, 1963, p. 3.
"Eastman Kodak: What Makes It Click?" *Forbes*, April 1, 1963, p. 22.
"Quality at Kodak," *Dun's Review and Modern Industry*, June, 1963, p. 33.

Olin Mathieson Chemical Corporation

OLIN MATHIESON, a widely diversified corporation, had its beginning shortly after the Civil War. In 1866 Oliver Winchester bought the rights to produce the Henty repeating rifle, and in 1886 Franklin Olin started the Western Cartridge Company. These two companies operated independently until 1931; at that time Western Cartridge Company bought Winchester, which was at that time in receivership. The resulting divisions were organized under the parent company, Olin Industries.

Mathieson Chemical Company, originally formed in 1892, acquired Squibb in 1952. In 1954 Olin Industries and Mathieson merged and since that merger Olin Mathieson's history has been one of almost continuous merger, purchase, and sale of minor and major companies. Olin Mathieson merged with Brown Paper in 1955 and in 1958 formed a joint ownership called Ormet Aluminum with Revere Copper and Brass. There were also many smaller purchases. Its expansion was halted with the 1958 venture into the aluminum business.

The company has expanded into many diverse fields: chemicals (34% of sales), which include inorganics and organics; metals (18% of sales), which include aluminum, brass, and other nonferrous metals; packaging products (18% of sales), which include cellophane, film, kraft paper, and fine paper; Squibb pharmaceuticals (18% of sales), which include vitamins, antibiotics, and steroids; Western-Winchester (12% of sales), which includes firearms and ammunition.

This expansion has been costly; one writer described it as being a "slap dash" expansion. While it is true that Olin Mathieson sales between 1953 and 1964 increased from $468 million to $816 million, its operating margin fell from 18.8% in 1953 to 14.1% in 1963.

Generally, however, Olin Mathieson is making good progress. Earnings had fallen from a high of $3.21 in 1955 to $2.47 in 1961. Earnings have increased from this 1961 low to $3.16 in 1964. The finances, in spite of the company's problems, are sound. The 1964 ratio was 3.5 to 1 and profits are at a steady increase.

In general, the major problems of the chemical and drug industry seem to be large capital investment in process plants, rapid obsolescence from technological competition, and susceptibility to price competition problems. The problems have resulted in characteristic behavior by the members of the industry:

1. The capital problem:
   a. many joint ventures
   b. flexible capital structures
   c. large companies
   d. conservative dividend payments

2. The obsolescence problem:
   a. large research budgets
   b. high rate of depreciation write-off

3. The price competition problem:
   a. price fixing
   b. restriction of trade practices
   c. high tariff pressures
   d. pressure to increase plant productivity through technological improvements

Olin Mathieson has suffered from the chemical industry's problems. It has been forced to build new plants due to obsolescence, it has suffered from inadequate research for new products, and it has also been charged with price fixing and restriction of trade agreements.

However, it appears that most of the problems are caused by its rapid and diversified expansion. This expansion seems to have taken place on an opportunistic basis with a disregard for the problems of integrating each new part of the company to the whole. This may not be as illogical as it seems because Olin Mathieson was strong financially and it may have lost the opportunities had it stopped to consolidate its organization.

The last venture with Revere Copper and Brass may have been the deal that caused enough trouble to stop its expansion tendencies. The sum of $300 million was invested in Ormet and a rapid write-off of the costs was scheduled. Ormet was immediately faced with stiff price competition from the other aluminum producers and lost Olin Mathieson $.38 a share of earnings. In this case it erroneously applied its chemical industry tactic of rapid write-off in the metals industry.

In Squibb the company has taken over what is called an ethical drug company (one which sells only to doctors, hospitals, and laboratories), which has not provided for enough research funds. Squibb needs more consumer sales to get research funds; but it doesn't have products to sell, nor does it have the proper kind of marketing staff to sell consumer goods. Squibb also faces the fear that if it does succeed with consumer goods, it may ruin its ethical drug business.

Olin Mathieson has had much trouble with Winchester. One writer described Winchester's manufacturing equipment as being straight out of 1900. While Winchester holds 80% of the new firearm market, it was only the number two bidder on the Army's M-14 rifle. To make matters worse it was outdone by a nonfirearms manufacturer. The job amounts to $15 million of work for Winchester and the Army has announced that much of the work will be stopped because of obsolescence. Another significant fact about Winchester is that it has not produced an acceptable ordinance design since early in the Second World War.

In addition to the above problem of Winchester (which is a problem of poor management), it is also facing a declining market in sporting goods and ammunition.

Olin Mathieson appears to be fighting on two fronts to increase its profitability by modernizing its process and production facilities and by trying to expand its consumer sales possibilities.

Because of the company's great financial strength it has been able to make tremendous strides in plant modernization. It is co-owner of one of the most modern aluminum facilities in the U.S. and through a $225 million modernization investment has the nation's most productive brass mills. Also, because of its rapid write-off policies they will be very profitable plants in the future. Olin Mathieson has also done well in plant modernization for Winchester; the manufacturing areas have been reduced by 60% with an increase in production.

The most difficult problem area has been the marketing problems that the company faces. Squibb and Winchester are the divisions that lie at the core of these problems. Both divisions have been noted for their past conservatism in marketing and product design.

Squibb has marketed a toothbrush, toothpaste, and an antacid for the consumer, but it has not been very successful because of the extreme competition in these products. Winchester has just introduced a new rifle, but it is too early to tell how it will be received. It is contended, however, that Winchester doesn't need new rifles as much as it needs a larger market. Winchester has planned to try to promote the shooting sports in the same way as American Machine & Foundry and Brunswick promoted bowling, and this seems to be a very intelligent approach to its problem; but Winchester has not made very much progress with this plan and the cause of its inaction appears to be bad management and a sales force unequal to the task.

Recently, another problem has been added to the list of the sprawling company. In the latter part of 1964 managers of the various divisions sat down to bargain with some ten different unions. With the threat of more effective strike action, they immediately were confronted with a familiar package of pension and insurance demands. Since then, an Employee Incentive Thrift Plan has been approved, with the company's contribution rate fixed at 20%.

Olin Mathieson's problems can be outlined as follows:

1. *Chemicals:* Nothing very different than the industry's problems of large capital outlays, rapid obsolescence, and price competition.

2. *Drugs:* Lack of research, lack of consumer products, and a lack of consumer oriented sales force.

3. *Paper:* No serious problems.

4. *Metals:* Aluminum stiff-price competition; brass and other nonferrous metals' equipment obsolescence.

5. *Winchester:* Managerial weakness and declining market for sporting arms and ammunition.

In general, the company must add to its knowledge of consumer marketing to take advantage of its diversification.

FOR DISCUSSION

1. What problems does Olin Mathieson share in the chemical drug industry?
2. How has diversified expansion created problems?
3. What is the company's most difficult problem area? What decisions have been made relative to this? Do you believe the company has proceeded in the proper manner?

SUGGESTED READING

Burke, G., "Chemicals: The Reluctant Competitors," *Fortune*, November, 1963, pp. 148-153.

"Old Gun New Ramrod," *Business Week*, June 15, 1963, pp. 168-172.

"The Chemical Multiplier," *Forbes*, May 1, 1962, p. 16.

CHAPTER 8

American Tobacco Company

FROM THE EARLIEST DAYS of the settlement of Jamestown, tobacco changed the course of colonial development and became one of the prime forces in the lives of people and the affairs of state. People lived by it, and governments continuously sought to regulate the production and commerce in it. For more than three centuries tobacco has increased in importance as an agricultural product and an article of industry and trade.

Extending its operations to the various branches of the tobacco industry, the original American Tobacco Company was incorporated in New Jersey in January, 1890. It was this organization which the U.S. Supreme Court ordered dissolved on May 29, 1911. The Supreme Court found that this company had created a monopoly in restraint of trade under the Antitrust Law and ordered its dissolution or disintegration into fourteen separate and independent companies. By order of the Supreme Court The American Tobacco Company on May 29, 1911, was dissolved into the following 14 companies:

1. American Tobacco Co.
2. Liggett & Myers Tobacco Co.
3. American Snuff Co.
4. George W. Helme Co.
5. Weyman-Burton Co.
6. Conley Foil Co.
7. MacAndrews & Forbes Co.
8. Johnson Tin Foil & Metal Co.
9. J. S. Young Co.
10. R. J. Reynolds Co.
11. United Cigar Stores Co.
12. British-American Tobacco Co.
13. Porto-Rican & American Tobacco Co.
14. P. Lorillard Co.

In May of 1911 the American Tobacco Company, as it is known today, was established. Richmond, Virginia, became the base of operations for the new American Tobacco Company. Thus, a new era was beginning in the now competitive tobacco industry.

As early as 1911 the American Tobacco Company was pioneering in the field of tobacco research. It developed toasting processes, blending and aging techniques, and other advances in cigar and cigarette production, such as the cigarette rolling machine.

Complete dissolution of the old American Tobacco Company was not completed until 1915. In this transitional stage, Reynolds, Liggett & Myers, and Lorillard began introducing "blended cigarettes," which came prepackaged and prerolled. In 1916 the American Tobacco Company, which was slow in reorganizing, developed the Lucky Strike cigarette and began competing with such other brands of "blended cigarettes" as Tiger, Old Gold, Camel, and Chesterfield. It should be noted that prior to 1913, 95% of all cigarette smokers "rolled their own"; the remaining 5% smoked imported blends. The basic products of the tobacco industry at this time were pipe mixtures, cut tobacco for rolling, chewing tobacco, and snuff.

The American Tobacco Company did not have outright ownership of its manufactured brands; it was leasing ownership from the Tobacco Producers Corporation. In 1935 it commuted this lease and absorbed the Tobacco Producers Corporation and all its assets. Today, American is the second largest firm in the tobacco industry (Figure 8.1, Table 8.1). Its

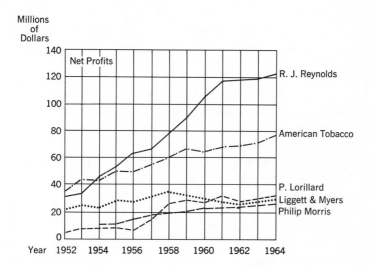

Figure 8.1

principal products are cigarettes—Pall Mall, Lucky Strike, Dual-Filter Tareyton, Montclair, and Carlton; cigars—Roi-Tan, La Corona, Bock y Ca., and Antonio y Cleopatra; smoking tobaccos—Half and Half, Blue Boar, and Genuine "Bull" Durham.

American's overall share of the market has remained steady at about 25%. The American Tobacco Company's profits in 1963 were 9% of sales

Table 8.1

SALES (Million)

	1962	1963	1964
R. J. REYNOLDS	1,627.5	1,672.4	1,613.8
AMERICAN TOBACCO	1,169.2	1,192.3	1,203.4
P. LORILLARD	516.1	516.1	466.8
LIGGETT & MYERS	500.0	507.16	502.67

which is about average for the industry (R. J. Reynolds had the high return of 13%). Sales in 1964 for American were $1,203,428,958; this compares with 1963 sales of $1,192,318,771—an increase of 1.2% over 1962. Again this figure approximates the industry increase of 1.4%. Up until 1961, sales for the industry were increasing from 3 to 4%. Since 1961, sales increases have been from 1 to 2%. The reasons for this declining trend will be discussed in another section. Earnings-per-share dropped from $2.53 in 1962 to $2.51 in 1963 although in 1964 they were up to $2.69. This drop has been industrywide. The most logical explanation is that the adverse publicity that cigarette smoking has received with respect to causing lung cancer and other bronchial diseases has pushed advertising budgets to all-time highs.

American has 90% of its cigarette sales in the nonfilter market, such as Pall Mall, Lucky Strike, and Herbert Tareyton. It has the largest selling cigarette in the U.S. with its Pall Mall brand. Naturally, Pall Mall is the largest selling cigarette in the nonfilter king-size market. Lucky Strike is second to Camels in the shrinking nonfilter regular-size market. The American Tobacco Company has recently entered the mentholated-filter market with its new Montclair brand. (The leader, by far, is R. J. Reynolds' Salem.) In the king-size filter market its Tareyton brand is ranked a weak sixth. American's newest brand to hit the market is in the filter-king field—Carlton. Carlton prints the nicotine and tar content of each cigarette on the back of each pack of cigarettes. American is hoping that Carlton will increase its share in the king-size filter-tip market. The filter-king market is growing and its profit potential is higher than in the non-filter markets.

In the cigar field American's Roi-Tan is the largest selling ten-cent cigar in the country. In pipe tobacco its Half and Half brand is a big seller in the low-priced field. Tobacco sales other than cigarettes account for about 12% of American's income. This figure is higher than the other members of the big five who account for from 2 to 9% of income on sales of cigar and pipe tobacco.

The American Tobacco Company has three basic problems. The paramount problem is one it shares with all other firms in the tobacco industry—the U.S. Surgeon General's report that cigarette smoking is a detriment to health and a major cause of lung cancer. The second problem, peculiar only to American Tobacco, is its failure to have an adequate competitive brand in the filter-tip king-size market. The third problem is one with respect to policy decisions—diversification and plant and equipment modernization. Succinctly stated, the overall problem is that of maintaining its share of the market and improving its profit position.

The American Tobacco Company does not face the problem of smoking and health alone; it is an industrywide problem. The Surgeon General's report was aimed directly at cigarette smoking. Cigarettes constitute 90% of all U.S. tobacco consumption. Last year the American public spent in excess of $8 billion on cigarettes.

The problem in its present form dates from the early 1950's, when studies correlating smoking and lung cancer first attracted nationwide attention. The biggest blow to cigarette manufacturers came in January of 1964 when the U.S. Surgeon General's Office came out with a report stating that cigarette smoking is a direct cause of lung cancer and probably many other lung diseases. The anticipated effect of this report is noticeable in the sales of American and other cigarette manufacturers. American's 1963 sales rose only 1.2%, breaking the trend of 3 to 4% increases.

Since the Surgeon General's report antismoking campaigns have sprung up all over the country. The American Tobacco Company, as well as other members of the industry, maintains that:

" . . . eminent scientists continue to come to different conclusions (about cigarettes being a cause of lung cancer) and this indicates that the final answers are not yet known. The president of the Tobacco Institute, commenting on the Surgeon General's statement, stated that the tobacco industry, which is already supporting research in this field, stands ready to increase that support . . . "

The American Tobacco Company has endorsed the position of the Tobacco Institute. In 1965 the Senate Commerce Committee approved a bill calling for a health warning on cigarette packages: "Caution: cigarette smoking may be hazardous to your health." This bill was passed. A warning on cigarette advertising may come in the future.

Another major effect of the health scare is seen in the record-high advertising budgets of American. Most of the advertising dollar is being spent to defend the company's products. American Tobacco is facing such proposals as labeling cigarettes as poison, the elimination of cigarettes from the market, restriction of cigarette advertising, and a long list of other plans dealing with the restriction of cigarette sales.

Concerning competition in the filter market, about 90% of American Tobacco's cigarette sales are in the nonfilter market. The nonfilter regular market is declining, the nonfilter king-size market has leveled off, and the filter market is experiencing growth and profit increases.

The American Tobacco Company was slow in entering the filter market. As stated earlier, Dual-Filter Tareyton, its largest seller, is comparatively weak in the market. Mentholated Montclair has failed to live up to the expectations of the company. Carlton sales, thus far, have been good but it still has to prove itself. The major disadvantage of the problem of weak sales in the filter market is the shrinkage of the regular nonfilter market. American will have trouble maintaining its market position unless it can offset losses in the regular market by gains in the filter market.

Another aspect of this problem is the opportunity to maximize tobacco leaf utility. The tobacco that filter cigarettes are made of is "homogenized" or "reconstituted." In this process, stems, scraps, and other parts of the tobacco leaf that were formerly discarded are utilized. The greater opportunity for such economies lies in the filter market. Examples would be R. J. Reynolds and P. Lorillard, who have 60 % and 95%, respectively, of their sales in filtered brands.

Pall Mall, Lucky Strike, and Herbert Tareyton account for 50% of all cigarettes sold in the nonfilter market. This indicates a high dependency on this market. Outside of cigarettes and minor interests in cigar and smoking tobaccos, American has few other interests. It does have 13% of the stock in Gahaller Tobaccos Limited of England. Diversification is not at all prominent in American Tobacco's structure. R. J. Reynolds, for example, has diversified by obtaining a fruit juice company and a tinfoil paper company. Phillip Morris Incorporated has gone into the manufacture of razor blades. The uncertainty of future expansion in the tobacco products field seems to indicate that a plan of diversification, by American, is in order. Failure to diversify may put American in a position where it cannot expand. This would be especially true if cigarette sales follow a declining trend.

The second area of policy decisions deals with plant and equipment improvements. At present, American's machinery and facilities are adequate. However, many new advances in equipment have been made, especially in the fields of production machinery, data processing, and computers. American Tobacco has overlooked many of these new advances preferring old proven methods. The failure to utilize new techniques may keep costs up and expansion potential down.

The problem of American Tobacco, then, is essentially this: Due to the problems of health connected with cigarette smoking, American faces a need to diversify. Vacillation in this area, along with the problem of competition, could ultimately put American in a very difficult position.

FOR DISCUSSION

1. What industrywide problem does American Tobacco face? What is the Tobacco Institute's position on this?

2. In your opinion, what is American Tobacco's biggest problem?
3. What should be the objectives of the company in its problem areas and what policies should be formulated to achieve these goals?

SUGGESTED READING

"American's Filter Troubles," *Forbes*, January 15, 1960, p. 24.
"American Tobacco Bucks Industry Downtrend," *Financial World*, November 4, 1964, pp. 5-6.
Maxwell, Jr., J. C., "Cigarettes: Still Bouncing Back," *Printers' Ink*, December 18, 1964, pp. 21-22.
"Passing the Sweets," *Time*, February 12, 1965, p. 84.
"Still Second," *Forbes*, February 1, 1962, p. 29.

Pabst Brewing Company

NOW THE NATION'S THIRD LARGEST PRODUCER of beer and ale, the Pabst Brewing Company originally started in 1844 as a local Milwaukee brewery. It was originally named "Best's" after the Best family which founded the brewery. At that time sales were limited to the immediate Milwaukee area. Around 1881 branches were founded in Peoria, Illinois; Kansas City, Missouri; and St. Paul, Minnesota. This marked the company's first period of expansion to its current position as a national brewer. Through the marriage of Captain Frederick Pabst to Phillip Best's daughter, the name of Best was changed to the present name of Pabst.

As the first of the great Milwaukee breweries, Pabst was recognized as leader in the industry for over half a century. It maintained this position until the end of 1952 when sales volume reached a level of $174.8 million. A Milwaukee strike in 1953, however, cost the company dearly. As a result of a basic loss of its market position, which at the time the company was unable to regain, sales began to fall steadily. By the end of 1957 sales had dropped to $112.1 million and earnings fell from $1.90 per share in 1952 to a deficit of $.70 a share. The stock during this period fell from a 1952 high of 22¼ to a 1957 low of 4¾. Pabst during this time fell from its position as leader of the industry to fifth place.

The outlook at this time did not look at all encouraging. Nevertheless, the company acquired Blatz Brewing in July, 1958, from Schenley Industries. The merger offered Pabst a young, aggressive management, which immediately initiated a vigorous rehabilitation program. Also, as a popular priced beer, Blatz opened new markets and substantially strengthened the company's competitive position.

Almost immediately after the merger, the Blatz Brewery in Milwaukee was closed and production was transferred to the four Pabst Breweries. Operations were fully integrated and costs were cut through substantially increased production efficiency. At the same time, management embarked on a comprehensive program to modernize and expand facilities in anticipation of increased business.

Following the Blatz merger, the company made an outstanding recovery. Beer sales have increased almost 50% from the 1957 figure of 3.9 million to 7.4 million barrels by the end of 1964. Net sales, in turn, have recovered from the depressed $112.1 million in 1957 to a record $227.6 million in 1964. Earnings have also rebounded to new heights (Table 8.2).

The company's total rated capacity is about 7,500,000 barrels. Brew-

Table 8.2

PABST BREWING COMPANY (DELAWARE) AND SUBSIDIARY COMPANIES: Consolidated Statement of Income and Earnings Retained For the Years Ended December 31, 1964 and 1963

	1964	*1963*
INCOME:		
Net sales	$227,610,189	$202,859,842
Cost of sales, federal excise taxes and		
operating expenses	206,666,109	184,981,138
Operating income	20,944,080	17,878,704
Other (income) and charges		
Interest income—net	(401,289)	(290,485)
Idle plant expense	697,999	703,128
Miscellaneous—net	226,148	339,302
	522,858	751,945
	20,421,222	17,126,759
Provision for federal and state taxes		
on income (Note 4)	10,400,000	9,100,000
Net income for the year	10,021,222	8,026,759
EARNINGS RETAINED:		
Balance at beginning of year	74,815,945	71,169,943
Cash dividends—$.50 per share	(2,369,510)	(2,337,866
Purchase of common stock warrant	—	(2,000,000)
Loss on sale of treasury stock		
under option plans (Note 5)	(27,012)	(42,891)
Balance at end of year (Note 3)	$ 82,440,645	$ 74,815,945
Net income per share outstanding at end of		
respective periods	$2.11	$1.71
Provision for depreciation included in		
above expenses	$6,742,235	$6,585,290

SOURCE: 1964 Annual Report.

ing operations take place in four strategically located plants in Milwaukee, Wisconsin; Peoria Heights, Illinois; Newark, New Jersey; and Los Angeles, California. Distribution is effected through wholesalers and distributors throughout the country serving well over 200,000 retail outlets.

In October, 1959, more than a year after the acquisition of Blatz, the Justice Department instituted proceedings against the company, alleging that the Blatz acquisition was in violation of Section 7 of the Clayton Act. The government charged that the merger severely lessened competition and that the company should be made to divest itself of the business and the assets of Blatz Brewing. The company did not feel that the suit had merit and therefore defended its position vigorously. On October 13, 1964, the Federal District Court in Milwaukee dismissed this suit, but the government on December 11, 1964 appealed to the Supreme Court. However, the appeal has not yet been completed. If it is completed, Pabst will continue its vigorous defense.

Pabst, after enjoying over half a century as the leader of the brewing industry, now ranks third. Sales were maintained until 1953 mainly because of its reputation as industry leader. However, at this time a Milwaukee strike and an unpopular product lost this long-held position. A four year decline ensued, bringing the company down to fifth place by 1957.

Overcapacity and intense competition have long plagued the brewing industry. The soft drink industry has made competition even more rugged than ever. Shortly after repeal, there were some 750 brewers in operation; however, demand failed to return to the high preprohibition level. As a result, there began a steady decline in the number of brewers so that by 1952 the total was cut down to 357. Over the last ten years, because of bankruptcies, sell-outs, and mergers, the number has been further reduced to an estimated 220 breweries in operation.

Because of the limited marketing area of a small local brewer, it is very difficult for these small brewers to compete effectively with the national companies. Since beer and ale consumption have remained relatively stable since 1945, the most logical way to increase sales has been to expand sales territory; thus, many companies have merged and consolidated operations in order to expand and to compete more effectively. It seems that the regional brewers will continue to feel the pressure of the large national brewer and that this trend toward consolidation and the reduction in the number of brewers will undoubtedly continue for some time. In the long run, this trend should help to bring capacity and production more in line and be of benefit to the whole industry.

Since the Second World War beer consumption has remained relatively stable, increasing only 29% from the 1946 low of 70.5 million barrels. The slowness of this growth rate is largely due to the distribution of population. The largest consumers of beer by far are the male population between the ages of 20 and 35. Over the past 20 years this group has not grown because of the low birth rate during the depression and the loss of youth sustained in both the Second World War and in the Korean Conflict.

By the late 1960's both per-capita consumption and total consumption should expand significantly due to the high birth rate after the Second World War. During the 1960's the number of people in this age group should show an uptrend. By 1970 this group should increase 14½% over 1960 figures, so looking at this it seems that the brewing industry and Pabst have a fine future.

Upon acquisition of Blatz Brewing, Pabst was able to obtain the old formula and dropped the "26 Blend" line. Original Pabst Blue Ribbon was then made and its success was fantastic. The public began to accept this product very well.

Pabst Blue Ribbon and Blatz are both nationally distributed, while East Side, a third principal product, is sold only in Southern California. Pabst has traditionally been known as a premium priced beer, but recently the company has embarked on a vigorous sales promotion campaign. Original Pabst Blue Ribbon is offered at popular prices in certain key markets. Public reception has been excellent and it looks as if the company will maintain this policy indefinitely throughout the country.

Table 8.3 shows the position of this industry in 1962. The 10 companies mentioned account for over 50% of the market output. Since then Pabst has been gaining by leaps and bounds. Executives of the company hope to pass Schlitz and hold second place soon, and of course the main objective is the enormous task of regaining its lost position as industry leader. At present Pabst is enjoying a demand which surpasses its produc-

Table 8.3

THE POSITION OF PABST IN 1962

Company	Barrel Sales 1962	Barrel Sales 1961	Change %	Market %
ANHEUSER-BUSCH	9035	8508	+ 6.2	9.9
SCHLITZ	6869	5767	+19.1	7.5
PABST	5844	5217	+12.0	6.4
CARLING	5359	5047	+ 6.2	5.9
FALSTAFF	5310	5128	+ 3.5	5.8
BALLANTINE	4550	4510	− 0.9	5.0
SCHAEFER	3778	3467	+ 9.0	4.1
HAMM	3724	3714	+ 0.3	4.1
LIEBMANN	2992	2987	+ 0.2	3.3
MILLER	2805	2707	+ 3.6	3.1

SOURCE: Reprinted with permission of *The Wall Street Journal.*

tion. Orders allow year-round total production and it seems that possible future expansion might be necessary. Although overtaking Anheuser-Busch is quite a task, it is certainly a feasible goal. With the fine management Pabst enjoys, market leadership could come in the future.

In the past Pabst has faced many problems. These problems cover almost every area: management, labor, product, and finance. Very few companies have ever had to face all these problems at once without going down in the depths of bankruptcy; very few companies have ever come back as fast and as effectively as Pabst has.

Following prohibition the Pabst Brewing Company came out with what was known as "26 Blend." This product was sold as premium priced beer. However, this beer was not the product that it was hoped to be; and because of it, Pabst lost its market position. It was far inferior to that of its competitors. Pabst, therefore, had as one of its greatest problems a product that would not sell.

Following the war Pabst enjoyed the industry's top market position. Management was slack and static. Its line supervision consisted of men promoted from the ranks and they had little education or training. As one might imagine, supervision and direction of the company was very haphazard and ineffective.

Labor in the industry has always been very strong. Wages of the brewery workers are very high, and education and skill are not required of the worker. Union policy has been to get as much as it can for the worker and strikes have been frequent, although Pabst since 1953 has been trying to avoid any strikes. Unions have gained so much strength that it is almost impossible to fire a man; so there has been an omnipresent labor problem for Pabst.

Financial problems were also faced by Pabst Brewing Company as a result of a poor product, static management, and a strong labor union. Table 8.4 shows sales, income, and per-share data for the years 1953-1962. Here one can see the seriousness of the financial problems during these 10 years.

It was a combination of these problems that led to the downfall of the Pabst Brewing Company. From the highpoint in 1952 things got worse and worse. Sales were down, profits turned into staggering losses, dividends ceased, standing in the market dropped to fifth place, and stock prices fell drastically. Insolvency and eventually bankruptcy seemed imminent.

In 1957 the board of directors of Pabst finally came up with a hopeful solution to the problem at hand. Although the purchase of Blatz Brewing would give them additional capacity, this is not what they were looking for in its acquisition. This company held a young and aggressive management, which was doing wonders with Blatz. Some have claimed that Blatz would have beat out Pabst if the merger had not come about. Also, Blatz

Table 8.4
SALES, INCOME, AND PER SHARE DATA

Year[a]	Net Sales[b]	Net Income[b]	Earnings	($) Per Common Share Dividends	Price Range
1962	$181.4	$6.45	$1.38	$0.50	18½ — 10
1961	175.5	5.09	1.10	—	18½ — 8⅞
1960	150.0	2.06	0.45	c	10⅛ — 7¾
1959	146.5	1.24	0.28	—	14⅞ — 9⅜
1958	140.8	(D) 0.56	(D) 0.13	—	11½ — 4¾
1957	112.1	(D) 2.87	(D) 0.70	0.20	8 — 4¾
1956	128.3	(D) 0.77	(D) 0.19	0.52½	11⅜ — 7¼
1955	134.3	2.38	0.58	0.70	16½ — 10
1954	145.0	2.08	0.50	1.00	20¾ — 13
1953	168.3	6.44	1.54	0.75[d]	22¾ — 16¾

a Year ended December 31
b In millions of dollars, including excise taxes
c 5% in stock
d Also 2% in stock
SOURCE: Reprinted with permission of *The Wall Street Journal.*

held the old Pabst formula which was very necessary to solve the product problem. If the merger could be made, Pabst could save itself from possible bankruptcy.

In 1958 Blatz merged with Pabst. The new young management immediately set to work to try to straighten things out; a management rearrangement came about, the best men of both companies coming out with the top positions. Blatz management fared very well, landing many of the high positions; static management was either fired or bumped down. The end result was a very capable management anxious to get something done.

Line supervision at this time was kept the same. Brewery school training was established as a prerequisite but formal college training was not needed.

Management immediately dropped the "26 Blend" product and began using a new formula. It then began a vigorous sales campaign to get the new product into the public's eye. A sales campaign selling "Original Pabst Blue Ribbon" at popular prices was launched. The public response was almost immediate.

Management and labor helped one another out and resolved problems. Although wages have been rising moderately, there has not been a strike since the merger. Workers have also had many opportunities to work Saturdays or overtime to meet product demand; thus labor-management relations have improved greatly.

History has been made since the merger. The new management has brought about cost savings and an increasing amount of better equipment, which in turn accounts for lower costs and increased production. New facilities for increased production were begun. Sales promotion campaigns paid off and orders began pouring in. Within one year profits were being made. Market position was raised to third place and stock prices began to climb as the result of management's accomplishments. Pabst began to come out of its decline and started to progress in a manner never seen before. Continuously, management has worked and planned for the future; constantly, it is working toward its ultimate goal as industry leader.

Pabst is now becoming an increasingly progressive company. In recent years more automation has been added and the future calls for even more data processing equipment than is now being used.

Line supervision policies have changed. Newly hired men must be either college graduates or experienced men from other breweries. For the college men brewery school is necessary. Pabst success has really been a result of its superior management. The past five years' sales records can vouch for this.

What about the future at Pabst? Will these advances continue? The future will be good for both the industry and Pabst. With a great increase in the market potential, everyone in the industry should do well. Company executives feel that it will soon overtake Schlitz in the near future. There is no way of telling whether it will ever surpass Anheuser-Busch.

Many persons feel that the company's advertising is extremely poor and backward. It is, they claim, not eye catching or appealing to the younger people who are the backbone of the market.

This poor advertising must change in order to bring the company to the top. If this is accomplished, a pressing struggle for first place is inevitable. Pabst then will have what every firm could ever desire—fine management, good labor relations, and a fine product that is appealing to the market.

FOR DISCUSSION

1. What are the problems of the brewing industry in general?
2. What were the primary causes of the downfall of Pabst in the 1950's? Could this have been avoided by policy decisions?
3. What decisions and factors were responsible for the improvement of Pabst's position?
4. What policies have been changed at Pabst; what specific area needs policy change in order for the company to reach the top? Can you suggest any policies in this area?

SUGGESTED READING

"Pabst Is Making Greatest Comeback," *Advertising Age*, September 11, 1961, p. 139.

Seagram (Joseph E.) & Sons, Incorporated

DISTILLERS CORPORATION-SEAGRAM LIMITED had its meager beginnings forty years ago when Samuel Bronfman, at twenty-one went into the hotel business in Quebec. After noticing that the most profitable part of the hotel business was the sale of liquor, he and his brother went into the mail-order liquor business.

In 1924 he set up Distillers Corporation Limited to operate a new distilling plant he purchased in La Salle, Quebec. This was his first distilling operation. Four years later they joined with England's Distillers Limited in buying out Joseph E. Seagram and Sons Limited. Seagram had already established a reputation for good whiskey. Then in 1933, at the height of the depression, Bronfman bought out his English partner; thus, was the large complex family-run business of Distillers Corporation-Seagram Limited on its way to becoming the largest of all the distillers in the world.

From 1933 on, the company has followed a policy of acquisition and diversification. It currently has 40 wholly owned subsidiaries, most of which are in the liquor production business. Seagram is now a holding company that owns 3 main subsidiaries which in turn own the rest. Joseph E. Seagram & Sons is the main U.S. subsidiary. The second subsidiary is the House of Seagram, a Canadian branch. The third is the international branch of the main corporation. From these main subsidiaries and the other wholly owned companies, 150 types of gin, whiskey, rum, and wine are produced. Among the main brands are Seagram's 7 Crown, Seagram's V. O., Calvert Extra, Four Roses, Kessler, Wolfschmidt, Martell, Mumm's, Myer's, Leroux, Brolio, and Kijafa.

In 1943 Seagram began branching into businesses other than distilling. It purchased Franfort distilleries, which is mainly a pharmaceutical subsidiary. In 1955 it went into its first oil venture. This has been a very costly venture to date. So far it has written off $18 million of the costs. The payoff for this ventutre should begin in the next few years and is likely to be quite a profitable one.

The company is still controlled by a tightly knit family group. Samuel Bronfman's sons, Edgar and Charles, manage the two main subsidiaries

—U.S. and Canadian respectively. The board of directors is composed of Samuel, his brother Allen, his two sons, six Bronfman subsidiary executives, and a couple of "outsiders." One of these outsiders is Edgar's father-in-law.

Even with tight family control, one of the company's primary assets has been the depth of competent management it has been able to develop through the years.

Long term prospects for the industry are quite favorable. One of the contributing factors will be that the companies will be able to have better balanced inventories. The principal reason is the "All in Bond" proposal, which will be explained later.

A second contributing factor is a forecast rise in the adult population as well as a rise in disposable income. Liquor distributors as well as baby food producers will benefit from the post-war population explosion in the U.S. War babies are just now reaching the legal drinking age and will soon be consuming as much as the adult population is now.

The industry is fortunate to have an indicator with which it can predict the total consumption by the population. The following graph shows the relationship between disposable income and liquor consumption per person.

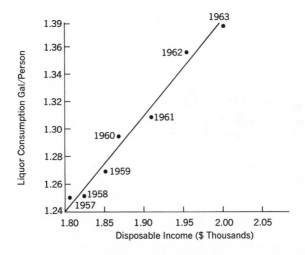

Shifts in age groups within the population don't affect the accuracy of the graph since it depicts per-capita data. With the recent tax cuts, predictions are for an increase in disposable income. There is no reason to suspect that the increase will not be accompanied by a similar increase in per-capita liquor consumption.

This handy relationship is valuable for long-range forecasts for the companies. By predicting long-range increases in disposable income, the industry is able to determine its long-range production requirements. This is necessary since whiskey must be aged a minimum of four years before it is suitable for sale.

As we have noted previously, Distillers Corporation is the largest of all the distillers in the world. It does 90% of its business within the United States. In 1964 its total sales reached a high of $897.1 million up from $864.5 million in 1963. Its leading competitor, National Distilleries had total sales of $776.87 million. The following chart is a comparison of the four largest distilleries. These four firms have 61% of the total liquor business.

(all figures in millions of dollars)

	SEAGRAM	NATIONAL	SCHENLEY	HIRAM-WALKER
Sales				
1964	897	—	405	—
1963	864.5	766.87	400.4	478.8
1962	820	775	370	469
1961	794	748	406	450
Profit				
1964	37.63	—	10.43	32.17
1963	34.26	22.81	10.52	29.64
1962	31.6	24.2	7.4	27.7
1961	30.9	23.2	12.4	26.3

It is interesting to note that although Hiram-Walker sold only half as much as Seagram, Hiram-Walker had almost as much profit. The major difference between the two companies is that Seagram has a large outstanding debt and Hiram-Walker is completely free of that type of capitalization.

Seagram has a large variety of liquor on the market. Seagram's 7 Crown and Seagram's V. O. are the largest selling items of the company. Total sales last year for 7 Crown were 7 million cases. This is 5 million more than any other blend of whiskey on the market. Of the top 11 blend labels on the market, Seagram has 5 of them. Its total sales of blends encompasses more than one-half of the domestic blend market.

The broad base of liquor has put Seagram far into the forefront of sales. The following chart shows the share of the market that the ten top producers have.

It is interesting to note that even though Seagram sells more than half of the total blend market, its total market is about one-fourth of the industry's sales.

One of the biggest headaches for the entire industry is the tax on liquor. On each gallon of liquor produced, there is a $10.50 federal excise

	Millions of Cases	Share of the Market (%)
SEAGRAM	20.5	24
NATIONAL	11	13
SCHENLEY	10.5	12
HIRAM-WALKER	10.5	12
RENFIELD	3	3.5
FLEISCHMAN	3	3.5
HEUBLEIN	3	3.5
AMERICAN	2.8	3
PUBLICKER	2.5	3
BEAM	2.2	2.5

tax and an average of $1.75 in state and local taxes. This is approximately half of the total retail price.

Several problems are presented by this extremely high tax, one of the obvious being the loss in total sales because of the high price. This is reflected not only in the price at the liquor store, but in the prices of mixed drinks at restaurants. One of the less obvious effects of the tax is that it unwittingly encourages moonshining. Industry representatives estimate that bootleggers market at 20 to 25% of total industry sales each year. This amounts to 50-60 million cases of liquor that is sold illegally each year. Government estimates of moonshining are half that of the industry estimates. Regardless of who is correct, the loss of sales to bootlegging is phenomenal.

Another industrywide problem is the control of proper inventory levels of aging whiskey. During the Second World War the levels of whiskey inventories were drastically low. This was due to limitations imposed on the companies by wartime production restrictions. Around 1950 inventory levels were about back to normal levels; however, several companies became afraid that wartime restrictions were going to be put on the industry again by the government. This led them to overstock their inventory levels.

Now, when the inventories are aged properly, these companies find that it is expensive to keep the excess in inventory. To alleviate their predicament, they do one of two things. Either they sell it to small stores for use in private labels, or they dump it for blending with grain neutral spirits. This blending cuts right into the heart of Seagram's primary market.

This past year an industry representative has been working on a proposal that very well may save the industry a great deal of money. It is called the "All in Bond" system. The government has vetoed one proposal already, but methods to overcome its objections have been devised. The industry has great hopes for implementation of this proposal in the near future.

The federal excise tax of $10.50 per gallon must currently be paid at the time of bottling. This means that working capital for any liquor that is in the company's warehouses (bottled) is tied up. The new proposal calls for tax payment at the time of shipment rather than at the time of bottling. By allowing this proposal, the government would be losing the revenue for about 4 to 5 days, the time difference between bottling and shipping.

Under the current tax payment system, the companies are forced to produce their major brands just before they're ready for shipment; thus, with the seasonal demand for liquor most companies must have larger plants than necessary and work a lot of overtime in October and November. During these peak production periods, there is a lot of strain put on the company's equipment. Under the "All in Bond" system, the companies would be able to schedule their production throughout the entire year for inventory in the bonded warehouses. They would also be able to eliminate the need for overtime during seasonal peaks. Both of these cost reductions would increase the industry's profits. Longer production runs for inventory would lower the break-even point on each item. One side effect would be that the distilling companies would not need as many large capacity plants as they now maintain for peak period production.

Another benefit of the new plan is that it would accrue to wide-based distributors such as Seagram. Items that are slow-moving could be produced in larger batches, which would lower the break-even points of these items. The working capital of the company is thus not tied up for tax purposes until the actual inventory is sold.

The primary disadvantage of the proposed system for distillers is that they must have more warehouse space; however, the benefits, according to industry analysts, far exceed the costs of the plan to producers. The less diversified companies and those companies that depend on a wide variety of brands will benefit most by the new proposal. Seagram stands to benefit greatly in the reduction of its costs. With this reduction Seagram's profit margin stands to increase from its currently low position.

The industry's problems are very much a part of Seagram's problems. It faces large taxes, it suffers from the excess inventories dumped onto the blend market, and it has increased costs because of the method of paying federal excise taxes; yet, as in any business, it has several problems uniquely its own.

One of these problems is the relatively low profit margin of 9.4% of sales. This figure is indicative of a costly operation in maintaining and selling the brands that Seagram does. Seagram has five distinct and decentralized sales organizations to handle the large number of items the company produces. The company realizes that it is sacrificing a certain amount of profit in order to maintain its broad base in liquor stocks.

Probably the major problem for Seagram in recent years has been the shift in drinking habits. In 1947, just after the war years, the market for blended whiskey was 88% of the total whiskey sold. In 1960 the blended whiskeys were 44% of the total with the difference primarily being made up of straight whiskeys (no grain neutral spirits added). Part of the change in drinking habits has been in other types of drinks. In 1950 sales of vodka amounted to one-fourth of 1%; in 1960 vodka sales were 8% of the total.

Seagram has always been heavily dependent on blends for its sales. It is just beginning to become established in the straight whiskey market. Straight whiskeys are more expensive for the consumer than blends and are more profitable for distributors. Some market analysts suggest that as disposable income rises, not only does the amount of liquor consumed rise, but tastes become more expensive. In other words, as disposable income continues to rise, the percentage of the market drinking straight whiskey and exotic drinks as opposed to those drinking blended whiskey will also rise. The following graph shows the trend in the past few years:

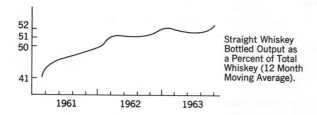

Straight Whiskey Bottled Output as a Percent of Total Whiskey (12 Month Moving Average).

To attempt to combat this trend, Seagram has done two things: first, it has eased itself into the straight whiskey market; second, it recently put out a new "soft" blended whiskey in the form of Calvert's Extra. This new blend has been its prime focal point in advertising. So far, the company has had a great deal of success with this new introduction. Whether or not it will reverse the trend back towards blends remains to be seen.

As any leading corporation in an industry must, Seagram has to continually be on its guard against being classified as a monopoly. In the fall of 1963, the Justice Department brought a price fixing suit against Seagram in Florida. It charged Seagram and its co-defendants of seven specific violations of the antitrust and Federal Trade Commission acts since 1938. Seagram of course denied all of the counts of price fixing; the charges were later dropped.

In summary, while prospects for increased sales look very good for the industry and Seagram in the future, the industry is still faced with the major problems of taxes and inventories; however, the "All in Bond" proposal may go a long way to alleviate some of the costly production practices that must be carried on by the companies. Seagram with its large variety of brands stands to benefit a great deal financially by the move. Other problems of low profit margins, the shift in consumers' buying habits, caution against being classified as a monopoly by the government, will provide Seagram's competent management with many opportunities to prove itself.

FOR DISCUSSION

1. What problems are basic to the distilling industry? What procedures have been taken by the distillers to overcome these problems? Do you think that the "All in Bond" proposal will accomplish its purposes?
2. What major problem is Seagram facing at the present time? What decisions have been made to combat this?

SUGGESTED READING

"Liquor Industry's Family-style Empire," *Business Week*, October 20, 1962, pp. 194-196.

"Perplexed Liquor Industry," *Fortune*, August, 1961, pp. 118-122.

CHAPTER 9

American Can Company

THE HISTORY OF THE AMERICAN CAN COMPANY dates back to 1901, when some of the original organizers of U.S. Steel brought together over 60 independent manufacturers and formed the company. Today, the company is one of the two large producers of cans and has 110 plants and 70 offices throughout the United States, Canada, and Puerto Rico.

American Can (Canco) was the first large manufacturer in the can industry, and it made several major advancements in containers during the first forty years of its existence. Some of the important "firsts" that it was responsible for were: producing a double tight friction cover for paint cans, putting beer into cans, large scale manufacturing of paper milk cartons, putting motor oil into cans.

By 1941 it was the giant of the industry. It accounted for 75% of the container business; of the 12 billion cans sold that year, 9 billion were produced by American Can. The company's facilities expanded to 60 plants throughout the United States, Canada, and Puerto Rico. It faced no grave problems and its competition was meager, with Continental Can offering the greatest challenge. The others, National Can, Crown Container, and Owens-Illinois Can, were far behind.

American's position was summed up by *Fortune* magazine in January, 1941: "In the path ahead of American Can Company, it is hard to spot a pitfall big enough to trap a hippopotamus."

But less than ten years later, the pitfall did occur. On June 22, 1950, a United States District Court in San Francisco handed down an antitrust ruling which stated that the company couldn't exclusively lease its can-closing machinery (which in effect forced customers to buy cans from the company) but had to sell the machinery outright and that it couldn't give a quantity discount to large customers, but had to charge the same price to all. This decision changed the entire operation of American Can and ended the free ride that it had enjoyed for so many years as the dominant company in the industry. The full effect of the decision can be seen from the following resulting conditions: American's share of the metal container market fell from 50% to 33%; competitors grew in number from essentially one to over a hundred; its sales pattern changed from 10-20 year exclusive contracts to day-to-day battles; with the increase in competition it lost the large quantity discounts on the tinplate purchases; Continental Can took over the number one spot in the container field with its wide diversification in glass, paper, and plastic. Not all of these conditions occurred immediately, but the court decision was the starting point. At the present, the company is just beginning to overcome the problems and difficulties it was faced with in 1950.

American's leadership in the industry held up for several years after the court ruling, but this was because it had such a large headstart on its competitors. In 1952 it still retained 50% of the industry with sales of $555.2 million. Continental Can, American's nearest competitor, had sales of $397.8 million; but American's profit margin was twice that of Continental Can. The company had by no means stopped growing, as evidenced by the $75.5 million it spent on expansion that year.

However, by 1956 American's share of the market had declined to 45% and Continental's share had risen to 25%. American was still expanding, but not nearly at the rate of its competitors. With its program of wide diversification, Continental was growing 200% faster than American. Right after the Second World War Continental Can expanded rapidly into several areas of the container industry, while American Can was content to stick with its profitable advantage in the metal can field.

Lack of diversification left American Can with few places in which to expand, and as a consequence Continental soon took over the leadership in the can industry. In 1960 American had sales of $1.06 billion as compared to Continental Can's sales of $1.12 billion. However, a unique factor involved here is that its profit was $7 million more than that of Continental Can.

By this time the competition in the container industry was limited to a battle between the two giants—American Can and Continental Can. The other manufacturers in the field were lost in the shuffle. In 1961 when both companies were showing sales near $1.12 billion, their nearest competitor, National Can, had sales of only $120 million. The others in the industry were far behind.

After 1960 American Can started to close the gap between itself and Continental Can, and as of 1964 both were about equal in their leadership of the industry.

The financial picture has always been bright at American. Even in the years when Continental Can maintained the leadership of the container industry, its profit volume was always higher than that of Continental; in all the 60 plus years of its existence American has never missed a dividend.

Earlier decline in profit in 1964 was attributed to heavy price-cutting in the paper cup and milk container industries and a stepped-up consumer production program to introduce paper products such as toilet tissues and cups into new market areas; but at year's end American's position in the industrial market was 43rd, ahead of Continental which had dropped to 45th position. In 1962 and 1963 American had ranked behind Continental in the "Billion Dollar Sales Club."

American Can, an extremely stable company, has awakened to the fact that expansion and diversification are necessary to stay ahead of competition. While progress is expected to continue at about the same rate as overall economic growth, there will be some squeeze on its profit position because of the switch from metal cans to other packaging materials; however, a large boom in the sale of composite cans (foil covered fiber) and plastic top coffee cans is expected, with Canco producing a large share of the total.

After a long drought American is showing again the technological progress and leadership that it did during the first 50 years of its existence. Some of its latest achievements are: (1) blow-molded aluminum cans that are shaped to the customer's design—the operation is an attempt to achieve product identity for the customer; (2) the first really inexpensive ready-labeled disposable bottle for soft drinks; (3) new electrostatic printing process for labeling irregular packaging surfaces. With continued advancement and the full force of a diversified company behind it, the management of the company is expecting to maintain its position in the can industry.

Many problems that face the company today have plagued the company for the last decade. In the first 50 years of its history it was the "big cheese." It had no appreciable competition and through the practice of making 20 year contracts with its customers, business was assured in the future. After the antitrust ruling in 1950 its comfortable future was changed into one of stiff competition. One of the immediate problems was the decision by many customers to make their own cans. Since American Can could on longer offer large quantity discounts, these companies found it cheaper to self-manufacture their own containers. An outstanding example is Campbell Soup Company, which is now the third largest world producer of metal containers. The only way the company could regain its lost customers was to make the price of its cans so low that these companies couldn't afford to keep on producing their own cans. In 1959 the company cut its can prices and raised operating efficiency in order to price its can attractively, but in doing this it had to knock $20 million off its profit volume. This strategy enabled American to regain a large part of its lost business.

One of the concerns of any company is cost reduction, but with a can company it is a matter of extreme importance. In 1960 a metal can cost about $.03, of which $.021 went to the steel companies for the tinplate used. This left the can manufacturers with $.009 with which to make a profit. Tinplate, being the biggest expense, really became a concern when its cost started to rise. Since 1950 the price of tinplate has risen about 43% while the cost of the metal can has risen only 32%. American like all the other can companies had a real problem balancing the budget.

Since developing its own steel plant or buying a ready-made plant involved too large a capital investment, American concluded that metal can packaging with tinplate was at its peak and that new materials would be used for packaging in the future. Aluminum was already being used for some cans and the development of foil-covered fiber cans was under way. The other remedy was to see if it could perform any of the necessary operations cheaper than the steel companies could. It was on this basis that American decided to buy tinplate in huge coils and do its own sizing, sorting, inspecting, and cutting. This simple decision has saved the company between $7 and $10 million annually.

When the antitrust decision forced the company to give up its exclusive contracts, the future of the company was uncertain. Before, it was guaranteed business for 10 or 20 years ahead; but after the court ruling, competition was on a daily struggle basis. Since that time it has been seeking new ways of securing its business for the future, at the same time trying not to run the risk of having another antitrust suit against it.

One method is the use of contract packaging. In July of 1961 American Can started a new division—Custom Packers. This division fills cans for carbonated soft drink bottlers. The arrangement has been reasonable only recently since the big boom of soft drinks being sold in cans. Custom Packers is under contract with the bottling companies to fill American cans with their particular product. The success of this operation depends on making the cost low enough so the bottlers can have Custom Packers fill the cans cheaper than they could themselves. In this way the company sells the cans and assures itself of a market for the future.

Another technique is to enter into joint ventures with food producers to build a can producing and filling plant. In this way American will be the company that supplies all the cans the producer needs. With the joint investment the food company can't afford to buy its cans elsewhere, which gives American the exclusive market but also means less cost for the food producer. Two examples of this type of arrangement have gone into operation recently. American Can entered a joint venture with George A. Hormel & Company to build a plant at Austin, Minnesota; another venture was with the Lindsay Ripe Olive Company to build a plant at Lindsay, California, with a capacity of 60 million cans per year. American Can would like to set up several more joint operations. Whether the government approves of this practice is something it will know at a later date.

Probably the biggest problem the company faced was the lack of adequate diversification in the container industry to meet the rapid advancement of new techniques in the packaging market. This problem really came to light in 1950 when the aggressive action of Continental Can began to wake up the people at American. Something had to be done or Continental would run away with the market. At about this time a new president took office for the American Can Company—William Stolk. Under his leadership the company took on a new outlook with aggressive planning for the future. One of his first concerns was the diversification problem. To be prepared for the future expansion into new materials, it would need some foothold in the fields of plastics, glass, and paper.

To accomplish these tasks, American took steps to acquire several existing companies. In 1956 it bought the Bradley Container Corporation and the Sun Tube Corporation, which were formed into the Bradley-Sun Division. This move gave it a position in the field of plastic containers and thin metal tubes. In 1957 it purchased Marathon Corporation and Dixie Cup, which gave the company a position in the paper products field. In 1962 it purchased the Metal & Thermit Corporation, which was renamed M&T Chemicals Incorporated. This company is involved in the production of paint and coatings. The diversification story doesn't stop with the purchase of other companies because most of the expansion has come from within. American Can's original development of the paper milk container has resulted in the formation of the Milk Container Division, with plants across the country. Another entirely developed division is the Glass Division with plants in Indiana and Minnesota. This division has been particularly active in research and development, with a breakthrough in 1962 of a new type of glass mug used for bottling beer. Originally, in early 1960 when the company was expanding to try and meet the greater diversification of Continental Can, American's management stated that it wasn't going to follow Continental into the glass business since all major technological advancements were going to come in the plastics field. However, two years later American formed a glass division and it made a breakthrough with the new beer mug; the twist is that just recently Continental Can has completed its plans to get out of the glass business.

There is every indication that American is continuing with its policy of further diversification and expansion. These are the major steps it must take to overcome the competition of Continental and resume leadership of the industry.

FOR DISCUSSION

1. What was the primary reason why American Can lost its position in the can industry?
2. What is American's major problem? What is the nature of the decisions that will be necessary to combat this?
3. What has the company done to achieve the objectives it seeks? Do you agree with these methods?

SUGGESTED READING

"Canco's Team of Men in Action," *Business Week*, October 24, 1959, pp. 78-80.
"Fight for 9/10 of a Cent," *Fortune*, April, 1961, pp. 149-157.
"New World of American Can," *Forbes*, January 15, 1960, pp. 19-22.

Continental Can Company, Incorporated

CONTINENTAL CAN COMPANY was incorporated on January 17, 1913, acquiring the assets of Continental Can Company, the Export and Domestic Can Company, and the Standard Tinplate Company. The real beginning of Continental Can Company. Incorporated, began back in 1904. In that year Edmon Norton resigned from the board of directors of American Can Company because of a disagreement which broke into open conflict over the policies which had directed the activities of American Can since its inception in 1900. With initial capital of $500,000, he formed Continental Can Company and in 1905 Continental Can shipped its first cans from the factory assembly line. This marked the entrance of a great and highly competitive firm into the packaging industry. Continental Can was to plague American Can forever in the developing packaging industry.

After its incorporation the Continental chain continued to grow. Tinplate plants for the fabrication of tin containers were built, acquired through merger, or bought outright. During this period until 1942, the company selected each new plant on two criteria; location in relation to market, and addition to capacity to produce various lines of cans. In total, it had purchased or absorbed 28 independent can companies by 1942.

In 1942 Continental Can took its first steps in its plans for diversification and decentralization. It purchased the assets of Boothly Fibre Drum Company, Fonda Container Company, and The Container Company of Wert, Ohio. This allowed Continental Can to become a diversified manufacturer in the packaging industry with the addition of these lines. The diversification or market mixing continued into kraft papers, glass, plastics, and paperwear containers. In July of 1964 the company made a substantial investment in Jagenberg-Werke of West Germany, a producer of milk containers and paper converting machinery. Continental also granted a license to the company for the production and sale of paper cups in West Germany.

The company is now the second largest producer of metal cans with 57 plants operated by the metal container division throughout the U.S. Glass and plastic operations are carried out at 31 plants; the paper products group consists of 42 plants, and in addition, the company has 3 equipment manufacturing centers and 5 research and development centers. The steady growth of Continental Can has resulted in a status that few companies have been able to achieve.

In 1964 Continental Can Company held the 45th position on Fortune's "500." This position represented a decrease from the previous year by five and from 1962 by nine. American Can also showed a decrease of two from 41st in 1963 to 43rd in 1964.

The third major producer of containers, National Can Company, rose from 377th in 1963 to 365th in 1964. This helps to explain why Continental Can, along with American Can, has been slipping in the container market. However, Continental and American together compose first and second in the industry, each fighting to gain on the other.

Sales and earnings in 1964 set records, sales rising to $1,198,120,000 from $1,154,024,000 in 1963 and net earnings-per-share of $3.97 exceeding 1963 earnings by $.70. Paper operations continued to contribute heavily to sales and profit, while sales on the West Coast were down somewhat due to the strikes against California brewing companies, hurting sales of cans, bottle crowns, and carriers for beer containers.

On a market basis the food industry is the company's largest customer, accounting for slightly more than 40% of U.S. sales. Beverage customers take approximately 20% of U.S. volume; household, automotive, personal care, and clothing follow in importance.

All large corporations, even the most successful, have problems which can greatly affect the profitability of the firm. Continental Can has problems which are unique to its own industry and mode of operation and problems that can be found in all industries. Of special interest to the board of directors are four problem areas which have plagued them for almost a decade. These four areas are: competition, return on expenses, legal aspects, and conservative management.

In 1963 Continental Can outsold American Can by less than 1%. American Can on the other hand had a better net corporate income picture by outstripping Continental Can by 10%.

Sales do not always reflect the true problems of competition. Competition comes from market mix, expansion, efficiency, and other related problems. American Can has produced better net corporate income through more efficient operations. In another area, American Can has been more conservative in that it has released less profit to its shareholders. Continental Can with its diversification program into the different areas of the packaging industry has cost the company more money.

Concerning return on expenses, as a young company Continental grew fast; but growth along diversified lines costs money. It has always been plagued by operating efficiency. In a low margin industry, one period of improper planning can cost the company all its profits.

As an example, a #303 can for peas has a selling price of $.03 per can to the packer. Of this $.03 the company spends $.021 for the metal and soldering materials to produce the can. With the remaining $.009, it has to manufacture, pack, ship, and make a profit. This shows the importance of operating efficiency and the problem of trying to realize the greatest return on expense possible for every dollar.

Continental's management has probably had its greatest headache in the area of legal entanglements. The Justice Department has been dogging Continental Can business for almost two decades. The Justice Department has repeatedly brought suit against the company contending violation of both the Sherman and Clayton Acts.

In 1950 the Justice Department brought suit against the industry involving the principle of long-term discounts to quantity customers. The case was tried with American Can as the defendant, and with Continental Can agreeing to abide by the decision. In 1956 two suits were brought against the company contending violation of the Clayton Act in connection with the mergers into the company of the Hazel-Atlas Glass Company and the Robert Gair Paper Company, Incorporated. On April 16, 1963, the district court entered its order dismissing the complaint. The Department of Justice, however, appealed this decision to the Supreme Court, where it is still pending.

The latest encounter with the Justice Department came in 1963. At that time, a suit against the company and several other companies in the corrugated container industry was filed claiming violation of the Sherman Act in connection with the conduct of business in that industry.

History has shown how Continental Can, prior to 1942, had conservative management. Up to this time its board of directors was an integral part of the management system. The board of directors had developed policies along the lines of static concepts. It was a company that was number two in its industry and had been so for 40 years. The management was trying to become number one by using old unchallenged concepts. It didn't believe in overextending itself or expanding and diversifying along lines of dissimilar competition with its chief competitors.

The advent of progressive management, the demands of a wartime economy, and the postwar explosion of gross national product has brought about many changes at Continental Can. Some of the inherent problems of the company have been solved, but solution of these problems has also presented new challenges to management—challenges which have been acted upon to help Continental Can grow and find solutions to its problems.

As part of its program to become the leader in its industry, Continental Can has become a large diversified enterprise. Acquisitions contributed importantly to this growth.

The solution to closing the gap in sales on its chief competitor came from external development; but trying to be number one can have its downfalls. Continental Can has had to pay for external development through less efficiency. In spite of this, Continental has been overall a profitable company. Much to its investors' pleasure, the company has never had an unprofitable year. It has been able to solve its problems with external development while American Can has been successful in making a larger profit on a smaller sales base. American Can has done this by sticking to the business that it knows best—internal development of tin containers.

In the diversification-expansion program at Continental Can, two points have been recognized as important in the solution of the competition problem: control of sources of supply, thus stabilizing production and also realizing greater profits; and diversifying along dissimilar lines with the strongest competitors so there is no direct competition with them.

As an example of the first point, Continental's management decided to buy coil steel from the mills and have the company cut it to specifications itself instead of relying on the mills to do it. This insured scheduling and planning for future production. On the second point Continental acted by mixing the market. The market mix includes containers of steel, glass, plastic, and paper. Further diversification has led into services and machinery manufacture.

The ability of management to create containers for new products, to improve old styles, and to furnish customers with the fastest, most reliable closing machinery possible, has helped to solve the problems associated with competition at Continental.

In present day industry, automation has played an important part in competition for Continental. Automation has provided solutions to the problems of return on expenses through cutting of costs and stabilization of manpower. Automation has allowed for expansion because it has created a base large enough to spread costs. Labor has become relatively unimportant in this intensive industry.

Continental Can has cut costs by changing packaging materials, threatening suppliers with backward integration, and stabilizing labor requirements. It was the first company to make aluminum cans, and it was able to cut costs by replacing steel with this cheaper material. Recently, Continental reported substantial progress on a method for directly converting gases into plastic coatings for containers. This process could save the can-making industry 75% of its current annual outlay of about $30 million for coating materials; however, the process is not expected to be completed until at least 1966.

Automation has also allowed Continental to stabilize employment even though its largest consumer of cans is in a seasonal industry.

Most companies who tangle with the Justice Department have to change policies or business practices to satisfy the courts. To the Justice Department, Continental Can indirectly owes its gratitude for being first place in its industry.

In the 1950 case with American Can as the defendant, the Justice

Department won the verdict which forbade long-term quantity discounts. This decision solved Continental Can's problem of getting to American's big cash buyers. This decision favored Continental by putting all sellers of containers on a more competitive basis. On this basis, Continental has been able to capture much of American's old business.

The case involving the Hazel-Atlas Glass merger enabled Continental to gain an insight into the direction it can take in expansion of its firm, but it has found that winning decisions in antitrust fights can cause new problems in the definition of competition in today's multi-product economy. Many solutions have been offered on both sides, but complete agreement seems to lie in the future.

Dynamic management inherited the problems of Continental Can in 1950. This progressive management is reflected in one man—Retired General Lucius Clay, 63, who became chairman of the board and executive officer in 1950. With his interest in the grand strategy of business, Clay has achieved grandeur for Continental largely through acquisitions, leading the company to package diversification while the management of American Can pondered the wisdom of it.

With the development of the aluminum can by Reynolds Metal Company, a new area was open to the packaging industry. Continental, under Clay's able direction, was able to capitalize on this development faster than its competitors. It developed oil and frozen juice can-making machinery and tested it before its competitors realized the value of the move. Clay directed the conversion of four plants in Florida to make Continental the major producer of the 750 million concentrate cans sold each year.

But for Clay this was not enough. He realized the importance of aluminum in cost cutting. With his interest in grand strategy he shook the research and development of the steel industry by threatening to develop aluminum to its fullest extent as fast as possible. Steel, fearing that sales would drop in an area where it had been practically king, developed a new tinplate called "skinny plate." Clay's strategy worked. He achieved a 14% price reduction, dropping the price from $8.05 per base box to $6.90 per base box.

Along with Clay the rest of Continental Can's management has reevaluated itself stating its ideas and objectives in future dynamic concepts. It has come to see competition in terms of the evolution of marketing and organizational methods and as a flood of new products created by research and development. The philosophy of the present management expresses determination to solve problems and to propel Continental Can into the forefront of U.S. business.

According to Clay, the company's diversification is now broad enough to provide growth in profits while stabilizing imputs. Efforts must now be concentrated on the different markets that the company participates in. Constant analysis is necessary. Product lines of the past must be thrown out; present moneymakers must be updated; and products which will satisfy customer needs must be developed.

In summary, while diversification has solved many problems, the company has also inherited new problems. Only continued growth will provide the solutions.

FOR DISCUSSION

1. What problems does Continental Can share with the industry?
2. What decisions, major and minor, have been important in solution of the competition problem?
3. What are the problems inherited by diversification?
4. In what way did the Justice Department indirectly help Continental Can to attain first place in the industry?

SUGGESTED READING

"Antitrusters Lose Test Case," *Business Week*, December 17, 1960, p. 29.
"Continental Can's Big Push," *Fortune*, April, 1955, p. 119.
Drucker, Peter, "Care and Feeding of the Profitable Product," *Fortune*, May, 1964, p. 133.

The Owens-Illinois Glass Company

THE OWENS-ILLINOIS GLASS COMPANY, long a leader in the glass container industry, was first incorporated in New Jersey in 1903 and later in Ohio in 1907 under the name of the Owens Bottle Machine Corporation. The name was changed to the Owens Bottle Company in 1919 and to its present name in 1929 when it merged with the second-ranked Illinois Glass Company. The merger proved to be advantageous to both parties concerned as it combined the machinery rights of the Owens Bottle Company with the know-how of the older, more profitable Illinois Glass Company. This combined company made glass containers, including beverage and milk bottles, and some special glass products, such as insulators. In the 1930's its product line was expanded to include glass tableware and tumblers as the result of its acquiring Libbey Glass. Other additions to its products line during the 1930's included metal containers and plastic bottle caps.

In keeping with its traditional spirit of diversification the company pooled its resources with those of the Corning Glass Works and formed the Owens-Corning Fiberglas Corporation in 1938. As of 1964 Owens and Corning Glass each owned 2,009,927 common shares apiece, with the remaining shares owned by the other 8,000 stockholders. Of Owens-Illinois holdings, some 574,954 shares are reserved for exchange for its preferred stock.

The repeal of the Volstead Act in 1933 and the beginning of the war created tremendous demands for Owens' containers. In addition to the demands from the now booming beer, wine, and liquor industry, the lack of domestic tin created demands from the food processors. Management expended an all-out effort to meet the critical shortages by preventing operating stoppages whenever possible and by maintaining operations at near capacity 24 hours a day. Furnaces were rebuilt on a shift basis, thus preventing down-time from exceeding 30 days. Despite these efforts some stoppages did occur due to lack of raw materials, particularly soda ash and natural gas. Other hardships encountered during the war were lack of personnel, extraordinary transportation costs, and high raw materials costs. Despite these and other problems the company was able to meet the demands of most of its customers and equitably distribute its production. The standardization of container size and shape by the government proved to be an invaluable aid to the company in meeting its war commitment. The high efficiency was attributed to the company's loyal and hardworking personnel, experienced and competent supervision, and modern equipment design.

Owens emerged from the war with a substantial backlog of orders in all its major product lines. The shift from wartime to peacetime operations was made rapidly since there was essentially no change in the product line. The only changes which were made were quite small; for example, some of the machine shops which were used for war production were reorganized for the company's own use.

Observing that the conditions were ripe for expansion, the management embarked on an all-out expansion program in all its major product lines. To aid in this planned growth, marketing research was coupled with engineering skill. The Packaging and Process Research Department was enlarged and subdivided into three areas. The Engineering Department was also enlarged and divided into two main divisions; one to aid in long-range planning and the other to aid in the day-to-day production problems. Expansion was undertaken in the product areas of glass containers, closures, Libbey-ware, glass blocks, and other building materials.

The major strategy in this new expansion effort was to buy out existing operations. In 1946 Owens acquired the Kimble Glass Company, maker of specialty glass products. Soon after, it bought into plywood, paper, paper coatings, and injection moldings. In 1953 Owens-Illinois bought a 50% interest in the Plax Corporation and in 1956 it acquired the National Container Corporation, a major producer of paperboard and corrugated containers. These acquisitions brought opposition from the Justice

Department, who charged antitrust violations. As a result Owens-Illinois was forced to sell its interest in Plax Corporation to Monsanto Chemical Company for 325,000 shares of Monsanto common. A suit was filed in 1956 protesting the merger of Owens with the National Container Corporation, and as of 1963 the company will have to divest itself of a container board mill and five corrugated shipping box plants. In addition, in July, 1964, Owens said it was ready to proceed with the sale of some of its Forest Products Division properties as required under an antitrust consent decree entered into in July, 1963.

As a result of these and similar suits, Owens-Illinois has shifted its tactics. Instead of buying out existing plants it is progressing on its own, building its own plants. An example of the extent of this new growth can be seen during the period of 1960-1962 when it opened 15 new plants in 12 states. Another example of Owens-Illinois' rapid growth can be seen in its expansion overseas, where it has operating plants in 10 foreign countries. Ray H. Mulford, president, sums up the foreign situation in this statement:

The international situation is one of our most promising areas of expansion. We can take our relatively mature technology into the international field—in glass manufacturing ability, for instance, and find we are far advanced over what exists in those countries. We can upgrade, do good for the country involved, and make a higher profit than we can expect to make at home.

In keeping with its aim of supplying a variety of containers to several thousand customers, Owens pioneered the development of the plastic container. Owens-Illinois started the development and design of equipment for manufacturing blown plastic polyethylene and polyvinyl chloride bottles as early as 1950. Several different types of forming machines and processes were developed before a finalized design was decided upon in 1954, at which time a pilot machine was developed and tested. A number of these machines were manufactured in the machine shop at Godfrey, Illinois. The production of plastic bottles actually began in 1958 at Glassboro on a small basis, first with 2 machines and later with 6. In 1959, 6 more machines were added for a total of 12. Six machines were placed in the St. Charles Plant. At that time both plants were engaged in the production of closures for the various glass containers and were thus familiar with injection molding equipment and the materials involved. By 1962 the Plastic Products Division had become a separate division from the Closure Division in the organization.

The multiplicity of new plants, products, and manufacturing processes is all in an effort to stay ahead in the competitive struggle which characterizes the container industry. In the container business it pays to be big. Products such as glass and plastic bottles, metal and plastic closures, and corrugated and fiberboard shipping boxes have a low unit price, thus making long-haul transporting prohibitively expensive. Since customers do not want to maintain large inventories of these products, they nearly always want "overnight service." This situation has forced Owens to decentralize its operations so that it may continue to be number one in the glass and plastic container business.

In glass containers Owens produces 40% of the industry total with the next producer accounting for 16% of production. The table below shows the big four producers of glass containers. This gives only a rough idea of the company's standing as there is really no company which has a similar product mix or that competes in identical products; for example, Continental Can, which merged with Hazel-Atlas, devotes 50% of its production to metal containers and only about 16% of its production to glass and plastic containers while Owens' production is about 60% glass containers.

SALES
(millions of dollars)

	Rank	59	60	61	62	63	64
OWENS-ILLINOIS	1	552.7	561.0	596.4	627.8	654.0	693.5
ANCHOR-HOCKING	2	141.1	142.9	145.1	150.3	155.0	—
CONTINENTAL CAN	3	1146.5	1170.0	1153.3	1182.9	1185.0	—
THATCHER GLASS	4	49.9	51.4	55.1	53.4	55.0	42.9

In the manufacture of plastic containers comparative figures such as the ones above are even more confusing in that the producers do not itemize their sales by product lines and even the product lines are not clear-cut. There are many firms and potential firms in the field. It is important to note the potential firms since the plastic bottle business is not as stable as glass, requiring much less capital to get into business.

In 1964 Owens-Illinois set records in sales and earnings. Sales reached a high of $693,560,200 while net earnings increased to $42,660,501 from the 1963 figure of $35,116,247.

Because of the ever-present problem of competition, Owens-Illinois' marketing and engineering teamwork is constantly on the alert to the opening of new opportunities to get an edge on competitors. The traditional expansion procedure of starting from the ground and building a plant site suitable to new operations has largely been abandoned in the interests of gaining an initial jump on competitors. In the case of Kansas City, Chicago, Newburyport, and St. Louis, the company was able to lease existing buildings and revise or change them over in order to make them suitable for its operations. By leasing existing buildings it is possible to save anywhere from five to six months of time in starting a new plant at these locations. In locating other new plants suitable buildings were not available, but flexibility was facilitated as much as possible by contracting with a lease-builder to construct a building of suitable dimensions for the company's operations. Flexibility is also realized in several of its operations which are located in available space at other Owens' plants. Other divisions such as its International Division are also using the same kind of strategy. The Canadian operation at Toronto, which produces plastic bottles, is also a leased building.

The quality of raw materials, which varies greatly from one vendor to another and from one shipment to the next, has presented a problem in that it is difficult to detect such variations and to screen raw materials. Stress cracks and other defects in the finished product may result when operations are not adjusted for variations in material characteristics; for example, variations in the density of raw materials tend to cause some plastics to be flexible while others are quite brittle.

In addition to having to cope with variations in material quality, manufacturing management must also contend with other production problems. Job changes are quite frequent and management must train people on a continuing basis if important rush orders are to be filled. Also, changes in equipment to adjust for container size, shape, weight, and volume present a constant challenge. Color changes and other chemistry problems add even more complexity to the situation.

With so many plants, 74 in total, plus Owens-Illinois' sand and natural gas interests, dispersed as they are, the company is unable to realize any savings that are associated with centralized operations. The greater the number of plants the higher the costs of capital equipment, start-up costs, and labor. The result is that management expends much of its effort coping with costs and building greater efficiency into operations.

Management has attempted to cut some of these costs by centralizing its various staff units and utilizing staff equipment on as broad a basis as possible. Recently, for example, Owens has located a RCA 301 computer in Champaign, Illinois. This computer is utilized by three of Owens-Illinois' largest container plants for solving various inventory, accounting, and payroll problems. This facilitates a large savings for the company in that each of the plants involved have access to a large computer while the costs are divided three ways. This also provides for better utilization of equipment. Other regional processing departments are also being planned.

The grand strategy of all this expansion and computer utilization seems to be one big effort to stabilize the container industry by making it a high capital cost industry instead of a medium cost industry. Entry into the plastic container industry is becoming more difficult every year and competitors have been forced to either refinance or get out of the industry while Owens has been able to keep its debt/equity ratio at a constant level.

In essence, while in a very good financial position, quality of raw material and production problems will always be of concern to the company. In addition, Owens-Illinois must always be alert to competitive situations, especially in the area of plastic containers.

FOR DISCUSSION

1. What problem characterizes the container industry? What has Owens done concerning this?
2. What are the problems connected with production? Are they major or minor?
3. What seems to be the objective of expansion and computer utilization? What is the nature of the policies needed to accomplish this?

SUGGESTED READING

Kiggins, G. M., "Comparing Two Leaders in the Packaging Field," *Magazine of Wall Street*, February 23, 1963, pp. 82-85.
"Squeeze Relieved," *Forbes*, April 15, 1963, pp. 39-40.

CHAPTER 10

American Telephone and Telegraph Company

WITH THE COMMUNICATION of the first sentence on Bell's telephone in March, 1876, emerged the beginning of one of the most powerful industries in the United States. Today, American Telephone and Telegraph Company, with its twenty operating subsidiaries and two associated but noncontrolled companies (Southern New England Telephone and Cincinnati & Suburban Bell Telephone), is the telephone industry! It controls almost 85% of all the telephones in the United States, has 85% of the total telephone plant investment, receives over 88% of the gross telephone rental, and employs over 85% of the total number of telephone employees (Table 10.1).

Table 10.1

1962 COMPARISON OF A. T. & T. TO ALL INDEPENDENTS

	Telephones		Plant Investment		Gross Revenues		Employees	
	Number (000)	% Total	Amount (000)	% Total	Amount (million)	% Total	Number	% Total
A. T. & T.	68,392	84.3	$28,691,712	85	$9,194	88.2	578,403	85.4
INDEPENDENTS	12,715	15.7	5,050,000	15	1,230	11.8	99,200	14.6

Initially financed by Gardiner Hubbard and Thomas Sanders, who had each invested half of the necessary funds for an equal share of Bell's patent rights, the experiments led to the formation of the American Bell Telephone Company.

In 1880 Mr. T. M. Vail was hired as general manager of American Bell. His sound business policies, methods, and procedures have remained fundamental in the present-day policies of the A. T. & T. Company. Through his leadership the company was able to become victorious over Western Union (a comparative giant of that time) in obtaining the patent rights that established A. T. & T. as a monopoly, and was able to absorb the majority of the independent competitors.

Up until 1881 the Bell companies had obtained their telephone instruments from various independent shops, but in 1882 the American Bell Company organized the Western Electric Company Incorporated. They transferred all their interests and gave Western Electric the exclusive manufacturing rights under the telephone patents owned by American Bell.

From 1885 to 1900 A. T. & T. was engaged principally in long-distance communication. At this time it was a subsidiary of the controlling company of the system, American Bell Telephone company (Figure 10.1).

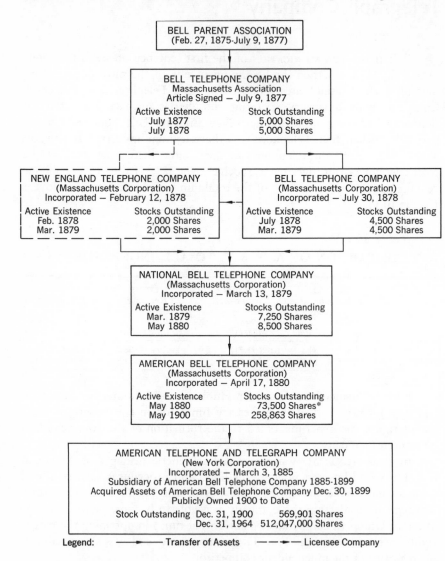

Figure 10.1
Historical Chart of the Parent Organization of the Bell System

NOTE: All stock is $100 par.
* Includes 14,000 shares of trustee stock held by National Bell Telephone Company.

However, since 1900 A. T. & T. has been the holding company of the giant Bell System network as well as the long-distance operating company.

By about 1906 A. T. & T. had eliminated any serious competition in the telephone field. It had control of all long-distance calls, as well as control of about 70% of all local calls. A. T. & T. also controlled Western Electric, which by this time had an essential monopoly on all telephone equipment for the industry. In 1925 Western Electric split one of its divisions and established Bell Telephone Laboratories (under the joint control of A. T. & T. and Western Electric) for the purpose of research, (Figure 10.2), thereby assuring the Bell System of its number one position through its further patent developments and research.

Since the telephone industry was essentially a monopoly, many state commissions were set up to regulate the company and its rates. However, since A. T. & T. was a holding company operating between all states, the only regulation it really had was from the Interstate Commerce Commission. In the mid-1930's the ICC set up the Federal Communications Commission, which had as one of its functions the regulation of interstate telephone communication. Over the 30 years that the FCC has been in existence, it has established a system of standard accounting procedures for

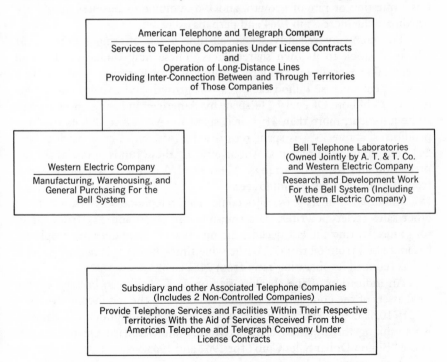

Figure 10.2
Principal Functions of A.T.&T. Company and Major Affiliated Companies

all telephone companies, but has essentially done little else in its regulation of A. T. & T. This has been mainly due to the size and complexity of the company, in addition to not having the money, staff, and authority to do the job. Of course, the positive image which has been created by A. T. & T. has not made any radical action by the FCC necessary.

However, A. T. & T. is constantly being harassed by government in attempts to break or limit its monopoly position. In 1956 as a result of a consent decree, Western Electric and A. T. & T. were forced to make all of its patents available to anyone who wanted them. This was the result of an antitrust case which had sought to completely separate the two giants from each other. The negligible results would seem to partially indicate the power and authority that the company has gained and been able to maintain over the more than 80 years of its existence.

In the 1964 annual report Chairman Frederick R. Kappel of A. T. & T. told 2.6 million share owners that the Bell System has been "experiencing exceptional growth in the demand for telephone service." In April, 1965, he stated that whether or not the economy pushes ahead with the same strength as that of 1964 the demand for communication services will still be enormous. There is no question of the growth of A. T. & T.; rather it is a question of rate of growth, and 1965 volume of business should approximate the increase in 1964 and perhaps exceed it.

The company recently set an all-time stock offering record of $1 billion of stock to its own shareholders. These new funds will be used for capital expansion and modernization. For over 9 straight years A. T. & T. has spent over $2 billion each year on growth and expansion. In 1964 it spent $3 billion. Of every $14 spent by American industry on new plant and equipment, more than $1 of it is spent by A. T. & T. Of its total expenditures, about 58% is spent on growth, 16% improving services, and 26% on public requirements. About 60% of these funds comes from depreciation and retained earnings. Another 33% of the new money comes from the sale of stock to employees.

About 90% of its gross sales come from telephone services, 5% from other sales (teletypewriter, data transmission, etc.), and 5% from directory sales. During the last decade, the number of telephones per employee has increased from 68 to 117. At the same time, during this period A. T. & T. has reduced its operating ratio from 74% to 68%.

An indication of the absolute size of A. T. & T. can be seen by the total assets of the company of $30,906,295,000 and the net income for 1964 of $1,710,623,000. Another indication of its size throughout the country is its ranking third behind General Motors and Standard Oil for 2 years in the "Billion Dollar Sales Club" for 1962 and 1963.

A comparative idea of the growth of A. T. & T., and the telephone industry as a whole, can be seen when the 137% increase in total Gross National Product over the last 15 years is compared with the increase of

816% in the net income of the telephone companies during the same period (Tables 10.2, 10.3).

Table 10.2
BELL SYSTEM GROWTH, 1950-1964

	1964	1960	1950
TELEPHONES	72,043,823	60,735,073	35,343,440
Percent Equipped for			
Direct Distance Dialing	84%	48%	None
AVERAGE DAILY CONVERSATIONS[a]			
Local	249,776,000	209,950,000	136,186,000
Long Distance	12,305,000	9,143,000	4,596,000
OVERSEAS CONVERSATIONS			
(Total for Year)	6,377,000	3,713,000	1,000,000
NET TELEPHONE PLANT[b]	$25,594,735	$18,825,273	$ 7,275,277
OPERATING REVENUES[b]	$10,305,993	$ 7,920,454	$ 3,261,528
CONSTRUCTION EXPENDITURES[b]	$ 3,518,896	$ 2,658,381	$ 891,000
OPERATING TAXES[b]	$ 2,382,809	$ 1,847,702	$ 499,451
EMPLOYEES			
Telephone Companies	589,667	580,450	523,251
Western Electric	157,626	143,352	73,458
Bell Telephone Laboratories	14,318	12,009	5,757
TOTAL WAGES[b]	$ 5,022,527	$ 4,174,500	$ 2,007,216
A.T. & T. SHARE OWNERS	2,674,141	1,911,484	985,583

a On basis of present classification between local and long distance.
b Thousands of dollars.

Table 10.3
GROWTH OF THE TELEPHONE INDUSTRY

	TELEPHONE INDUSTRY			
	Total GNP (billion)	Operating Revenues (million)	Net Income (million)	Number of Phones (million)
1962	$554.9	$9,512	$1,567	71.8
1947	234.3	2,356	171	31.3
% Increase	137%	304%	816%	129%

The fields of public relations, governmental regulation, and internal problems are three basic or possible problem areas of some concern to A. T. & T.

The least of these problems would seem to be their internal difficulties. Within the scope of this problem area is the need for top managers, the income limitations of private use (growth slowdown), and the means of obtaining the capital necessary for its continued expansion.

The difficulty of obtaining top managers for its organization is probably A. T. & T.'s major internal concern. Because of its size and complexity, a great number of well-trained managers must be ready to fill vacated positions at all times.

This type of organization (electrical) requires individuals trained in technical areas; but the heavy emphasis of A. T. & T. on public relations, and human relations in general, requires that individuals be able to fit its image. This type of management position requires a special type of well-rounded individual, capable of learning and adjusting to the company's image and its centralized leadership. To meet these ends, A. T. & T. has set up elaborate screening programs for all its positions, but in particular its management jobs. To insure that the proper individual is ready for the position, A. T. & T. has set up extensive training programs and consistently emphasizes promotion from within the organization.

Its two minor internal problems of growth and money to grow are virtually insignificant in the long run since the company has such a broadly based enterprise and has the necessary machinery to perpetuate itself at an excellent growth rate for many years, at least on paper!

One of A. T. & T.'s real problem areas is government regulation. Within the scope of this problem are the regulation by the FCC and the restrictions on any further monopolistic efforts by A. T. & T.

Bell System companies have to negotiate rates with regulatory commissions in 46 states and the separate cities of Texas, and the FCC for interstate telephoning. The profit that Bell companies are currently allowed to earn from the states range from 6.6% to 8%. The FCC allows 7½% on interstate calls. The basic idea behind these rates is to allow A. T. & T. and its operating companies a profit large enough to attract investors without being too high. However, it has been pointed out that in 1957, for example, if A. T. & T. were listed on the basis of rate-of-return (6.72), it would rank in 424th place among the nation's 500 largest companies. This would have been the case, even though it had a record high earnings that year.

A more serious threat to A. T. & T. comes from the constant intervention by the federal government. Mainly influenced by pressures from other companies in related industries, the government attempts to keep A. T. & T. from growing larger (vertical or horizontal) and/or to break apart the present Bell System monopoly.

One of the recent attempts to break up the Bell System occurred in the antitrust case which involved an effort by the government to separate A. T. & T. and Western Electric (already mentioned). The case was started in 1949 and was finally decided through a consent decree in 1956, with no real effect on their relationship.

Continued efforts to limit the power of A. T. & T. have manifested themselves in the battle that the Justice Department and other government officials have fought against overparticipation by A. T. & T. in the space communication program. They fear that the communications satellite program will be in the hands of the 10 international communication companies, which are 80% dominated by A. T. & T.

In still another area, voice-data communications, the FCC in March, 1964, turned down A. T. & T.'s request for permission to transmit printed as well as spoken communications through its transatlantic cables, which are capable of carrying both; in fact, the FCC gave this advantage to A. T. & T.'s rivals: RCA, Western Union International, and International Telephone & Telegraph. This new business area already brings the Bell System $90 million a year in U.S. sales alone.

However, the most serious problem or threat to A. T. & T. is public opinion. This is an area that the company has been aware of and has been working on, very successfully, since the early 1900's. Due to the nature of the organization (its size and monopolistic position), this will probably remain an area of great concern to A. T. & T. management for many more years.

The mere size and everyday involvement of the company has caused the public to be extremely sensitive to any and all changes which A. T. & T. makes, for example, the recent controversy caused by "All Number Calling," which replaces the names of exchanges with numbers. About 18 million phones have already been switched, and all will be changed within the next 4 years. In California, opposition to "All number calling" has been dramatized by the Anti-Digit Dialing League.

A. T. & T. has always been extremely aware of the feelings of the public and has made every effort possible to build a positive image in their eyes. It realizes the power that the public commands and knows that a hostile population could very easily topple it from its lofty number one position. Big business is always in a precarious position as far as public acceptance is concerned, and the Bell System is in even worse condition because of its monopolistic position. If government ever got the backing of the public, A. T. & T.'s monopoly would be broken up to such an extent that it would never again be recognizable.

To develop in the public's mind a picture of a company that is responsible and public-spirited, the Bell System spent $51.4 million on advertising last year and still more on public relations. Last year, employees interviewed 50,000 stockholders concerning their feelings toward the business.

Along the same idea, A. T. & T. works hard at courting the politicians, who determine its fate. A. T. & T.'s lobbying in Washington is aggressive and effective. State commissioners are brought to Bell Telephone Laboratories to be impressed by the research work done there. And it was no accident that the first Telstar telecast, which was programmed entirely by A. T. & T., featured a collection of politicians.

Direct responsibilities in public relations include customer relations and new service, public affairs, long-range planning, contributions, press relations and services, labor and bargaining information, revenue information, satellite communications, science-research-defense activities, studies of customer attitude and similar subjects, Bell System advertising and promotion, advertising and sales promotion, contacts with other Bell companies, radio and television activities, exhibits, displays, general information for employees and public, films, community relations, school relations, talks, and visits to the company premises.

The company has 78, and the associated companies 390 people working in public relations, not including secretaries and clerical help. This may not seem to be a large figure when the size of the company and the job to be done are taken into consideration, but A. T. & T.'s greatest strength lies in this: It would be hard to find an important executive, or any employee for that matter, from the long-distance operator to the repair man, who is not conscious of the importance of the general public's good will toward the company.

The long view of the company can be seen from the fact that N. W. Ayer & Son has been A. T. & T.'s advertising agency for information and sales advertising for 55 years, and Cunningham and Walsh has handled Yellow Pages advertising for 35 years. The outstanding example of stability in its public relations activities is Pendleton Dudley of Dudley-Anderson-Yutzy, who has been a consultant on public relations to A. T. & T.'s executives since 1912.

A. T. & T. is proof that a company can have a good profit position and still spend time, money, effort, and thought on its public relations, government regulation, and internal problems. From its first general manager, T. M. Vail, to its present chairman of the board, F. D. Kappel, management has constantly recognized that as powerful as it is, it must never forget that it functions only with the consent of the public and government.

FOR DISCUSSION

1. What would you say is A. T. & T.'s major problem? What is the company's attitude toward this?
2. What major and minor problems are inherent in the broad area of internal problems?
3. What has A. T. & T. done in the area of public opinion? What are the general and specific objectives relative to this?

SUGGESTED READING

"Antitrust boss takes new swipe at AT&T," *Business Week*, August 12, 1961, pp. 31-32.

Brooks, T. R., "People, vitality, and AT&T," *Dun's Review and Modern Industry*, April, 1963, pp. 53-55.

Burck, G., "Is AT&T playing it too safe?" *Fortune*, September, 1960, pp. 132-135.

Coon, Horace, *American Tel. & Tel.*, Toronto, Longmans, 1939.

"Cutting in on the line," *Time*, March 27, 1964, p. 75.

Danielian, N. R., *A T & T-The Story of Industrial Conquest*, New York, Vanguard, 1939.

Golden, L. L., "Lesson of AT&T," *Saturday Review*, June 9, 1962, p. 49.

Gottlieb, D., "Does the FCC have AT&T's number?" *New Republic*, April 6, 1963, pp. 17-19.

Kappel, Frederick R., *Vitality in a Business Enterprise*, New York, McGraw-Hill, 1960.

Moskin, J. R., "World's biggest business," *Look*, August 28, 1962, pp. 22-26.

Perelman, Norman, *What Price Telephones?* New York, League for Industrial Democracy, 1941.

CHAPTER II

M. D. King Milling Company

THE HISTORY AND GROWTH of the M. D. King Milling Company of Pittsfield, Illinois, is typical of many American businesses. The company was founded in 1869 as a small flour mill. It operated until 1899 when it was completely destroyed by fire; then in 1900 the company rebuilt a modern 600 barrel per day mill and installed one of the first banks of steel roller mills in the U.S.

In the years to follow, the company built a 100,000 bushel elevator and also acquired other line elevators in surrounding towns. The firm expanded its capacity during the First World War, and local Pike county wheat was milled into flour for shipments throughout the U. S. and several foreign countries. The mill brands of Crystal Gem and Golden Rod were quality products used in many homes throughout the midwestern and southern states.

With times changing and flour milling moving into large terminal mills, the company recognized the growing demand of commercial feed for livestock. Only feeds of outside manufacturers were handled at first, and then gradually the firm began stocking protein ingredients. By 1937 the feed business had grown to proportions where the company decided to introduce its own line of feeds.

Limited production of Golden Rod feed started when the firm installed a hammermill and mixer. During the period of the Second World War, demand for livestock feed increased tremendously; and in 1947 the decision was made to build a modern feed mixing plant, including equipment for making pellets and a molasses type of feed.

This modern plant allowed the firm to expand its feed production to include all types of livestock and poultry feed, and its brands soon became recognized throughout western Illinois and eastern Missouri.

Opportunities in the feed business convinced management that full time should be devoted to the feed and grain business, and the decision was made in 1950 to discontinue the flour milling operation. The flour milling machinery was sold and a 150,000 bushel concrete elevator was built that year.

The demand for King feed outstripped production facilities in 1955 and 1956. After a careful survey of the market and the potential demand for commercial feed in the area, the decision was made in 1957 to construct a modern "push button" type bulk feed mill. A professional engineering firm was employed to survey the market and to advise management upon the type of mill to be built.

The new feed mill not only had to be capable of producing more than the old one, but also it had to be efficient and be able to handle a large percentage of incoming ingredients in bulk. It had to utilize a minimum of labor and at the same time be a flexible mill, capable of serving the farmers with their individual needs and requirements.

A new feed warehouse with a capacity of 300 tons (of pellets) was designed and built; bulk storage bins were constructed to hold incoming bulk ingredients. Facilities, with a capacity of 40 tons per hour, were designed and constructed to unload bulk ingredients from either cars or bulk trucks. Machinery was installed to transfer these ingredients from the eight 50 ton storage tanks into smaller 15 ton bins built within the mill building.

Complete automation in the batching and mixing system was not practical, so the engineers designed a "push button" panel board allowing the operator to assemble as many as 18 different ingredients into a two ton scale hopper. Provisions were made to add medications, antibiotics, and other specialized types of additives in small quantities.

Two pellet mills with a capacity of 10 tons per hour, equipped with 100 horsepower electric motors, were installed. A Wenger horizontal-type cooler was installed under one mill and a California vertical-type cooler under the other. With this cooling equipment, all types of pelleted feed could be manufactured, including high molasses pellets and various types of roughage pellets. Each pelleting system was equipped with its own elevation legs, screening and sifting machines, and individual spouting. In this way each machine could be in operation on a different type of feed.

In order to handle the large percentage (40% in 1960; 70% in 1963) of bulk orders, a series of twelve bulk bins were included in the design for the new mill. Either pelleted or meal feed can be spouted to any of these bins. A self-cleaning rapid discharge belt collects feed from under these bins and dumps it, at the rate of one ton per minute, into a spout leading to the bulk trucks.

By October, 1959, this "push button" feed mill, costing $240,000, was producing pelleted bulk and sacked feed. This new mill has had success. Labor was reduced from 32 men producing a maximum of 75 tons in 24 hours down to 10 men producing 110 tons in 8 hours. Direct labor cost dropped from $7.50 per ton to $2.54 per ton.

The King Milling Company is presently looking for a site to build a new feed mill. An extensive study was made by the management with cooperation of the Department of Agricultural Economics of the University of Illinois, concerning the number of livestock in the northwestern counties of Illinois. The results of this study revealed a very good potential, with low competition, for King Feed in the area 100 miles north of its present mill. This "satellite" mill will be a separate corporation, the King Feed Company (not to be confused with the M. D. King Milling Company of Pittsfield) of which the M. D. King Milling Company will purchase $100,000 in stock. The amount of $50,000 will be purchased locally.

Management is currently negotiating for the sale of the Hull Elevator Company, valued at $65,000, for $85,000. The proceeds of this sale would be used to purchase stock in the new corporation.

The present feed mill with two pellet mills is now operating at 50% capacity producing 25,000 tons of feed per year. The long range expectation for top production of the Pittsfield plant is to reach a production of 35,000 to 40,000 tons per year on a two shift basis. A 10% increase per year in tonnage is anticipated and has held true in the past.

Prior to 1958 the King Milling Company operated a farm supply department, which sold merchandise to other feed dealers. In 1958 a separate corporation was formed, the Arrow Farm Supply Company, which has opened a new source of profits for the King Milling Company. This company is a wholesaler that sells farm supplies to many retail dealers in the area. Sales have increased to over $800,000, a 400% increase over 1958 gross sales.

The King Milling Company competes with the major national mills, which operate through individual dealers and a few grind mix dealers. However, King's biggest competition is with smaller individual mills operating on a similar procedure.

Since 1960 tonnage has continued to expand. Bulk feed continued to increase, reaching 70% of total volume in the fall of 1963. Eight additional bulk bins, together with a truck loading scale, were installed in 1962 to handle this increase in tonnage. This equipment permits the customer to have his truck loaded while on the scale, assuring him of getting the desired amount. In addition, a new warehouse, 40 feet by 100 feet, was built in the summer of 1963 to handle the increased demand for sacked feed.

In financing the present mill, the company has made a payment each year in excess of the required $25,000; therefore, the bank has allowed the company to make expenditures for fixed assets in excess of the $10,000 limit stated in the agreement. Fixed asset expenditures for 1962 and 1963 were $18,547 and $19,807 respectively. The bank has also given the company permission to invest up to $100,000 in a new "satellite" mill.

The feed industry's largest problem is finding an efficient method of distributing its commercial feed. Feed is distributed in three basic methods:

1. "Captive business," which consists of major feed manufacturers who own hatcheries, broiler plants, turkey farms, and cattle farms. These industries

have entered these businesses mainly as a side line activity to increase their feed volume. Recently, a few of the larger producers, such as General Mills and Pillsbury Mills, which have been manufacturing feed for this "captive business," have sold all of their interests because it did not prove to be profitable.

2. National mills, which manufacture feed in large volume and sell through dealer organizations.
3. Individually owned mills, such as the King Milling Company, which sell directly to the feeder and usually operate within a 100 mile radius of their plant.

In 1954 the King Milling Company made a complete survey of the western Illinois and eastern Missouri cattle and hog area. The results of this survey led to management's decision to sell directly to the customer. Eight salesmen were thereby employed to cover this area. Prior to 1954 the company had been selling through dealers.

A long-range problem which the feed industry and the King Milling Company must keep in mind is: In the future where will feed be manu-factured, at a mill or on the farm? A few large farms have installed a feed mix plant, which enables them to buy a premix and add this to their own soybean meal and grain. A premix consists of antibiotics, minerals, vita-mins, growth stimulants, and other additives of small amounts.

The largest account of the King Milling Company, $75,000 in yearly sales, recently installed a feed mix plant of this type. Consequently, instead of buying feed supplements from the company and mixing them with its grain, it is buying only the premix which the King Milling Company pro-duces. This has led to a 50% reduction in tonnage on this account.

Management feels that the large scale sale of premix is a long way off, but it sees its possibilities and now has premixes for sale. Growth of these feed mix plants on farms will be slow because of the capital investment needed, $30,000 to $50,000; and only the large producers can justify this type of investment.

The company's main problem is decreasing grain sales. The main reasons for this are that the company cannot compete with the river elevators with their low barge transportation costs and the decrease in government storage programs. For the past few years profits in this de-partment have been constantly declining:

1961	$18,000
1962	$19,000
1963	$16,000
1964 est.	$12,000

The management of the company recognizes this problem and believes grain department profits will level off about $10,000. By stressing other parts of the business, mainly the feed aspect, King Milling should be able to cope with this decrease in grain sales.

FOR DISCUSSION

1. What problem is common to the feed industry? What procedures have been employed to deal with this problem?
2. What is King's main problem? What factors are responsible for this? Do you feel that the company is moving in the right direction toward a solution of this problem?

SUGGESTED READING

"Agricultural Development Potentials," *Sixth Agricultural Industries Forum*, University of Illinois, January 23, 1964, pp. 1-13.
"Breathtaking Pace of Trade Cited at Midwest," *Feedstuffs*, March 28, 1964, pp. 1-73.

A. E. Staley Manufacturing Company

ON NOVEMBER 6, 1906, A. E. Staley incorporated the starch business he had started in 1898 in Baltimore, Maryland. He had rented a small loft and had a supply of fancy packages printed up with a "Cream" corn starch label on them. He had purchased a few barrels of corn starch which he put into his packages. He developed the sales of his "Cream" corn starch until he felt he was ready to manufacture his own starch, financing his enterprise by selling stock to his old friends and customers.

In 1909 he used the capital acquired from stockholders to buy a defunct starch plant in Decatur, Illinois. Three years were spent rebuilding the plant and in March of 1912 operations began. The company had a good business in the United States but also developed a very strong export business. The First World War took away this export business and had a great enough effect to force the plant to close down. Mr. Staley couldn't borrow from the banks; but his old friends and stockholders again purchased bonds issued by the company; and when the company reopened fifteen months later, the war demand increased domestic business.

After the war Mr. Staley began to interest midwestern farmers in the possibility of increasing their soybean production and at the same time secured the interest of the Illinois Central Railroad and the University of Illinois in the crusade to have increased soybean crops. The increase in soybean production also saved the land from wearing out due to over-production of corn. From 1922-1923 the mill processed 60,000 bushels of beans, which was more than twice as many as had been raised in the entire state of Illinois in 1921. Soybean crops today yield more than 470 million bushels per year. 100,000 bushels of grain are processed daily by the Staley Company. This growth has made the Staley Company one of the largest corn and soybean processors in the world.

March of 1961 marked the completion of the new Staley Research Center at the Decatur plant. Here developmental research seeks to create new products and experimentation to uncover future applications of existing products.

The future potential of soybean and corn products is tremendous. In order to continue its accepted mode of diversification and to maintain the competitive structure within the industry, the Staley Company has stressed one plan continually in the last few years—expansion. Since 1946 the company has spent more than $100 million on new construction, modernization, and product and process technology. The company plans to compete in the future by increasing expenditure on research. The new research center located at the Decatur plant provides the most modern facilities that are available for studies of new products and new applications of the many products already being produced.

The UBS Chemical Division has new plants at Marlboro, Massachusetts, and Lemont, Illinois. Polymers are used in many manufacturing industries such as paint, paper, and wax; in addition, new distribution centers have recently been added and more are planned in the future. There has also been an emphasis on the expansion of foreign markets and activities. This is a very important step in keeping ahead of competition.

In Illinois most plants process only soybeans. There are a few plants, including Staley's, which process another oil producing seed or grain. This element of flexibility can be very important. If there is a shortage of any particular oil crop, a plant can still produce at full capacity by relying on its other crop. Staley is located in the heart of American soybean and corn producing land; therefore, while this dual production is probably intended to widen its scope of final products, it is at the same time a sort of safety device.

One of the best measures of the competitive position of a processor in the soybean industry is the crushing margin. This is the difference between the price paid for the soybeans by the processor and the price he receives for the meal and oil after the beans are processed. The top competitors in the soybean industry are those processors in the states of Illinois, Iowa, and Minnesota. The oil yield per bushel of soybeans processed in Minnesota is one pound less than the yield per bushel in Illinois and one half pound less than the yield in Iowa. Since this means that Minnesota and Iowa soybeans have higher meal yields, the advantage or disadvantage is decided by the prices of meal and oil.

Decatur is used as a base point in the soybean industry. This puts the Staley plant in Decatur at a long-run disadvantage. The freight price charged on all sales by processors is based on the charge from Decatur to the point of sale. The difference between the freight charge from Decatur to the point of sale and the freight charge from the processing plant to the point of sale becomes an additional profit to certain processors. Because Decatur has a central location in the U.S., all processors west of Decatur have an advantage on sales made in the West. The same is true for the North, South, and East.

Nevertheless, Staley has managed to maintain a good position in the industry. It is a leading manufacturer of products derived from corn and soybeans. There are nine companies which make up the industry. The Corn Products Company is a gigantic concern which dominates the entire industry. Staley is next, followed by Penick and Ford Limited, Incorporated. Corn Products' net sales for 1963 were $856.9 million. Staley's net sales were $185.1 million. Net sales of Penick and Ford Limited, Incorporated were $58.8 million. The other companies in the industry are considerably smaller.

In 1963 sales of the chemical division increased. Polymers for floor polish and other uses are in great demand. The soybean division had a good year although there is somewhat of a shortage in the supply of soybeans. This is the only major farm crop not in surplus supply. The corn division is expected to maintain Staley's expansion plan. Its research center has discovered a new method of making dextrose which is in great demand by the food industry as a sugar substitute. In addition, it plans to spend about $10 million in the near future for the erection of a new crystalline dextrose plant.

Staley, like most other firms, has its own unique problems and also problems which might be expected in any firm in the industry. Marketing is an important aspect of any manufacturing company. The products do not show a profit until they can be successfully placed in the hands of customers, but marketing is a complicated phenomenon. One of the marketing problems faced by Staley is that of constantly changing markets; for instance, many of Staley's products have a derived demand. If the demand for another company's product falls off and Staley supplies the firm with an intermediate product, the derived demand for Staley's product will fall. Its market for this product has changed. Consumer markets fluctuate to a great extent also. Consumer tastes, preferences, and incomes may cause them to demand less or more of Staley's products, for example. Attempts to solve such problems are undertaken by the marketing research department. This is a problem that can never be completely solved, but the problem has been of sufficient magnitude to warrant more attention by Staley in the past few years.

The marketing program at the Staley Company was altered in the fall of 1963 when a new distribution division was created. This move resulted in the centralization of the old distribution services. This move was also made to bring about more specialization. Salesmen had been devoting time to duties that are now performed by specialists on the distribution team; now they will devote more time to selling, and long-run sales should increase. Selling costs have been too high, but the new system should be more efficient and therefore reduce costs. It should also reduce the inventory-control problem. Since the company is becoming more centralized, there will be integrated decision making. Each man had been making decisions in the interest only of his own section of the company. Now each man will be presented with a more thorough understanding of what is happening in the entire organization and can make his decisions accordingly.

The Staley Company is a member of an industry which finds itself in an overcapacity situation. The problem has plagued the corn and soybean processing industry for many years. The industry simply developed too fast. As a result, competition has been keen and profits smaller than would be the case if the overcapacity situation did not exist. There is nothing that Staley can do to erase this problem. The only defense is to work hard enough to withstand its competition.

Starches are being imported in increasing quantities each year. Most of these imports are coming from Thailand. These imports are definitely putting pressure on the Staley Company and other domestic starch producers. The imported starches are now being sold at prices much lower than those of the domestic starches. Appeals to the government to restrict such imports have been the main attempt to solve this problem. At present, however, the government refuses to accommodate these appeals because this would lower the economic activity of the countries producing the starch. These countries are not generally well-developed, and the government feels that such actions would be harmful to our international relations as well as damaging to the economies of the affected countries.

In recent years another problem has arisen in the grain processing industry. Staley has been hurt because raw material cost has been rising. Both corn and soybeans are now price supported by the government. Staley has not been able to compensate for these price increases by increasing the prices of its products. If the company did increase the prices of its products, it might lose a lot of sales and would be worse off than before. While sales have been increasing, with a few decreases over the last ten years, net earnings have not increased proportionally. This indicates that costs have been rising faster than sales. Rising labor costs have also been a factor in this problem, but it still is not feasible to raise prices immediately to combat these rising costs; however, if this trend continues, it will definitely be necessary to make some adjustment in the future.

The Staley Company has been a leader in the research and development phase of the industry. This has given the company a good reputation for being progressive and also an admirable position in the industry; but at the same time other companies often take advantage of these developments without spending their own money on research. This is an industry with relatively easy entry; therefore, small firms may enter with the aid of methods and processes which other firms have spent thousands or even millions of dollars to develop. Patents eliminate part of this problem but not all of it. However, it is still worthwhile to be first in discovery of new products or processes; and research expenditures are paid back many times, even if other companies benefit just as much from the research.

Another problem in this area is that of measuring the return from these investments. While it is obvious that research and development are important, there is no way to calculate the exact return on investments in this facet of business. While Staley Company attributes much of its success to its emphasis on research and development, the problem will always exist since it has no clear-cut solution.

There are no serious personnel or labor problems in the Staley Company, but certain problems have arisen due to technological advances in recent years. The Staley Company is highly automated. In the last ten years output has risen tremendously while the number of employees has remained about the same. This automation has caused increased worry about job security.

Employee relations have always been good at the Staley Company. During the first fifty years of the company's existence, the employees staged no labor strikes; however, as each negotiation session now gets under way, an increase in the possibility of a prolonged strike is more evident. This is another problem resulting from the fact that the Staley Company is in a period of transition, with organizational structure becoming more centralized and automation rapidly taking place. Another noticeable change in the company is its increased emphasis on grocery products. This change is being accented by increased advertising.

This transitional period is a result of growth, accelerated by the expansion program which was initiated in 1956. However, although expansion brings many problems, this is the course that Staley must take to achieve future success.

FOR DISCUSSION

1. What procedure has Staley used to continue diversification and sustain competition.
2. What problems have been common to Staley and other similar firms? What has been done about these problems? Can you suggest any other procedures?
3. Evaluate Staley's marketing program.

SUGGESTED READING

"Expansion," *The Staley Journal*, February, 1964.
"Reluctant Expansion," *Forbes*, October 1, 1963, p. 18.

CHAPTER 12

Armstrong Cork Company

TODAY'S HIGHLY SUCCESSFUL ARMSTRONG CORK COMPANY began with a one-room shop containing several sharp knives and cutting tools, and a supply of cork. In 1860 the founder, Thomas Morton Armstrong, a youthful Pittsburgh shipping clerk, invested his entire savings of $300 and formed a partnership with John D. Glass. They worked together in this one-room shop, manually cutting the cork into bottle corks.

By 1862 the partners realized the importance of mechanization and purchased their first machine for cutting cork stoppers. Mr. Glass' death in 1864, a disastrous fire in 1878, and increasing competition in the infant cork industry were taken in stride by Mr. Armstrong, and the company continued to grow.

In 1891 Armstrong Cork Corporation came into being with Thomas Armstrong as president and his son Charles as first vice-president and general manager. Under this structure and leadership Armstrong began to diversify its interests. Using shavings from the stopper machines, several new products were developed. Cork tile for the home, gaskets for the newly-born automobile industry, cork board, cork pipe covering, and cork mats of various applications were soon introduced into the product line. The most significant development of all, however, was the manufacturing of linoleum, a product which at that time consisted largely of cork.

After his father's death in 1908, Charles became president. One of his first major decisions was to build a linoleum plant in Lancaster, Pennsylvania, in 1908. Although linoleum was not a new product (it had been first produced in England fifty years before), Armstrong's creative approach was an American first. Armstrong was the first company to produce a linoleum that was attractive as well as functional. It was through this initial production of linoleum that Armstrong Cork began its industrial growth, a growth that has been characterized by conservative corporate policies and a sincere interest in humanity.

Since the erection of its first factory in Lancaster, Armstrong Cork has been growing steadily. From a struggling corporation of 53 stockholders in 1900, to a respected industrial leader with over 5½ million shareholders in 1963, Armstrong has built a strong corporate character.

Its five major divisions, aptly called "profit centers" by its current president Mr. M. J. Warnock, compete with the foremost corporations of our era. Competitive giants such as Du Pont, U.S. Gypsum, Johns-Manville, Celotex, and Sandura are just a few of Armstrong's strong competitors.

There are many reasons for Armstrong's continued prosperity among such adversaries. Probably the foremost reasons can be found in the stated corporate principles:

1. To respect the dignity and inherent rights of the individual human being in all dealings with people.
2. To maintain high moral and ethical standards and to reflect honesty, integrity, reliability, and forthrightness in all relationships.
3. To reflect the tenets of good taste and common courtesy in all attitudes, words, and deeds.
4. To serve fairly, and in proper balance, the interests of all groups associated with the business—customers, stockholders, employees, suppliers, community neighbors, government, and the general public.

This corporate personality is indeed a dynamic one. Thomas Armstrong built a deep sense of corporate pride into his company that has endured to today. He believed that people, not profits, were the prime concern of his company and that quality and dependability were the chief products.

A 1960 article in *Forbes* shows that this corporate personality created by Thomas Armstrong has persevered. "Rounding out its 100 years, Armstrong Cork Company clings to a humanistic tradition which weighs people against growth, reputation against publicity. Its earned watchword: Let's earn people's respect." Maintaining such a virtuous corporate image, however, is not a simple task. For example, the post-Korean War rush to produce plastic tile floors for the booming residential and commercial markets offered high profit opportunities. Armstrong, however, did not have a quality product ready for the market and did not offer one for several months. The company may have lost a chance to make a few dollars by that decision, but it would not produce a product it could not proudly put its name on.

One must admire such thinking, but overcautiousness can easily be a detriment. A close analysis of Armstrong's financial history reveals that, while long-run growth has been sustained, there have been several periods of stagnation. Their current capitalization, for example, includes no long-term bonded debt, a situation unique to modern enterprise. This is indeed a conservative structure and one which provides no opportunity for trade on the equity or gain from borrowed capital.

Despite the corporation's outstanding advertising system, which is headed by a vice-president with amazing corporate authority, and despite one of the oldest and most thorough sales promotion systems that works with a highly diversified product line, corporate earnings have been somewhat unstable.

During the mid-1950's, when many other industrial companies' earnings were soaring, Armstrong's lagged noticeably despite a steady growth in sales.

It was during this period, however, that Armstrong was making several significant changes. A vastly improved chemical department was beginning to provide synthetic substitutes for many of the raw inputs. Cork, linseed oil, and burlap, which previously comprised the bulk of the building material supply were being replaced by plastics and synthetic fibers. Not only did these new raw materials provide a constant and low-cost supply to manufacturing, but they also contributed to far superior finished goods. Resilient floors became easier to maintain and the variety of chemical compositions possible enabled dramatic new styling.

New acoustical ceiling tiles were manufactured with significant cost reductions, thus opening the market to the residential construction industry. Shortly after the initial production of these acoustical tiles, an improved product, Armstrong Acoustical Fire Guard, became available to the commercial construction industry. This fireproof tile was soon given the Underwriter's Laboratory seal as well as the praise of fire prevention organizations.

These innovations, plus increased emphasis on cost reduction in all areas of production, enabled the corporation to resume its earnings climb in the early 1960's. Its financial reports of 1955-1960 indicate that an increase in dollar sales of 33% contributed a net profit rise of over 61%.

At the end of 1964 net sales were up 5.5% to $360,768,000 from those of the year before and earnings were up 18% to $32,037,000; this reflected the combined effects of an active building market, the success of newer products, and aggressive merchandising efforts. The continuing program to reduce costs aided profit margins. Armstrong, though showing an unbroken rise in sales since 1957, has opted for profitability rather than volume. The biggest contribution to profitability has probably been made by the combination of three long-time Armstrong policies: (1) heavy consumer advertising, (2) a refusal to sacrifice product quality to price, and (3) a shunning of commodity-type products in favor of specialized innovations. These policies may have hurt Armstrong in the mass-building market but have made it strong in the huge, quality-conscious, largely recession-proof market for home repairs and modernization.

In a corporation which derives over 60% of its gross revenue directly from the building construction industry, and another 20 to 30% indirectly from such things as resins and industrial specialties, the future existence of the corporation is naturally dependent upon future building and remodeling projects.

Two factors, however, tend to negate future problems in this area. First, diversification of the produce line into the container and consumer product areas is well on the way. Armstrong's new one-step floor cleaner, has survived the market test quite well and more consumer goods are now in the final stages of marketing. The effect of this diversification can be seen by analyzing the present product line. In 1960, for example, one-third of the products were less than 10 years old, and what is more significant is that these products accounted for almost 50% of the sales volume. Second, the outlook for commercial and residential construction is favorable. Standard & Poor's states that although a moderate dip in demand for building products may be experienced in certain years, the long-pull outlook is favored by population growth and gains in per-capita income. The recent tax cut will release more funds for both private and corporate uses. This, coupled with the increased demand for "roomier" homes, should provide an increasingly favorable outlet for a great percentage of building products.

The products themselves, however, do not deserve all the credit. The sales or distribution system of Armstrong Cork is especially impressive. Armstrong's sales representatives are given an extensive five month training program during which each salesman learns not only the finer points of the products he will be selling, but also the qualities of the competitive products. While in the training program the sales representative becomes an integral member of Armstrong Cork Corporation—that is, he assumes a corporate personality. A New York flooring contractor said, "If you ever listen to one Armstrong salesman, you can pick out another Armstrong man anywhere you happen to find him."

According to M. J. Warnock, president, one of the most critical problems that industry currently faces is that of government intervention. It is his belief that the increasing restrictions of managerial action by governmental agencies is indeed a serious problem. Not only does the government have a strong lever over profits and taxes, but it also is quite firmly imbedded in basic administration. One particular area that Mr. Warnock is concerned about is the growing number of government questionnaires. Not only are these costly in management time and dollars, but they are dangerous in the extent to which they require more and more exposure of detailed company operations.

A solution to this problem is not apparent. Certainly, the U.S. Government has the betterment of the economy in general as its goal; but, there seems to be an increasing tendency for administrative agencies to enter into the sacred area of the Judicial Branch and directly regulate the activities of business without specific authority.

The future of Armstrong Cork Corporation looks highly favorable from all points of view. Since the company is well diversified, is managed by apparently capable young men (the average age of the top 500 management personnel is 45), has a highly capable sales force, and is thought of as a business leader, the several industrywide problems appear to be well prepared for.

SALES
(Million $)

Quarter	1963	1962	1961	1960	1959	1958
March	78.1	74.0	70.4	70.0	66.9	57.9
June	86.9	82.5	77.6	75.2	75.4	60.9
Sept.	90.5	84.5	78.2	75.5	76.9	63.7
Dec.		81.7	76.5	70.8	71.4	67.4

COMMON SHARE EARNINGS ($)

Quarter	1963	1962	1961	1960	1959	1958
March	1.00	0.81	0.71	0.75	0.83	0.50
June	1.39	1.07	0.96	0.96	1.08	0.61
Sept.	1.50	1.11	0.93	0.80	1.03	0.70
Dec.		1.00	0.90	0.56	0.74	0.78

FOR DISCUSSION

1. What is the nature of Armstrong Cork's general policies?
2. Where has Armstrong Cork shown its concern for ethical standards?
3. What problems is Armstrong Cork faced with? What is the outlook for the future concerning these problems?

SUGGESTED READING

Kay, Hubert, "To Live and Die for Armstrong," *Fortune*, March, 1964, pp. 125-129.

"Practice at Armstrong Cork: Special Report," *Printer's Ink*, December 9, 1960, pp. 25-28.

"Prudent Conservatism at Armstrong Cork: Special Report," *Forbes*, November 15, 1960, pp. 15-16.

Ashley Furniture Corporation

THE ASHLEY FURNITURE CORPORATION was an outgrowth of the Cambridge Furniture Corporation, which was started in 1945 by four stockholders with an original investment of $36,000. Cambridge was a selling agency, having a sales organization in 1948 of 30 traveling representatives. Cambridge represented 15 different factories. Its gross income was realized from a commission override on the sales of its representatives.

In 1948 the stockholders of Cambridge, realizing that the day of the selling agency in furniture was drawing to an end, established the Ashley Furniture Corporation in Illinois as a furniture jobbing company. The profit potential in jobbing was much greater than in a sales organization. Cambridge and Ashley operated through the same sales organization until 1950.

In 1950 Ashley Furniture Corporation purchased a 50% interest in the manufacturing operations of two of its suppliers and became, in effect, a furniture manufacturer. This was the turning point in Ashley's expansion in the industry, since within two years it was successful enough in manufacturing to discontinue active operation of the selling agency, Cambridge, which has remained a relatively dormant corporation.

In 1948 one of the original organizers of Cambridge and Ashley was bought out, leaving only three stockholders and officers. In 1954 another one of the original stockholders was bought out, leaving only two operating heads of Ashley Furniture Corporation.

Rapid expansion from 1954 to the present date has resulted in increased sales from $400,000 per annum in 1954 to over $2 million in 1963. Through the plowing back of profits the company has been able to conduct its business in the last eight years without the benefit of outside capital and has therefore realized substantial profits on its investment in each year, spinning off profits to its four subsidiary corporations.

Much of the success of this corporation can be attributed to its ability to change with the times and the demands of the furniture industry. During this same period when Ashley was expanding, similar companies in this highly competitive industry were falling by the wayside because they remained either as selling agencies or as drop-shipment jobbers, instead of projecting themselves into manufacturing as well as selling.

Since this is an industry of myriad small manufacturers, the industry has seen, in large measure, the demise of the jobber, because of the enormous flexibility of the various aspects of the industry to respond to consumer need and preference. The jobber is limited to what he can acquire, but the manufacturer is limited only by the physical equipment at his disposal. It only remains for the manufacturer to be perspicacious enough to work out the "niche" in the industry which he can best fill.

Because of its small size it was necessary for Ashley to develop new techniques and concepts in order to compete with highly automated plants that were situated in much more desirable labor areas than itself. In 1950 Ashley introduced to the table industry the concept of using high pressure plastic laminates with wood-grained finishes for occasional-table surfaces. Up to this time occasional tables had been made only with wood, leather, marble, or glass surfaces. This pioneering effort was well received, permitting the company to expand considerably in the next two years. Competitors, becoming aware of Ashley's success with high-pressure laminated tables, began to introduce this material in their products, so that today this type of surface represents approximately 30% of all occasional tables manufactured in the United States. Ashley has, however, been able to maintain its prominence in this field so that it is still one of the leading producers of plastic top tables.

Ashley has continued to lead the way in adoption of new plastic processes as well, for in 1963 it set up facilities to avail itself of a plastic material previously used only rarely in furniture. This material had been in use for some time in institutional settings and wherever enormously hard wear had been a factor; however, Ashley was the first to use it in a line of commercial tables. This new product, Fiberesin, is vastly superior to other limited plastics in that it can be made to have either smooth or textured surfaces, high-gloss or flat finishes, cut or shaped edges, and still be completely free from all rippling, bubbling, and peeling. Ashley had been using this product in a limited way for some time; but since the initiation of its greatly expanded use in the winter of 1963, it has contributed greatly to the expansion of Ashley's share of the market.

Continuous expansion and retention of profits are the keynotes to Ashley's progress. In 1963 Ashley set up an assembly plant and warehouse adjoining the manufacturing operation of its principal supplier of high-pressure plastic laminates. This permitted utilization of the manufacturing facilities and the machines and equipment of its supplier, without necessitating the tremendous investment in such facilities made by its competitors. In this way Ashley now has the capacity to manufacture products and styles which will enable it to compete with the giants in the table industry. With this system, together with its other manufacturing facilities, continued expansion seems to be the order of the day for Ashley.

Although we find the trend toward "bigness" existing in the furniture industry, it is not nearly as marked as in our other giant industries such as automobiles, steel, oil, etc. Since this industry produces one of our "style products" and does not necessarily require tremendous investment in plant and equipment, it will continue to permit the existence of many smaller manufacturers. This is the premise upon which the Ashley Furniture Corporation hopes to continue its progress and expansion.

The occasional-table industry, even within the furniture industry, has particular problems because in this same field there is competition between the giant case goods manufacturers who have moved into the field and the hundreds of small manufacturers. In order to maintain its place in this industry, Ashley found it necessary to become a style leader and pioneer. Occasional tables are sold on the basis of price, quality, style, and service. Ashley's existence and progress has depended on its ability to be competitive in price with the low cost highly automated giants of the industry; to maintain quality equal to that of these same giants; to give much better service to its customers than these larger corporations can; and to regularly introduce new and desirable styles, maintaining a position of leadership with reference to style. By continuing to do this, Ashley has been able to maintain a place among the first ten manufacturers of occasional tables.

An excellent example of this is Ashley's venture into the manufacturing of glass topped tables. Ashley originally went into this field some four years ago with a group designed to retail for $60 to $100, depending on the specific piece involved. Consumer response was excellent; thus a couple of selling seasons later, Ashley began introducing glass table groups to retail for about $30. This tried and true principle of marketing, testing high quality, high cost items first to see if the market is ready, proved successful once again, for the company's success with its less expensive glass tables has been so great that it now manufactures no fewer than six glass or glass type tables out of a line only slightly more than twice that large. Because of Ashley's multiplant operation, it is possible for it to, in effect, cover the market whenever it "hits" a well received design innovation, thus allowing maximum exploitation of the available market.

Obviously, a company such as this, relatively small in size and with limited capital, is faced with a number of problems in attempting to maintain its place in the industry and continue its policy of growth and expansion. The greatest problem faced by Ashley is the manufacture of products that will have a constant demand in the face of the stiff competition of the large manufacturers of the same type of product. It should particularly be noted that the location of each of Ashley's factories is in an area of high labor rates where labor is highly organized. Large competitive companies are all located in areas with low labor rates, where labor unions have not made great inroads. In the face of this, Ashley must maintain sales of approximately 12,000 tables per month. Concentration has been placed upon effective management, an alert sales force, employment of top designers, and maintaining a relatively low overhead operation.

Centralization of all clerical and management personnel has been an effective method of cost reduction and control. General offices are maintained in the American Furniture Mart in Chicago as a part of Ashley's sales showroom in that building.

In answer to a direct question concerning the major problems faced by the Ashley Furniture Corporation, the president of the company listed the following as problems that he must be aware of every day of its operation:

1. Continuing sales in volume in a highly competitive industry.
2. Manufacturing competitively in high labor areas.
3. The increasing demands of the labor unions and its effect upon Ashley's competitive position.
4. The necessity to constantly be in front of the field with new designs, new styles, and new ideas.

5. The difficulty of expansion to other product fields with limited facilities and capital.

In order to meet the first four of these problems, he has surrounded himself with very capable executive personnel, who give every indication of maintaining Ashley's position in the industry. The fifth problem has a more complex solution. A number of possibilities are being considered by Ashley, such as a merger with a larger related company in the industry or the listing of Ashley's stock on one of the stock exchanges, in other words, "going public" in order to attract equity capital and still retain control in the hands of the present management.

Ashley is now at the point where a step forward in expansion with reference to products, can trigger a rapid expansion of its business. At the present time it is necessary for Ashley to employ factory representatives who sell Ashley's products as well as the products of other noncompetitive firms in the same industry, such as case-goods and/or upholstered goods. The reason for this is that the salesmen cannot earn sufficient money (on a commission basis) by selling the products of Ashley alone. Ashley therefore does not control its sales organization. If it can successfully expand its facilities and the type of product it manufactures so that an exclusive sales force can be maintained, Ashley could effectively control its sales force and thereby double or triple its present sales within the next five years.

This is the direction now being taken by Ashley management—a direction necessary if it is to meet the demands of competition and expansion.

FOR DISCUSSION

1. What decisions has Ashley made relative to various fields of competition? How effective have they been?
2. Evaluate the factors responsible for Ashley's progress.
3. What characteristics set off the furniture industry from other industries? Are these advantageous?
4. What is Ashley's financial problem? What procedures does Ashley propose? Do you believe the firm is proceeding in the proper manner toward solutions of competition and financial problems. Can you suggest any alternative solutions?

CHAPTER 13

American Airlines, Incorporated

On April 15, 1926, a young aviator named Charles Lindberg stowed a bag of mail in his DH-4, waved to the bystanders at Chicago, and took off for St. Louis. He flew the trip for the Robertson Aircraft Corporation, holder of the second air mail contract that the government awarded to private operators. Robertson was one of some 85 companies that eventually became American Airlines, which last year carried more than 9 million passengers and flew 32 million ton miles of mail.

In early 1929 a giant holding company with a $35 million capital was formed to finance several young aviation companies. The Aviation Corporation bought companies in the northeast, midwest, southwest, and in the far west. With some of the airlines came bus lines, radio stations, and airport construction companies.

The acquisitions gave the Aviation Corporation a hodgepodge of routes and businesses that didn't fit together, a fleet that probably included at least one of every type transport plane that had ever been manufactured, and local managements that were unwilling to give up their control. To attempt to weld an airline system from this conglomeration, in 1930 all airline subsidiaries were incorporated into American Airways, Incorporated.

The first chapter of commercial airline history ended abruptly in February, 1934, with the cancellation of the air mail contracts when the government alleged collusion between airline and government officials. These charges were proven false many years later. Chapter two started later in 1934 with the reletting of new contracts. American Airways became American Airlines, and the new company emerged with a more integrated route system. In October C. R. Smith was elected president; he has been chief executive of the company since, except during the Second World War when he served as deputy commander of the Air Transport Command.

Though still dependent on air mail, American realized that the future of air transport lay in the development of the passenger business. The most important development of the mid-1930's was an airplane—the DC-3. Douglas Aircraft Company and American worked together on a project to design this brand-new plane, which eventually became the most famous plane in commercial air transport history. According to C. R. Smith; "The DC-3 freed the airlines from complete dependence upon government mail pay. It was the first airplane that could make money by just handling passengers." American inaugurated DC-3 service on June 25, 1936.

During the Second World War, American turned over almost half of its fleet to the Air Transport Command. American crews operated all over the world.

In 1943 American operated the first transcontinental all-cargo service. American Airlines today is the nation's largest airfreight carrier, last year hauling a record 166,000,000 ton miles of freight.

The end of the Second World War began what was undoubtedly American's biggest business mistake—an attempt to break into the international market before the traffic was available to support this operation. American Overseas Airlines operated for five years and resulted in an operating loss of $1,640,000 for the period. At the end of this time Smith sold his flight equipment to Pan American realizing a $1 million loss and cancelled an aircraft contract resulting in another $1 million loss.

To encourage more people to fly, American in 1948 conceived the Family Fare Plan. A year later American began to offer coach service in the most modern aircraft at convenient hours on long-haul routes. In 1949 American retired the last of its 94 DC-3's and became the first airline to be equipped with an all-postwar fleet.

American introduced transcontinental nonstop service in the DC-7 in 1953. Two years later the first order for the Lockheed Electra was placed. These turboprops were introduced over American's short and medium range routes in January, 1959. Also introduced in 1959, the Boeing 707 cut transcontinental flying time 40%. By January, 1962, the airline had fitted all of its conventional Boeing 707's with new turbofan engines. It also introduced, in 1962, the intermediate-range Convair 990. By the end of 1963, American had 68 long-range Boeing 707-123's, medium-range 707-720's, and 707-323C jetfreighters in operation over its system.

In 1964, American received 15 three-engined Boeing 727 jet aircraft, with 10 more to be delivered in 1965. In the last half of 1965 fifteen BAC 111 twin-engined jet planes will be delivered, with another 10 to be delivered in 1966. In the supersonic area American has reserved delivery positions for 6 U.S. supersonic transports and 4 Concordes, being built jointly by Sud-Aviation of France and British Aircraft Corporation. These planes are not scheduled for service until at least 1970.

In its first 10 years American Airlines carried one million passengers. In 1955 the 50 millionth passenger was flown; and 6 years later, on December 28, 1961, American became the first airline in the world to carry 100 million passengers.

American Airlines holds a foremost position in the domestic airline industry of the U.S. Because of the basic characteristic of the industry which is regulated by the Civil Aeronautics Board, there are at times fluctuations in airline statistics in relation to the overall economy; but within the industry the line is one of the top ten airline corporations and one of *Fortune's* top fifty transportation companies. Figures in 1962 show American as the third largest airline in operating revenue, ranking first in assets, second in invested capital, sixth in net income, and seventh in income as a percentage of invested capital.

Figures for operations in 1963 show much improvement over 1962. Illustrating the leverage generally found in the airline industry, American's net earnings in 1963 soared 142.4% to $17.2 million ($2.05 a share) vs. $7.1 million ($.83 a share) in 1962 on an increase of only 5.4% in revenues to $488.1 million. The increased return is a welcome change from the low levels of the preceding three years; but, American earned more than $21 million in 1959 and more than $19 million in 1956, and in both of those earlier years the capital investment was much lower.

According to Federal regulatory policy, American Airlines, as a trunkline carrier, should earn 10¼% on investment; but it earned far less than that in 1963—6.9% on the average investment for the year (stockholder equity plus long-term debt). The average rate of return for the domestic industry was even less, being about 4½% for 1963.

The predominance of the airline within the industry is clearly illustrated by some of the many "firsts" which have been accrued over the years by "America's Leading Airline." In the introduction of flight equipment American has been first throughout its history, such as in its recent introduction of the Boeing 727. It developed the concept of air freight in 1943 when the line began scheduled service. Over the years ground handling and packaging methods have improved air freighted service, and today the airline still ranks as the number one carrier in this field. Air freight, the fast growing segment of the air transportation business over the past two decades, has enormous potential. Freight ton miles for the industry in 1962 amounted to 898,100,000 ton miles, up 22.5% over 1961. In the 1952-1962 era air freight rose by 211.3% while passenger miles increased 180.1%. Still air freight accounts for less than 1% of the total freight shipped in the U.S.

Along with other domestic trunklines in general, American has faced rising depreciation expense, interest charges, and break-in costs in connection with the receipt of jet equipment. Expansion of the economy and population, along with increased public acceptance of air travel, indicate traffic growth ahead, in which American, as an industry leader, should participate fully. As it is also the leading domestic carrier of air freight, this activity should contribute importantly to revenues in future years. At the same time, as the jet equipment program draws to a conclusion, the overall cost base should become increasingly manageable. The Civil Aeronautics Board then should be able to successfully implement its new policies designed to widen profit margins and produce a higher plateau of earnings for American and the industry.

The problems which are found in the airline industry are so numerous and provide so many possible solutions, it is little wonder that the field is defined as speculative by investment authorities. Some general problem areas are: (1) problems of a regulated industry; (2) problems of defining the market area; (3) problems of safety; (4) problems within the corporate structure.

Working within a regulated industry, the airline operator must hold a certificate of public convenience and necessity before he may operate between any two cities. The regulatory body (Civil Aeronautics Board) also places limits on the rates he may charge a customer for freight or passenger service. The route structure which American now flies is adequate; fares will be discussed more fully in the marketing section.

American Airlines has made two recent attempts at mergers, one with National Airlines and a recent one with Eastern Air Lines; both of them, however, were disapproved. Both of these merger attempts and the application for the southern (Florida-California) transcontinental route were made to try to strengthen the present route structure, eliminate duplicating costs, and provide better utilization of facilities and equipment. L. L. Doty stated in *Aviation Week:*

Today's trunkline systems are in large part obsolete as a result of new technology. Basically, they were designed around the abilities of small pistonengined airplanes, such as the DC-3. They are not best designed to secure most effective use of large jet aircraft. Further, the industry is suffering from over-production and over-duplication, both in the air and on the ground.

In defining a market area and finding customers and competition, a firm must make a thorough analysis of the market, something which is clearly "up in the air" in the airline industry. One airline says that its market survey shows that fares should be reduced (Continental); another airline says that there should be a single class of service (United); American believes that there should be two classes, but that the separation should not be extreme.

In the past twelve years American has taken over 48 separate market surveys resulting in the action which the line is presently taking in planning for the future. Three of these surveys included 18,000 interviews and showed that 78% of the population of the U.S. had never flown.

The number of air travelers interviewed showed that 15% make more than five trips per year, 26% take two to four trips per year, while more than 50% take only one air trip per year. The 15% who did the greatest amount of travel accounted for 64% of all air trips.

The survey also found that businessmen made up the bulk of the heavy travelers and had an income of greater than $10,000 per year; of the 15%, 86% traveled on an expense account. The second largest group were vacationers, who made up 16% of the trips but totaled 59% of the air travelers.

Using this data, American has come to the conclusion that a wide spread between coach and first class will reduce revenues by causing businessmen to travel coach. In the words of C. R. Smith in the 1963 *Annual Report:*

American has long and consistently advocated a reduction in the premium for first-class travel. Others in the industry have opposed the reduction. This year the Federal Regulatory Agency permitted the reduction to go into effect as of January 15, 1964.

The premium for first-class travel was most onerous on long journeys, because the dollar value of the premium bulked large. The new January rates involved a substantial reduction in first-class rates for all journeys of more than 700 miles. Before the January reduction, the premium for first-class transportation from New York to California, for example, was $41.80. Following the January reductions, the premium was, and is, only $15.80. First-class transportation is now on a sound, saleable basis.

While our experience with the new rates has been short, the effect of the reduction appears to be salutary. Full-fare travel in the first-class section has increased appreciably and our average rate of fare return has improved.

The Air Transport Association had commented on this particular trend in their *Facts and Figures, 1963:* ". . . the trend toward coach showed no letup in 1962. Coach passenger miles increased 22.2%, and first-class decreased 12%. Accordingly, coach traffic accounted for 65.5% of passenger miles in 1962."

Another conclusion is that the business market is just about saturated and future gains will come mainly from vacation travelers. To reach this market, American has organized an installment credit plan with the American Express Company. Like the Universal Air Travel Plan, which American organized for businessmen, the system is a deferred payment credit card, but for 3, 6, 9, or 12 months rather than 30 days.

One area where the American policy of fare structure has been challenged is on the routes between New York-Boston and New York-Washington. Eastern Air Lines has established what it calls an "air shuttle," which requires no reservations, has no extra services, and provides a reduced fare. If one person arrives for a flight that is already filled, a second plane is called for and flown just for the one person.

American has as competition the "Captain's Deluxe Service" with a $2 surcharge above the regular first-class fare, which provides hors d'oeuvres, drinks, newspapers, and stock quotations, all served by three stewardesses. A preliminary financial report for Eastern shows that in 1963 the shuttle lost money, but so did American, because of the drain on its market.

A factor which keeps many a potential passenger out of the air is the fear of the unknown. As Mr. Smith stated in 1937: ". . . fear keeps many people from enjoying the advantages of air transportation . . . people are afraid of the things they do not know about . . ."

To overcome this obstacle and to introduce new aircraft, American Airlines runs what it calls "flightseeing" flights to familiarize the public with airplanes and air travel. The trips were originally begun some three years ago to restore confidence in the Electra, a plane which had been in several accidents; but the large percentage of the nonflying public which turned out (50% in Chicago) caused a continuation of the flights to promote vacation travel.

The greatest obstacle which must be overcome in the vacation travel market is the large amount of automobile travel between cities. In 1962 the airlines carried only 4.3% of the intercity passengers in the U.S. This obstacle is being overcome only with public familiarization with the advantages of air travel, such as those already described, and through the use of car rental agencies at the destination airport.

The second marketing analysis is of the air freight, cargo, express, and mail divisions. The extent of air cargo and its present development have already been described. American has been a forerunner in this field and has used various cargo handling systems to increase freight carriage. In 1961 a new tariff proposal was made and approved to "attempt to bring order and simplification into air freight tariffs," where several thousand commodity rates were then in effect. This proposal provided for tapered rates; directional rates; volume discounts with 1,000, 2,000, 3,000, 5,000, and 10,000 pound breaks; 500-1,000 mile, and greater than 1,800 mile distance rate reductions; off peak hour promotional rates. The *Astrofreight* system, which was introduced last year has a completely mechanized system which permits facilitated order handling and rapid cargo pick up and delivery, and a jet loader which handles loading and unloading of the plane (90,000 pounds) in 40 minutes and jet flight speeds which make the country "five hours long and two hours deep," according to Mr. Smith.

American has almost always led in the introduction of new aircraft, but when a plane is in service the actual performance is then evaluated. In almost every case the correct airplane has been selected for the routes to be flown, the one most recent error being the Lockheed Electra; but when this aircraft was selected, there were few more appealing alternatives. American, over the past few years, has tended to purchase long-haul aircraft as opposed to the Caravelle and Boeing 720, which United purchased. Now that the turboprop Electras are eligible for retirement, American has purchase orders for the Boeing 727 and BAC 111, both designed for a shorter stage length and a smaller unit volume of flight. Beyond these aircraft are the supersonic transport designs of the U.S. and Britain-France. Whether American will exercise its options on both of these aircraft will depend on several things in the next few years—yearly income, increase in the long-haul market, and financing available at that time, among others. These aircraft, which will cross the continent in two hours, must be studied carefully to prevent the overexpansion which occurred when the present jets were introduced.

Once a plane is introduced and is competitive with a similar aircraft of another airline, the competition will fall back on the all-important department of customer services, such as better baggage handling and electronic reservations systems to fill the new jets.

The area of safety is always an important point in any discussion of air travel problems. Although it may be statistically proven that a person is safer in a scheduled air transport than in an auto or (disregarding time) even in his own home, many people will not believe that the figures are correct. Every time there is an airplane crash it makes banner headlines around the world.

For this reason every aircraft is checked mechanically, and all flight personnel are checked physically many times each year. Rules and regulations are placed on flights which cause the airlines to lose much money each year, but the cost is disregarded in the interest of safety.

The goal in new aircraft, which may be achieved with the new Boeing 727 and BAC 111, is a reduction of the required ceiling and visibility restrictions on the takeoff and landing. By using a new radio altimeter, a better instrument landing system, and $200,000 approach lights in addition to the present facilities, many of the 61,000 flights which the Federal Aviation Agency estimates are cancelled each year could be flown. When landing ceiling restrictions were lowered from 300 feet to 200 feet, Pan American Airways found that it saved 250 jet flights or 15,000 passengers from inconvenience. The FAA expects to have twenty-three airports in the U.S. fitted for the low visibility approach by 1968, but the aircraft must now be equipped with expensive radio gear to use the new landing systems.

On February 28, 1962, an American jet crashed in Jamaica Bay, New York City, killing all ninety-five passengers aboard. While a mechanical defect was found to have caused the crash, many people blamed the rigid noise restriction requirements for causing the fatalities. Had the turn been made at a higher altitude, it is possible that the plane could have been stopped from crashing.

This discussion brings in another restriction which airlines are facing today—people building their houses up to the end of a runway and then complaining about the noise of jets flying overhead. The Idlewild runway 31L departure required a left turn at 800 feet and reduced power and speed seventy-five knots less than the best three engine climb speed. To overcome this hazard, a much greater program of public instruction is required; but neither American nor any of the other airlines have the money or facilities to handle this job.

Aircraft of the future may be even louder than those of today, although designers are trying to prevent this. In the meantime, such organizations as the Airport Operators Council call for a sharp reduction in the expected noise level of the U.S. supersonic transport.

While the fourth area of problems within the corporate structure may be the most pressing to a company in another field or to a financial or labor-stressed airline, American seems to be in fairly good shape internally. With few labor problems currently pressing since the solution of the Flight Engineers difficulties, the employees seem to be content.

The financial position of the company looks sound. In April, 1965, American reported net earnings of $2,794,000 for the quarter ended March 31, 1965, compared with $1,768,000 for the first quarter of 1964. Moreover, prospects for the future are good. Even greater, however, are the challenges of satisfying the public in the areas of marketing and safety, which will require greater financial resources on the part of the company and imagination on the part of management.

FOR DISCUSSION

1. What are the problems associated with a regulated industry such as airlines?
2. What are the causes of public apprehension of the airline industry? What is needed to overcome these ideas?
3. What specific policies has American formulated in the area of safety? On what resources does the success of its objective depend? In what way has American shown a regard for business ethics?
4. What are the obstacles American faces in the vacation travel market? What decisions were made to overcome them?

SUGGESTED READING

"Airport Unit Warns of SST Noise Level," *Aviation Week*, March 30, 1964, p. 28.

"American Airlines Reveals Data from Extensive Market Surveys," *Aviation Week*, February 26, 1962, p. 47.

Doty, L. L., "CAB Faced with Vital Merger Decision," *Aviation Week*, January 29, 1962, p. 36-B.

"Jet Crash Spurs Pilot Criticism of Noise Abatement Procedures," *Aviation Week*, March 19, 1962, p. 42.

Moffit, Donald, "Aviation Researchers Work to Raise Number of Crash Survivors," *The Wall Street Journal*, March 14, 1963, p. 1 ff.

Stryker, Perrin, "There's More Than One Way to Run an Airline," *Fortune*, February, 1961, pp. 96-101 ff.

United Air Lines, Incorporated

DURING THE FIRST WORLD WAR the American public was exposed to an entirely new mode of transportation. The U.S. had always been a transportation conscious country and the dependability of the new flying machine during the war caught the interest of many U.S. citizens. The airplane of today has progressed a long way from back in the early 1900's and air travel has become a large and influential industry in our modern economy.

The history of United Air Lines, Incorporated, today's leader in the air transportation industry, can be traced back to 1919, when the first commercial airline, as we know it today, began with a combination of the talent and finances of Eddie Hubbard and W. E. Boeing. The Boeing Air Transport Company was formed to fly mail for the federal government. In 1926 the Pacific Air Transport Corporation was organized on the West Coast. By 1928 four airlines served most of the continental U.S. They were Pacific Air Transport on the West Coast, Varney Air Lines in the Northwest, Boeing Air Transport from the Midwest to the West Coast, and National Air Transport from the Midwest to the East Coast. These four airlines made up what we now know as United Air Lines, Incorporated.

W. E. Boeing (Boeing Air Transport) also played a large role in the aviation industry as an airplane producer. The Boeing Airplane Company has been producing commercial airliners since 1926. The Boeing Airplane Company became a part of United Air Lines on October 30, 1928, when the formal United name was adopted. The United Aircraft and Transportation Company was formed as a holding company for Boeing Airplane Company, Boeing Air Transport, Pacific Air Transport, and Pratt and Whitney. By 1934 Varney Air Lines and National Air Transport were merged into United Aircraft and Transportation Corporation.

By the early 1930's the airline future looked promising. New, all metal, low-winged transports were entered into service. Passengers became the dominant income for the airlines and new services were provided for their comfort. United Air Lines pioneered stewardesses in 1930, and warm, comfortable cabins made flying enjoyable. Precooked meals were served to passengers as added incentives to fly.

In 1933 the roof fell in on United as well as other airlines. The government cancelled all air mail contracts. Passenger service income was not yet sufficient enough to support the expensive airline operation. To add to United's headache, the Federal Government broke up United Aircraft and Transport Corporation in 1934, claiming that it was collusion and restraint of trade to build, fly, and administer both airplane construction and air lines. The result of the dissolution was the formation of two new companies: United Air Lines, Incorporated became head of the airline section of the old company, and United Aircraft Corporation became head of the construction of airplanes.

Also in 1934 the reputation and future of United Air Lines was determined. On April 13, 1934, William A. Patterson became president of United Air Lines following his vice-presidency in the firm. United Air Lines grew to be the leader in the U.S. airline industry due solely to the efforts and ambitions of Mr. Patterson, who remained president until 1963 when he became chairman of the board. George Keck, former head of the engineering and maintenance department, became the new president.

Mr. Patterson shaped United Air Lines into the giant of the industry. His strict policy of promotion from within built security and stability into the workforce. Until 1948 Mr. Patterson visited each and every employee personally once a year. People liked working for United and as a result they did their best work.

The conservative nature of Mr. Patterson is reflected in United Air Lines. After the Second World War all domestic airlines attempted to get authorization for overseas flights except United. A study by Mr. Patterson's aides showed the international market to be too small for more than one or two carriers. United's competitors lost millions of dollars in their attempts to make a go of it in the international markets.

Safety and passenger comfort was another United Air Line concern attributed to Mr. Patterson. Mr. Patterson originated the woman steward (now called stewardess). He also gave all his support to flying aides, such as radar and other electronic equipment, which make flying safer.

United Air Lines had a difficult past, but the worst came with the introduction of jet airliners. In 1959 United received delivery of its first fleet of jet airliners at a cost of over $5 million apiece. Very few firms, especially in the airline industry, have resources enough to pay for nearly one-quarter billion dollars worth of equipment. The cost of the equipment plus inefficient operations, made evident by the big jets' reduced profits, left the airlines, including United, in poor financial condition.

In 1961 United tried to build up its deteriorating financial position by merging with the nearly defunct Capital Airlines, Incorporated. By this merger United gained a larger share of the market, thereby hoping to improve its profit.

In 1963 and 1964 United profits once again rose and reached new highs. The deteriorating profit position changed its course not only because of the merger, but mostly because of better managerial talent in all areas of the airline business. Instead of foremen, United used production managers and educated personnel to increase efficiency and create a rosy future for United Air Lines.

The airline industry is rapidly changing. What is new today may be obsolete in the future, and what is true today may be different tomorrow. Passengers consider many things in their choice of an airline. Some of these considerations are departure and arrival times, safety record, service, type of aircraft, and entertainment facilities (movies, music, etc.).

Once again United can boast leadership in these areas. Due to its size and number of aircraft United can place more flights to and from a city giving passengers more choice to fit their needs.

Its safety record has always been one of the best in the industry. Mr. Patterson has gone to extremes to insure safety for United's passengers. He has even put fewer seats in an airplane, at the cost of higher revenues, to allow for easier access to emergency exits.

Service includes meals and general comfort of the passenger. United pioneered serving hot meals on flights in 1930 and now has its own kitchens in most airports. Customer service is a trademark of United Air Lines. An example of how United tries to serve its people is in the instigating of a one-class service airplane. Mr. Patterson feels that one-class service would be ideal for the American public. Patterson noted that the one-class of service would have five abreast seating. He asked: "Is there undue crowding of passengers? Do narrow aisles and sardine seating provide for reasonable and adequate evacuation of jet aircraft in case of minor ground accidents? In good conscience, just how many passengers can you squeeze into a plane?" He indicated that the one-class service would be his answer to these problems.

United Air Lines also has all the latest and finest equipment available. Its jet fleet consists of 38 DC-8's, 29 B-720's, 20 Caravelles, and 7 B-727's with 33 more on order.

To rank airlines in numbered positions is very difficult. A few standards to go by are total miles, number of aircraft, total revenue miles, profits, reliability, safety, total passengers, and revenue ton miles.

United Air Lines is the largest domestic airline in the U.S. It has led all others in revenue aircraft miles, number of passengers, revenue passenger miles, revenue ton miles, number of employees, and number of aircraft.

In June, 1964, passenger traffic on United set a new single-month record. It flew a total of 995,700,000 revenue passenger miles, 2.2% higher than the previous record month of August, 1963, when it flew 974,563,000 revenue passenger miles, and compared with 929,300,000 in June, 1963. A revenue passenger mile equals one passenger carried mile. By the end of 1964 the number of revenue passenger miles totaled 10,060,980,000, an increase of 9% over the 1963 total of 9,190,879,000. The number of individual passengers carried also set a high, totaling 1,361,542 up 1% from

August, 1963, the previous record. At the end of 1964 the number of revenue passengers increased to 14,630,000 from 13,717,000 in 1963. Freight ton miles climbed to 14,110,000 in June, 29.5% above June, 1963, and just short of the previous record of 14,215,000 ton miles carried in May, 1964. At year's end freight ton miles totaled 171,493,000, an increase over the 1963 figure of 133,459,000.

Business Week declared in the March 28, 1964, issue that the airlines' golden age is here. It claimed that profits and financial conditions are at a high level and should remain so in the years to come. This bright outlook, however, will require an alert management with effective use of modern managerial tools.

One problem United Air Lines has been able to overcome is the over-indebtedness. With the purchase of forty or more jet aircraft United put itself deeply in debt. In 1960 and 1961 operating costs began rising faster than profits and United's management was beginning to wonder how its large debt would be paid off.

The problem of reducing costs was attacked on the ground. United's management felt that the airplane was operating efficiently, but ground personnel had room for improvement. Problems of boarding and providing exits for nearly one hundred people were solved at new, modern airports such as Chicago's O'Hare. All of United's nonoperating departments were moved to Chicago from Denver and put under one roof. The change resulted in more efficient operations and a greater profit. United has been able to meet all its payments and award a dividend to its stockholders as well.

Another problem created by jet aircraft is filling all the extra seats available on the big airliners. United feels that the answer to this problem is one-class service. By giving the passenger more room at a very reasonable price more passengers will be induced to fly. In a speech before the Economic Club of Chicago, W. A. Patterson said that he considers the "various fare gimmicks" designed to tap the mass market to be a "serious mistake." He noted that "everyone failed." Patterson said that the air travel market lacks the elasticity of markets for many other products and, in spite of advice from economists, the airline business is "quite unlike other industries." He said: "It's time for the industry to stop listening to so-called experts who are free to dispense advice without having to bear any responsibility for subsequent financial problems. We have got to stand on our own judgment."

The results of United's one-class service have been very promising. One-class service has been extended to all major cities on United's route. One-Class Red Carpet Service overshadowed all other developments in the 1963 marketing program. In offering a single high-quality service at reasonable fares without class distinctions, United Air Lines directly challenged the multifare, multiclass concept. Following limited introduction last March, One-Class Red Carpet Service was gradually extended to thirty-one cities, as justified by market demand. More than a million passengers have now traveled on one-class flights and such operations are producing 21% of revenue passenger miles. The one-class passenger Load Factor for the year 1963 was 58.5%, 14% higher than the dual-class jets, and in 1964 it was 53.3%.

The jet aircraft also created problems of maintenance. Depreciation on a jet adds up at a frightening rate whether it flies or not; so it has to keep flying, preferably full of people. Mechanical problems cannot be tolerated.

Although most people think of a jet as simpler than a piston aircraft, it isn't. While it is true that the turbine engine is far simpler, the accouterments that go with it make the plane more complex. This very fact has put the airlines on guard.

United's modern maintenance plants in San Francisco, Chicago, Denver, and Philadelphia are run by computers. The result is better maintenance and greater utilization of each airliner. The greater the utilization the lower the breakeven point on each aircraft. Preventative maintenance is a must for United so the maintenance must be perfect.

United Air Lines is still trying to increase its profits to give it more stability. One method attempted is the entry into the air cargo field. United purchased three all cargo jet airliners to add to its fleet of piston cargo planes. The changeover from piston to jet cargoliners is expected to increase revenue greatly. It is calculated that the jet freighters can do six times the work of piston freighters, based on tripling of capacity and doubling of utilization. Their ton-mile cost of operation should be about $.04, against about $.06 for CL-445. They are capable of 15-hour-a-day utilization and a breakdown load factor of 50 to 60%, while the industry average is now running about 75% on 9½ hour use. Passenger jet operations are considered good at 11 hours of utilization.

To further increase profits United must increase its total demand for cargo flights. Mr. Patterson stated:

I think the industry has made a serious mistake in the past in thinking that the only way for them to get freight was to be competitive with surface rates. I've always felt you must go in and study the methods of distribution, inventories, inventory controls of an organization and be able to show them where speed at air rate is an economy and saves them a substantial amount of money. Most of the penetration, as I see it, on air cargo has been made on American and United and others now falling in line, that we are selling cargo on that basis, not at a competitive price, but taking into consideration the speed, price, and savings.

The growing up of airlines is evident, but it remains the duty of management to stay one step ahead of developments.

A few miles from Chicago's O'Hare Field, at the headquarters of United Air Lines, is a chart room where the top executives gather at 10 A.M. every day to review the previous day's operations and make plans for the next day; for example, they plan for jets that are grounded by weather and planes that are in the "Barn" for unscheduled maintenance.

Jets are so expensive that airlines simply cannot afford to keep stand-by planes around as they did in piston days. Turnaround time has to be cut in half; thus if a flight falls behind, there is less fat in the timetable to let it catch up.

Even so, on-time performance is far better than in piston days. This is partly a result of improved maintenance techniques, but it is also a result of top-level planning and follow up.

The statistical compilations kept up to the minute at United are extremely impressive. In the course of a day the company flies some 1500 trips. Yet every morning at eight, the new president, George E. Keck, has on his desk when he gets to work the number of passengers taken on during the 24 hours ended the previous midnight, the number of seats occupied, and the equipment used. By 10 A.M. every day he has a profit and loss statement.

"The chief value in all this," says Keck, "is that it enables us to alter course much more quickly. We become aware of deviations from our forecasts almost immediately."

The airline industry has made great gains in improving its stability and profit position. In the future we can expect new problems arising from the installation of supersonic jet transports in the airline industry. The future, however, looks very good. Certainly United Air Lines, Incorporated will play a big role in the ever-expanding airline industry.

FOR DISCUSSION

1. Evaluate William Patterson's general and specific policies and decisions.
2. What problems have been created by jet aircraft? How does United plan to cope with them? Is it adequate?
3. What decisions have been made pertinent to increasing profits?

SUGGESTED READING

Coyle, Joseph S., "The Jet Bet," *Traffic Management*, August, 1963, pp. 16-19.
"Special Report on Commercial Airlines," *Aviation Week and Space Technology*, July, 1964, pp. 43-48.
"The Airlines Golden Age: Special Report," *Business Week*, March 28, 1964, pp. 52-72.

Cessna Aircraft Company

FOUNDED BY CLYDE CESSNA AND VICTOR H. Roos, the Cessna-Roos Aircraft Company was incorporated in Wichita, Kansas, on September 7, 1927. The company formed to produce the Cessna-designed "Comet," a four-place, full-cantilever wing airplane powered by a 120-hp. Anzani engine. On December 27, 1927, the firm changed its name to the present Cessna Aircraft Company, Roos having sold his interest to Cessna.

The "A" series, a four-place, full-cantilever high wing monoplane, fabric-covered and weighing 2,260 pounds gross, marked the beginning of Cessna's production models. It was offered with five engine options subdesignated as the AA, AW, AS, AC, and AF. Forty-six of these planes were produced in 1928. *Popular Aviation*, in April, 1928, carried one of the first Cessna ads for the "A" series. It was designed to interest prospective dealers as well as customers.

Cessna contracted to deliver fifty airplanes per month to Curtiss Flying Service in 1929. It purchased eighty acres southeast of Wichita, the site of the present commercial division Pawnee Road plant, and built five new factory buildings designed for volume production. The "crash" of 1929 saw Curtiss go into bankruptcy leaving Cessna without a market for its airplanes. Production continued, however, until 1931 when Cessna's inventory became so large that it was forced to shut down.

Between 1931 and 1934 Cessna sold an occasional airplane and produced some special-order racing aircraft. Cessna's son, Eldon, designed a small glider, which they built and sold in limited quantity. The company remained dormant until 1934 when Dwane L. Wallace, a newly-graduated aeronautical engineer, and Clyde Cessna's nephew, convinced the stockholders to reopen the firm. Wallace became manager with Cessna as president. In 1936 Clyde retired after selling his interest to Wallace in 1935; Wallace then became president.

Few airplanes were sold after the reopening in 1934; however, a new model, the C-34, did win permanent possession of the title "World's Most Efficient Airplane" in 1936. The major breakthrough came in 1939 when Cessna designed the T-50 Bobcat, a twin-engine, low wing, five-place aircraft with retractable landing gear. The firm's bank account had dwindled to $5.03 when Wallace persuaded the Canadian government to use the T-50 to train its bomber pilots. The United States Army Air Force followed in 1941 by ordering a large number of T-50's. In all, a total of 5,402 T-50's were built.

In 1941 Cessna purchased an additional 320 acres at its Pawnee plant bringing the total acreage to 640. An administration building and factory additions were constructed. A second plant was built in Hutchinson, Kansas, in 1942. For the Normandy invasion, 750 gliders were built here.

Just five months after the end of the war, Cessna introduced the Model 120-140 series of personal planes. They proved so popular that sales totaled nearly 4,000 units in 1946. The same year the firm began production of hydraulic units for International Harvester, Oliver, and John Deere, marking the horizontal integration of the product line.

In 1948 the 170 was developed—a large version of the 140. The four-place 170, with its additional seating capacity at little extra cost, spelled the end of the two-place series in 1951. The famous L-19 Bird Dog was developed from the 170 in 1949. It is still used today as the United States Army's chief fixed wing observation plane.

Cessna became a recognized leader in the business aircraft industry in 1950 with the opening of its third plant located on Wichita's southwest side. New aircraft tailored to varying business needs was added to its aircraft line. On April 11, 1952, Cessna acquired the entire capital stock of Seibel Helicopter Company, thus marking its entrance into the rotary wing field. An extensive sales and advertising campaign followed.

Development of the Air Force T-37 jet trainer began in 1953, marking Cessna's initiation into jet aircraft production. The company, believing the market has not developed for a large-scale acceptance of the jet, has not offered this plane commercially. The Air Force has also purchased a number of the popular twin-engine Model 310 planes introduced in 1953.

The Model 172, a tricycle gear version of the 170 with "Land-O-Matic" landing gear, entered the market in 1955. The 172 is acclaimed the most popular airplane in civil aviation today.

The National Aero Finance Company was incorporated by Cessna as a wholly owned subsidiary in 1956. It was designed to help finance aircraft sold to dealers and distributors in the United States and Canada. Cessna's first and only four-engine prototype, the 620, made its maiden flight the same year. It was designed for feeder airline and corporate use. Due to the introduction of the jet airplane to the airline industry and to the accompanying oversupply of its low-priced, used twin-engine aircraft, there was no market for the 620. In 1957 development was halted and the prototype was broken up for scrap.

The Aircraft Radio Corporation, Boonton Township, New Jersey, was acquired by Cessna for 209,731 shares of common stock on February 2, 1959. Due to a growing demand, Cessna reentered the two-place airplane market with its Model 150. The National Aero Finance Company started financing retail aircraft sales on December 1, 1959.

In 1960 Cessna bought 49% interest in Reims Aviation, Reims, France. McCauley Industrial Corporation of Dayton, Ohio, manufacturers of aircraft propellers, was also added to the fold. On March 4, 1960, Cessna issued a three-for-one stock split with each share having one vote. A new subsidiary, Cessna Industrial Products Limited, Scotland, was opened in June, 1961, to manufacture industrial hydraulic equipment for the United Kingdom.

Due to the lack of a military or a commercial market, the helicopter program was taken out in late 1962, after eleven years of development. Cessna bought back the helicopters it had sold, considering it a moral obligation and not wanting a scattering of its orphans in the field. The cost of getting out of the helicopter business was written off in 1963 at $750,-000 after taxes.

A letter contract estimated at $5 million was received October 31, 1963, from the United States Air Force for T-37B jet trainers. Production is scheduled to extend through December, 1965. On November 8th Cessna received an additional follow-on contract of $3,288,109 from the United States Army for ammunition dispensers and storage containers. Cessna holds subcontracts to supply assemblies for the McDonnell F-4B and F-4C, Phantom II fighters, and the Republic 105 Thunderchief. It also has a contract with Boeing Aircraft to supply the transporter for the Minuteman missile, marking Cessna's entry into the missile field. Reims Aviation started producing 172's in France in 1963, providing Cessna with an access to the European Common Market. Fuji Heavy Industries of Tokyo has been licensed to produce L-19's for the Japanese government. Cessna recently opened a branch office in Geneva, Switzerland.

Cessna is currently producing the following aircraft:

Two-place	Price ($)	Five-place	Price ($)
150	7,775	310	62,500
		Skynight	74,950
Four-place			
172	10,245	Six-place	
Skyhawk	11,995	Skywagon	19,495
Skylark	13,775	205	22,295
180	15,950	Skymaster	39,950
182	15,490		
Skylane	17,950		
210	23,450		

Cessna markets its aircraft through 500 retail outlets located worldwide. There are approximately 100 export dealers and sales representatives covering 60 foreign countries excluding Canada. In fiscal 1963 Cessna sold 3,257 commercial aircraft, of which 22% were exported.

Cessna accounts for 45% of the total industry unit shipments compared to Piper's 35% and Beech's 13.3%. It controls 36% of the industry's dollar volume compared to Piper's 24.4% and Beech's 25%. It also delivered 3,257 commercial airplanes in 1963 compared to Piper's 2,177 deliveries and Beech's 1,061 deliveries. In the first quarter of fiscal 1964, Cessna had delivered 1,145 planes worth $18,500,000.

CESSNA SALES DISTRIBUTION, 1961-1963

Area	1961	1962	1963
DEFENSE	24%	16%	15.9%
COMMERCIAL	54%	60%	59.3%
INDUSTRIAL	11%	12%	15.3%
AVIATION RADIO CORP.	10%	11%	9.5%
McCAULEY INDUSTRIES	11%	1%	

The emphasis Cessna puts on the commercial market is shown in the above table. It makes up over half of the industry's total sales, taking up the slack from decreasing military orders. This helps explain why Cessna has led the industry in sales of commercial aircraft for the last seven years.

McCauley Industries Corporation was dissolved September 30, 1962. Sales from the McCauley Division of Cessna Aircraft Company are reported along with the commercial sales. This accounts for the decreasing sales distribution figure in the table while the McCauley Division's sales to outside firms have increased from $793,159 in 1961 to $1,332,000 in 1964.

Dwane L. Wallace, president of Cessna Aircraft Company, feels that new entries seem to widen the aircraft market instead of creating more competition. Wallace estimates business prospects in the U.S. at 395,000 firms based on business income, percentage of budget spent on travel, etc. He claims that the general business market penetration is 20% at the present time. The Aircraft Owners and Pilots Association claims that there are some 39,000 corporate owned aircraft in use in the United States. By exploiting this market, Cessna has become the leader in the light plane industry. Eight of the last ten years' sales have increased, including 1964 with sales up 27%. Cessna's 50,000th airplane was produced in 1963.

What does Cessna see in the crystal ball? Dwane L. Wallace claims, "The turboprop is coming, but it's quite a way down the road." There is a narrow market for the pure jet business airplane in the $1 million to $750,000 class. The trend toward greater instrumentation will continue, but simpler instruments are on the way. The Federal Aviation Agency claims that the general aviation fleet will increase 26.2% by 1970.

Cessna has few labor problems. From December, 1935, to December, 1964, it had only six cases disputed before the Labor Relations Board. The last case concerned the International Association of Machinists in 1959.

Developing new airplane models or design changes often produces unexpected costs. Significant design changes, such as the fuselage to fit the new "Omni-Vision" wrap-around rear windshield, produce abnormal expenses. The redesign of the 182, Skylane, and 210 in 1962 are good examples. With its growing line of aircraft, Cessna incurs the extra costs of developing new models, thus reducing profit margins for the year.

The Booz-Allen-Hamilton firm made the first scientific studies of the light aircraft market potential in 1954 for Cessna. A very thorough study was undertaken to answer the following questions: (1) What is the size of the potential market for the Cessna-type plane? (2) What are the characteristics of purchasers? (3) Is Cessna's distribution system properly set up to exploit the market? (4) Are Cessna's sales tactics sound?

Based on the data collected, the firm found potential sales prospects of 151,000 broken down as follows:

	Potential Prospects	Estimated Penetration	Potential Buyers
COMPANY PLANES			
multi-engine	16,000	50%	8,000
single-engine	15,000	50%	7,500
EXECUTIVE PLANES	20,000	25%	5,000
PERSONAL PLANES	80,000	10%	8,000
FARMERS	20,000	25%	4,000
		Total	32,500

This is a relatively conservative estimate compared to some other predictions made.

Professional and technical people, farmers and farm managers, managers, officials, and proprietors, 72% of which have incomes of $10,000+, account for 68% of all personal plane owners. The probability of plane ownership is an increasing function of income. A man with $25,000 income is eight times more likely to purchase an airplane than a man with an income of $7,500.

The light plane ranks as follows in comparison with regular airlines, pullman, air coach, railroad coach, bus, automobile, and private airline: first in prestige; second in high speed in transit; second in flexible departure; third in comfort; third in terminal convenience. It follows that the best sales prospects are those who place high emphasis on prestige, speed, and flexibility.

Private aircraft sales resistance is listed by order of weighted importance: (1) high cost of ownership; (2) not sold on usefulness; (3) objections of family; (4) have not given serious thought to the matter; (5) question safety of light airplane; (6) fear or discomfort of flying. The best sales prospects, then, are people who can afford and who can use the airplane effectively.

Cessna must work hard to eliminate two major misconceptions: (1) flying is something dangerous and difficult to do; (2) the cost of flying your own airplane is excessive. To do this, Cessna has increased its sales and advertising expenditures from $300,000 in 1951 to $1 million in 1960. During the same period sales rose 180%. The Gardner Advertising Agency, St. Louis, is Cessna's advertising agency.

Cessna has changed its advertising theme from "Who, me fly?" to "Look who's flying." The ads are brief, business-type articles aimed directly at the busy executive. The format usually stresses time spent, business accomplished, and cost, using the split-screen technique. They usually portray actual case histories. Two executives in St. Louis have business engagements in Chicago. The first man arrives in Chicago late in the afternoon, attends his engagement, spends the night in a hotel, and drives back the next day. He arrives back at the office tired and hungry. The second man goes to Chicago by Cessna, attends his meeting, and arrives back home refreshed in time for dinner the same day. The ad ends with the question: "How Much Is Your Time Worth?" Other ads stress the ability of the airplane to speed the executive to the right place at the right time to close the big deal. These points make sense to the busy executive.

Cessna ads are carried in four military and aviation magazines. Regular ad series are run in *Time, Newsweek, Sports Illustrated, Fortune,* and the *Wall Street Journal.* Trade schedules are run in seven aviation business papers for plane oriented people. Cessna also advertises in the following foreign publications: *Vision, Revista Aérea, Life en Espanol,* and three foreign editions of *Time.*

The fledgling businessman is offered a bargain on flight training with his purchase of a new Cessna. While he is taking lessons at the regular price, his wife can learn how to fly for half price. His dealer also has a special trophy for him when he solos. While the executive is learning to fly, he can be making his business trips by air, thus killing two birds with one stone.

Cessna is laying the groundwork for a new light plane by pushing the pleasure aspects of flying. A two-place sport plane costing between $4,000 and $4,500 is in the making. It should offer cheaper flying to general aviation, being priced at a little over one-half the cost of a Cessna 150.

Cessna has an optimistic outlook toward the future because it produces a quality product and has the determination to succeed. Its efforts in advertising, however, must not let up as popular misconceptions continue to be an area of concern.

FOR DISCUSSION

1. How would you evaluate Cessna's position in the industry?
2. What conclusions do you have concerning its potential?
3. Can you suggest any methods for improving sales goals or quotas?
4. What effort is important to a solution of major problems?

SUGGESTED READING

"Cessna Acts to Widen Twin-Engine Sales; Foresees Industry Growth," *Aviation Week*, March 18, 1963, pp. 76 ff.

"Small Planes Find Sales Target; the Flying Business Man; Cessna, Beech, Piper, Step Up Ads," *Printers Ink*, March 4, 1960, p. 18.

"Time Study (Car vs. Plane; Cessna Ad Story of Two Business Trips)," *Printers Ink*, October 27, 1961, p. 40.

Delta Air Lines, Incorporated

THE EARLY DEVELOPMENT OF DELTA AIR LINES was the work of Collet E. Woolman. While working with the Agriculture Extension Department at Louisiana State University, he came into contact with cotton production problems brought about by the boll weevil. Woolman and several associates became interested in the problem and its possible solution through the use of airplanes to dust crops with weevil killing agents. In 1925 he organized the Huff Baland Duster, the world's first crop dusting organization. Because of its success the operations spread across the Southern United States and extended into Mexico and South America.

The expansion into Peru in 1926, the first crop dusting operation in South America, led to Woolman's establishing the first airline below the equator in 1927. It was an international carrier—mail and passenger—along the western South American coast. The route was later sold to Pan American Grace, becoming the basic structure for the present Panagra Airlines route.

The early success in South American air transportation brought about the expansion of Delta's crop dusting services in the U.S. and in 1928 the company's name was changed to Delta Air Service. On June 1, 1929, Delta inaugurated its first scheduled passenger service between Jackson, Mississippi, and Dallas, Texas. Shortly thereafter, this service was extended to Atlanta and Birmingham.

On December 31, 1930, Delta Air Service was incorporated in Louisiana and in 1945 it changed its name to the Delta Air Corporation.

In 1953 Delta merged with the old Chicago and Southern Air Lines, Incorporated. When it absorbed Southern, each share of the latter's stock was exchanged for $21 of Delta's twenty year convertible debentures. All debentures have now been redeemed or converted.

In 1934, when Delta was awarded its first U.S. Mail contract, the major emphasis focused on providing air transportation services. At that time, the crop dusting activities began to play a decreasingly important part in Delta's activities. Today, its dusting operations are a very insignificant part of Delta's services.

To serve its markets, Delta has a force of sales and traffic managers located at key areas throughout its system. Insofar as passenger markets are concerned, the airline provides its customers with seven methods of procuring tickets: cash and carry at any of its 98 ticket offices; by mail; air travel plan (monthly billing for those who travel a lot); airscrip (monthly billing for those who write their own tickets after reservations are confirmed); book ticket stock, particularly for companies (tickets issued whenever necessary); teletype tickets (ordered and received by Western Union); travel agents at over 2,200 authorized agencies throughout the U.S.

In order to induce potential passengers to use these plans, Delta has carried on extensive advertising programs during the past decade. Presently, its advertising budget is approximately $6 million. When the southern transcontinental route was inaugurated in 1961, it had to expand to national coverage, which cost nearly a million dollars in itself. Delta has had great success in the service it offers and it has further capitalized on it by using as its advertising focal point the theme of service and southern charm. The employer's job is to sell Delta; however, he will not sacrifice the quality of its service despite the fact that it might lead to the loss of a customer. For instance, Delta's management has stressed that a clerk is to recommend a better flight on a competing airline, if one exists, for a potential customer. The idea is, of course, that it would sacrifice an immediate sale rather than its characteristic service.

To a very great extent, much of the credit for Delta's success belongs to the man who has been at the company's controls since its founding. C. E. Woolman, president and general manager, has guided the company most skillfully through the past years. His shrewd business sense and his ability to motivate his employees to work at peak capacity have been the components of his success.

Further testimony to the quality and stability of the management team Woolman formed when Delta merged with Chicago and Southern is the fact that there has been only one major top management change since the early 1950's at the time of merger and reorganization. It was then that Woolman blended the available officials to form an equally balanced, highly effective management team.

Woolman's effective guiding hand can be seen in the future enterprises of the company. The flight equipment has now reached a stable point with only four more Fan-Jet DC-8's scheduled for delivery by 1966. However, in 1966 Delta will be the first airline to receive the new twin jet, short range Douglas DC-9. This year Delta ordered 15 with an option for 15 more of the planes that could well become the workhorse of tomorrow as the DC-3 was in the 1940's and early 1950's. These planes, of course, will insure a more economical service at high speed to the numerous "short hop" cities located within Delta's system.

Another Delta advance is presently being made with the installation of an IBM computer system. The computer will handle reservation requests from nearly 300 system sets scattered throughout the United States. The new system will handle within seconds, from any of the 300 remote sets, tasks of reserving, cancelling, confirming spaces; moreover, it will process reservations requested on other airlines. Special arrangements such as car rental, special meals on flights, and connecting flight information will also be handled by the IBM system.

Another aspect of Delta's improvement program is the continuance of its maintenance operations. Just completed in Atlanta, the home base for the airline is a gigantic 30 acre jet base. Buildings housing the engineering, inspection, overhaul, and maintenance departments cover 9 acres themselves. This is further testimony to management's desire to improve its equipment performance reliability through proper maintenance and overhaul.

The final area for definite future action appears to be in promotion. Delta made a big play for tourist traffic to the New York World's Fair which opened for two years in the spring of 1964.

It initiated a plan whereby the public could purchase travel stamps ($1 each) to save in a special book and use whenever they choose for a trip to the fair. This was a type of easy-payment/lay-away plan that would seem to play upon the modern American mania for collecting stamps.

Moreover, Delta is continuing to develop its traffic particularly in the western and Caribbean areas.

Delta Air Lines, being a common carrier and subject to certain amounts of governmental control, is in a position where it cannot radically alter its market niche as easily as members of other industries. Its present position is set to a great extent, and it must work to expand this niche to its greatest potential.

As a common carrier, Delta provides air transportation service to the public and government alike. It engages in the transportation of passengers, freight, express, and mail as speedily as possible. In order to accomplish its goals, the company has developed, through the Civil Aeronautics Board, a route and scheduling system that will best serve its purpose.

Insofar as passengers are concerned, Delta has the customary rate differential which provides first class, coach, and economy night coach service. This serves to attract a full range of would-be air travelers.

The big advantage offered by any airline is speed. Delta is no exception and has been conscious of this fact. As a result, over one-half of its jet fleet is composed of Convair 880's, the fastest commercial jet in operation. The route system includes international and domestic flights. It has flights that cover great distances nonstop (1,000 miles plus) as well as shorter flights that may cover as few as 40 miles. The system is a 14,000 mile network that serves the financial and government centers of the East and Midwest, the growing Southwest and West Coast areas, and the vacation areas of Florida and the Caribbean. On this system are sixty-four cities, large and small alike.

In March, 1961, the Civil Aeronautics Board made Delta a transcontinental airline by issuing a certificate to operate from its then most western point, Dallas, to the West Coast. This action gave the airline a system that stretched from Puerto Rico and Caracas westward to San Francisco, Los Angeles, and San Diego. Its northern limits remained at the focal points of Chicago, Detroit, and New York.

The Board's action served to strengthen Delta's route system as well as to give it long range operations that are most feasible in this "jet age"; moreover, the decision took the South—an area that is advancing more rapidly economically than the rest of the country—and tied it to the growing West. In so doing it gave Delta the position of being a vital air linkage between the expanding space age industries and facilities located in the South, Southwest, and West Coast areas: Orlando (Cape Kennedy); Huntsville, Alabama; New Orleans; Houston; Dallas; San Diego; Los Angeles, etc. This expansion increased the system by 25%, and is one of the reasons for Delta's improved operating results during 1962-1963.

As was characteristic during the previous few years, Delta in 1963 again led the industry in traffic performance. From January to July in 1963, Delta's overall Load Factor (amount of passengers and freight carried relative to amount of seats and space available) was three and a half points better than second place American Airlines (Table 13.1). The 60.79% is even eight points better than industry average. Anytime a carrier can reach the 60% mark in overall Load Factor performance, it is doing exceptionally well; for instance, since the beginning of the jet age the industry average has steadily dropped to 46.5% in 1962.

Table 13.1
DELTA'S OVERALL LOAD FACTOR PERFORMANCE

Traffic Performance   January-July, 1963

Carrier	Overall Load Factor		1st Class Load Factor		Coach Load Factor		% Revenue Passenger Miles	
DELTA	(1)	60.79%	(2)	52.95%	(1)	65.85%	(8)	65.80
AMERICAN	(2)	57.08	(1)	53.66	(2)	59.11		
NORTH EAST	(3)	55.31	(3)	51.98	(4)	57.20		
BRANIFF	(4)	53.08	(4)	47.39	(3)	57.86		

SOURCE: *American Aviation*, October, 1963, p. 68.

Astoundingly enough, in each of those years Delta's overall Load Factor remained relatively stable and was always above the average. During the past two years, however, Delta has begun to forge ahead, leaving it in the number one position for trunkline carriers.

Also to be noted is Delta's ranking as the top carrier in the passenger (coach) Load Factor. Its lead here is a substantial six points over American. On the other hand, it has slipped to second place in First Class passenger performance and is about three-fourths of a point behind American.

Although it has a much smaller system than each of the four larger trunklines (United, American, TWA, and Eastern), Delta again shows its class with the third largest percentage increase in Revenue Passenger Miles and the second largest increase in Revenue Passengers during the first half of 1963 (Table 13.2). Without a doubt Delta's traffic performance indicates it has a strong system despite its lack of size relative to the "Big Four."

Table 13.2
DELTA'S PERFORMANCE IN REVENUE PASSENGER MILES

Domestic Air Traffic   January-July, 1963 vs. 1962

Carrier	Revenue Passengers Miles	% Change	Revenue Passengers	Up
UNITED	$4,800,000,000	4.8	$6,800,000	1.0
AMERICAN	4,000,000,000	7.1	4,700,000	1.1
TWA	3,000,000,000	18.2	2,700,000	14.5
EASTERN	2,700,000,000	15.3	4,381,000	23.7
DELTA	1,800,000,000	12.3	2,400,000	14.7

SOURCE: *American Aviation*, October, 1963, p. 68.

In the industrial market Delta's air freight and air express ton-miles have increased approximately 900% and 500% respectively since 1950. In addition, the amount of mail carried by Delta since the same year has increased 900%. Combined, these figures give a 750% increase in Delta's air cargo since 1950.

Air freight, which in 1962 comprised approximately 64% of its total ton-miles of air cargo hauled, is usually delivered in one day and is applicable to most products. The air express operation is a division of the Railway Express Agency, which contracts with Delta and other airlines to transport the express business that is secured by either partner. It usually is faster than air freight because it is carried aboard all regularly scheduled flights. One advantage to Delta is the fact that Railway Express picks up the shipment from the shipper and delivers to the receiver; moreover, it takes care of all insurance and rate problems. As a result, the airline receives an easy source of income through this form of cargo.

The Woolman policy of strict cost control in all phases even extends to the point of spending millions of dollars just to cut future costs through efficiency; for instance, next year Delta will spend $10 million to replace the present turbo-jet engines in the first six DC-8's with new, much more efficient turbo-fan engines.

Chief engineer A. C. Ford personally keeps close tab on the performance of each 880 and DC-8 flying for Delta. If anything shows up on his up-to-the-minute charts that indicates an aircraft should be operating more efficiently, that plane is brought in as soon as possible for a thorough inspection.

This big push on maintenance is one reason for Delta's outstanding equipment reliability record. Actually, this reliability is needed more with Delta than the larger companies due to its smaller jet fleet.

The following advantage has been obtained through close scheduling and equipment usage control. Unlike competitors, Delta has not greatly and expensively expanded its force of jets. Woolman's belief was that it should concentrate its relatively few jets on the routes offering the least competition and on those that are most productive. As a result, Delta has achieved a tremendous degree of efficiency. Its DC-8's operate at a 64% passenger Load Factor, while the 880's carry a 67% average. United and National (the other two airlines using DC-8's during the second quarter of 1963) obtained only 46% and 51% respectively. As for the 880's TWA has a passenger Load Factor of 59%; and the other carrier flying 880's, Northeast, possesses a 54% level.

Delta's position is highly regarded in the financial world. The retained earnings are steadily rising while the long-term debt is steadily being depleted. The first six months of 1963 also demonstrate why Delta is so highly regarded. Despite being approximately one-third the size of American's system, Delta is only $1 million off American's leading operating profit figure of $17 million. The third place carrier had $7 million less (Table 13.3).

Table 13.3

U.S. TRUNK FINANCES: January-July, 1963

Operating Profits

AMERICAN	$17,000,000
DELTA	16,000,000
WESTERN	10,000,000
NATIONAL	8,000,000
UNITED	8,000,000

SOURCE: *American Aviation*, October, 1963, p. 68.

Without a doubt, Delta Air Lines probably is the most financially sound trunkline carrier. With its favorable sources of private long-term credit, ready whenever needed, Delta has behind it the confidence of the business world. By 1966 the company will use additional credit availability when it receives the first DC-9's on order from Douglas Aircraft. There is little doubt, however, all things remaining equal, that Delta will look just as healthy then as it does at the present time.

In spite of Delta's relatively strong operating position, the company has a major operating problem in its on-time departure record. During the past few years, Delta's "black sheep," so to speak, has been its poor record for dispatching flights on time. Unfortunately, Delta's management is put in a bad position by these late departures. On one hand, they are a blot against Delta's name, while on the other hand it must be taken into consideration that 27.8% of its revenue is derived from connecting service (20% from its own connecting flights, and 30 to 35% from interline transfers). If it were to dispatch flights on time regardless, there is a great possibility that the "costs" would be greater than those presently sustained. Briefly, these include loss of passengers by their not waiting for late inbound flights and loss of a portion of its service reputation. As of June, 1963, Delta had fallen to seventh place, only one place ahead of American and two other trunkline carriers.

Mr. Woolman believes that another problem of major concern is overcompetition. This, however, is a complaint of all executives in the air industry. They contend that the Civil Aeronautics Board, in its policy of competition expansion, during the early 1950's awarded certificates to too many competitors over certain air routes between certain cities. By and large, considering the present economics of air transportation in the jet age, this contention is true and the C.A.B. is beginning to realize it. As Woolman points out, on many routes each competitor must fly a large number of flights (creating a large available capacity figure) in order to remain competitive. Consequently, when flying with overcapacity, a line naturally is not operating as efficiently as it might. Any correction to this situation, however, must come from the Board, and this explains why lately it has been generally receptive to the idea of airline merger proposals.

One of Delta's marketing problems has been the slow development of its international traffic. Of course, it received a setback during the last couple of years when service to Cuba, Haiti, and the Dominican Republic was suspended due to political instabilities. Consequently, Caracas, Kingston, and San Juan, are the only stops presently made outside the U.S. Recently, Jamaica authorized Delta to fly east (to San Juan) along with the southern route to Caracas. This, of course, adds an important link between two major resort areas and will be highly beneficial to Delta.

Furthermore, Delta hopes to improve its showing now that its system extends to the West Coast, particularly in light of a recent survey. The results of this survey showed vast potential traffic from California all the way to Puerto Rico. Briefly, the number of hotel reservations in Puerto Rico from the State of California was second only to the State of New York. Delta, of course, has its eyes on this lucrative cross-country traffic.

One big problem that Delta faces in its management is concerned with Woolman. At seventy-two he cannot be expected to carry much longer the tasks inherent within the self-made power position that he has held since Delta's creation. In other words, who is in line to take over when the time comes? By and large, Delta appears to be a one man organization despite the quality of its top management personnel.

In 1961 Woolman expressed complete confidence in his team and indicated that Delta would not have to go outside the company for his successor. He wouldn't name any likely possibilities, however.

That was in 1961. On June 30, 1963, Delta's Todd Cole resigned to transfer his services to competitor Eastern Airlines. This was the first and only incident of change. Cole was an industry renowned financial strategist, whom many considered as heir apparent to Woolman's position.

At the same time, Woolman announced the name of the person to step into Cole's vice-presidential position. He was none other than General Dynamics' successful president, Earl D. Johnson. Because Woolman had tried unsuccessfully to land Johnson when the latter went to General Dynamics from the Air Transport Association in 1955, the speculators now believe he is the "crown prince," so to speak, of Delta. As for Johnson, he doesn't give that impression. He maintains that there are more capable men on the team at his level—men who are more qualified than he. Meanwhile, he has been helping out wherever he can with his administrative and financial knowledge.

What the change will mean to Delta's management team remains to be seen. Naturally, it could have adverse effects on their dispositions. However, with Woolman's ability in human relations, the team should remain close and effective regardless of which one of them succeeds him.

All in all, however, the future looks brighter than the present for Delta, especially with its increased domestic route system to the West Coast. With the high quality of management throughout the organization, the company is in a good position to overcome its major problems in marketing, operation, and management.

FOR DISCUSSION

1. How effective has C. E. Woolman been as president and manager of Delta?
2. What decisions are being made for successful action in the future?
3. Evaluate the consequences positive and negative of Woolman's self-made power position.
4. What has Delta done in its major problem area of marketing?

SUGGESTED READING

"Delta A Big Little Airline," *Business Week*, November 25, 1961, pp. 62-64.
"Delta's Program Pushes For Reliability," *American Aviation*, October, 1963, pp. 68-70.
"Delta's Success—A Look Behind The Scenes," *American Aviation*, September, 1963, p. 55.
"Early Profits Indicate Further Delta Gain," *Aviation Week*, October 22, 1962, pp. 39-40.

CHAPTER 14

E. J. Korvette, Incorporated

Now said to be one of the nation's most successful discount store chains, E. J. Korvette, Incorporated, had a simple beginning in 1949 when Eugene Ferkauf opened a store in a Manhattan loft building with a stock of discount-priced luggage on an investment of $4,000. Previously, Ferkauf had worked in a luggage shop run by his father. At a customer's suggestion, he branched out into appliances and rode along with the boom in appliance selling that came in the 1950's.

In December, 1955, the month-old Korvette Corporation acquired for 1,000,000 common shares the properties and assets of nine store corporations organized by Ferkauf up to that time and changed its name to E. J. Korvette, Inc. In 14 years Ferkauf developed his investment into a nationwide chain of stores with $330 million in annual sales. Of the 4 million outstanding shares, Ferkauf owns about one-third, worth about $57 million.

Korvette now operates some 30 promotional department stores, almost all in suburban shopping centers. The stores are concentrated in the East, but have recently expanded into the Midwest. There are now 3 stores in the Chicago suburbs. Seventeen of the stores are Korvette Cities which are large stores and include a beauty salon, leased furniture, carpet, and tire centers; about 20 include company-operated food markets. The department store area of the Cities is usually around 180,000 square feet, and total area is usually about 265,000 square feet. Since it is important to provide for customer parking, 5 or 6 times the selling space is allowed for parking.

Korvette is recognized as a leader in new techniques of merchandising. It has forced into submission some of the biggest manufacturers who were determined to "fair trade" at list prices. It was the first to jump from hard to soft goods when the appliance market became saturated. Korvette converted early to a supermarket type of operation, and was probably the first to enter the proprietary drug field on a large scale. There was a trying period in 1957 and 1958 as the hard goods boom receded, but Korvette enjoyed a strong comeback.

Best described as the maverick of the discount business, Eugene Ferkauf is largely responsible for the explosive growth of Korvette; he may also be the seat of many problems in the future. A hard worker, Ferkauf puts in a twelve hour day, six days a week. He shuns his office, brags that he has no secretary, and doesn't write business letters; he feels that he can do business quicker and more effectively over the telephone. He spends his days prowling the stores, making decisions along the way. Although now on the board of directors, he is still very much "in charge." Analysts refer to President William Willensky as one of Ferkauf's "mouthpieces."

Korvette is striving to change its image from that of a discount chain to a promotional department store chain. To demonstrate the change, Korvette opened a chic new store on Fifth Avenue in New York. To the relief of the "old guard" on the Avenue, Korvette's styling and tone were muted, and the emphasis was on a dignified and restrained appearance. The old Sloane Building was completely modernized, using 23 foot aluminum grills and new show windows on the exterior; and on the interior a double set of escalators; complete air-conditioning, individually controlled for each floor; all new fluorescent and incandescent lighting utilizing fancy lighting fixtures; composition tile and carpeted floors; and new display fixtures. Special features are peripheral stock areas hidden behind curtain walls and display fixtures for the quick replenishment of stocks, and an inside unloading dock to avoid causing traffic tie-ups. The total area of the store is 180,000 feet; and the cost of remodeling, excluding fixtures, ran about $1,750,000, which was substantially above what Korvette has spent in the past for remodeling a store. At the Korvette City in the Black Horse Pike Shopping Center and in other stores, charge accounts have replaced the former policy of cash and carry, and piped music and carefully chosen pastel decors are in evidence. Delivery and package wrapping services are also available.

All of these changes are causing pervasive and potentially dangerous consequences. Construction now runs more than $12 per square foot; fixtures are running three times what they did in the past; and fancy, expensive concealed lighting is now used exclusively. Stock turnover figures have been changing too; in 1956 the turnover was 10 to 12 times, but by 1960 the turnover came down to about 7 times. Annual sales per square foot of selling space has been going down, too, from $360 per square foot in 1956 to $260 in 1960; however, this is still more than the $98 per square foot figure achieved by the big department stores. Profits are approximately the same as for the big department stores—2.2% of sales compared to 2.4% for the big department stores. Korvette claims that it shoots for one half of the conventional retailer's margin, which would give Korvette 18%. At least one analyst believes that the markup is now 26%, and this represents a hefty rise over the years.

Korvette is still in the midst of a three-year expansion program begun in 1962 which will double the size of the chain and extend geographical diversification. President Willensky forecasts $750 million in sales volume by 1965, a 55% increase over 1963. There are 15 Korvette Cities now being planned or built. This includes centers at Bethesda, Maryland; Fairfax, Virginia; and West Orange, New Jersey.

As Korvette grows, several changes are being forced on it; for example, where previously Korvette saved money by paying for its stock on a cash basis (since turnover was so great), it now has to finance the stock. Further costs were cut by having only one advertising department for the chain and by not having big warehouses; instead they bought centrally and shipped direct from the seller to the stores.

Korvette is gradually increasing the percentage of soft goods in its line and decreasing the percentage of hard good items. Competition and a semisaturated market meant that the party was over for appliances, so Korvette had to expand its lines in order to survive. In 1961 hard goods still constituted 52% of sales, soft goods were 35%, food items accounted for 8%, and drugs and toiletries made up 5%. In addition, more higher-priced lines were being added along with more sales help per square foot and full department store services.

Things seemed to be rosier at Korvette, but along came the April quarter of 1963 when Korvette showed a loss of $218,000. It was explained that the loss was due to the number of new stores opened and that the April quarter has traditionally been low. The food operation, which Korvette had been pushing, had failed to yield a satisfactory profit. Retailers figure it takes one year for a new store of the size and type of Korvette to break even. Korvette had 6 such stores out of a total of 21 in April, 1963, but one of the six (on Fifth Avenue, N.Y.) was nearly a year old. Also, in the same quarter a year before, when the company made money, it had almost as high a percentage of new stores (4 out of 16). Moreover, operating costs, written off as incurred, should not have been greatly higher this year because only one new store was opened in that April quarter. Executive Vice President Joseph Lamm offered the defense that all new stores have made *operating* profits without allocating central office overhead. Korvette's common stock in 1963 sold for less than one-half the 1962 high, though still at 20 times 1962 earnings and 4 times book value.

Korvette's first year on the *Fortune* directory of the 50 largest merchandising firms in the U.S. was 1963. Korvette's $235,420,000 in sales placed it 48th on the *Fortune* list. Its assets of $52,447,000 brought it a ranking of 46, its net profit of $5,229,000 ranked a healthy 36, and its invested capital of $28,146,000 ranked 46th. On the *Fortune* profitability comparison, Korvette's ratio of net profit to invested capital of 18.6% earned an astounding 2nd place of the 50 giants! In 1964 sales rose to $485,257,003, an increase of $154,847,470. Net earnings and special credit were $7,477,304 which compared with net earnings of $6,377,535 for the previous year.

E. J. KORVETTE, INCORPORATED Income and
Balance Sheet Data

Year Ended July 31	Net Sales $Million	% Oper. Income Of Sales	Oper. Income $Million	Net Income $Million	Per Share Earns.	Divs. Paid
1964	485.25	—	—	6.75	1.52	—
1963	330.41	3.5	11.45	6.05	1.45	—
1962	235.42	4.4	10.38	5.30	1.27	—
1961	180.21	4.3	7.75	4.03	1.02	—
1960	157.51	3.6	5.62	2.74	.74	—
1959	114.89	3.7	4.25	1.91	.54	—
1958	105.76	1.8	1.94	.79	.23	—
1957	71.07	3.9	2.75	1.19	.34	—
1956	54.85	5.9	3.23	1.56	.42	—
1955	36.29	6.2	2.24	1.18	.39	—

Year Ended July 31	Gross Prop. $Million	Current Assets $Million	Current Liabs. $Million	Current Ratio Assets to Liabs.	$ Book Value per Com. Share
1964	—	72.59	24.06		
1963	24.54	61.58	29.76	2.1 — 1	8.54
1962	14.24	31.96	21.41	1.5 — 1	6.91
1961	8.49	22.38	11.32	2.0 — 1	5.60
1960	7.46	20.11	10.69	1.9 — 1	3.94
1959	5.92	13.93	6.80	2.0 — 1	3.13
1958	5.64	15.79	11.19	1.4 — 1	2.57
1957	3.59	13.93	9.00	1.6 — 1	2.35
1956	3.98	11.50	6.87	1.7 — 1	1.89
1955	.60	9.01	6.41	1.4 — 1	1.10

SOURCE: Standard & Poor's, January 31, 1964.

Korvette's swift growth has brought several comments from industry spokesmen, competitors, and analysts. Some of these comments are:

"A lot of highly successful merchants run into trouble when they try to become chains." (competitor)
"For on-the-spot management they have to substitute skill in communicating with subordinates a thousand miles away."
" . . . expanding sales lead to overbudgeting?"
"Suburbia overstored?"
"Additional discount department stores will probably first divert business from other discount department stores."

E. J. Korvette, Incorporated, whose philosophy is that everyone loves a bargain, has come a long way since its humble beginning; but it looks as if the next few years should tell whether Korvette can prove that it can successfully wear bigger pants. In the fire are various cost reductions that could possibly be obtained by installing push button warehouses and through inventory control via electronic data processing.

As one official said, "It's no picnic working for Korvette, but it's exciting!"

FOR DISCUSSION

1. What is the major reason for the success of E. J. Korvette?
2. What was the nature of decisions concerning the company's image and how effective were they?
3. What changes in policy were necessitated by the growth of the company?
4. What is the nature of decisions which will be necessary in the future if Korvette is to maintain its position?

SUGGESTED READING

"Chasing Rainbows?" *Forbes*, June 15, 1963, p. 14.
"Discounter Goes Posh," *Business Week*, June 2, 1962, p. 34.
"Korvette Plans Prestige Centers," *Chain Store Age-Exec.*, June, 1963, p. 20.
"Problems and Prospects of Discount Department Stores; Abstract," *Management Review*, April, 1962, p. 52.